LABOUR AND THE NORTHERN IRELAND PROBLEM
1945–1951

LABOUR AND THE NORTHERN IRELAND PROBLEM

1945–1951

The Missed Opportunity

Russell Rees

Foreword by
PAUL BEW

IRISH ACADEMIC PRESS
DUBLIN • PORTLAND, OR

First published in 2009 by Irish Academic Press

2 Brookside,
Dundrum Road,
Dublin 14, Ireland

920 NE 58th Avenue, Suite 300
Portland, Oregon,
97213-3786, USA

www.iap.ie

British Library Cataloguing-in-Publication Data
An entry can be found on request

978 0 7165 2970 5 (cloth)

Library of Congress Cataloging-in-Publication Data
An entry can be found on request

Printed by MPG Books Group, King's Lynn, Norfolk

Contents

Acknowledgements

The principal sources for this work are the cabinet and departmental papers from the period at the Public Record Office of Northern Ireland in Belfast, the United Kingdom National Archives (formerly the Public Record Office) in London and the State Paper Office at Dublin Castle. Staff at all three institutions were invariably courteous and helpful. My research has also benefited from time spent at the National Library of Ireland, the Public Record Office of Ireland and the Linenhall Library in Belfast. I would like to record my thanks to staff at all of the above for their assistance. I would also like to express my appreciation to all of those who gave me interviews and engaged in correspondence. Their names appear in the bibliography.

My early interest in Irish history was stimulated by the teaching of Professor J.L. McCracken at the University of Ulster, Coleraine. Subsequently, I was very fortunate that Professor Tony Hepburn agreed to supervise my doctoral thesis. His insight and perceptive questioning persuaded me to consider new lines of enquiry, and he was a constant source of support and encouragement. At the same time, his genuine interest in my work, his great enthusiasm and his eternal good humour made the many hours spent in his office both a privilege and a pleasure. I also owe a special word of thanks to Dr Éamon Phoenix who took the time to read the entire draft. His suggestions and friendship were invaluable. Professors David Harkness and Henry Patterson also made important comments on the original thesis, and these prompted me to clarify a number of the arguments. My understanding of the post-war period has also been enhanced by conversations with Dr Eugenio Biagini, Professor Seán Connolly, Dr Christopher Finlay, Mr Torrens McFetridge, Professor Alan Sharp, Mr David Shiels and Mr Ken Ward. At Omagh Academy I should mention the contributions of my colleagues Mr Michael Murphy, who had the courage and the patience to read the entire manuscript in his usual meticulous style, and Miss Audrey Hodge, who in the past two years has found me even more disorganized than usual. Technical input was supplied by Mr Andrew Blacoe, Mr Jonathan Bower and Mr Johnny Crutchley, each of whom did well to hide their incredulity and frustration with my ignorance of all things associated with the computer. I am also indebted to Professor Paul Bew who, in spite of the many demands on his time, took the trouble to read the manuscript and point me in the direction of new research, particularly in the inter-war period. For many labouring in the field of modern Irish history he remains an inspirational figure. To Lisa Hyde at Irish Academic Press I should express my gratitude for her patience, professionalism and organizational ability. It has made my task much more straightforward and enjoyable.

The Department of Education for Northern Ireland provided the necessary funding for my postgraduate research in the form of a Major State Studentship, and my family has consistently supported my studies. Gordon and Clark have helped in ways that will not be apparent to them, and my mother and father, to whom the book is dedicated, have been unstinting in their support. My greatest debt is to Jean, my wife, who typed both the original thesis and the final draft of this book. Without her constant encouragement, devotion and commitment, this book would never have been written.

Foreword

On the 8th of February 1939 Sir Richard Hopkins, the Treasury Controller, wrote to a senior colleague, Sir F. Phillips, on the subject of Northern Ireland's economic place within the United Kingdom:

> When the Northern Irish government was set up it was expected that their revenues would be sufficient both to meet their expenses and to provide a substantial contribution to Imperial services (defence, debt, &c.). This expectation was realised, at first fully and later in a diminishing degree. Since 1931 Northern Ireland has been in effect a depressed area. So far from receiving any imperial contribution, we have invented a series of dodges and devices to give them gifts and subventions within the ambit of the Government of Ireland Act so as to save Northern Ireland from coming openly on the dole as Newfoundland did.

Hopkins's note implies that the general position of Britain and Northern Ireland within the world economy was not subject to control by the Stormont government. Other documents in his name make it clear that this was in fact his view and explained his willingness to resort to 'wangles' and 'fudges' to help the province : 'The fact is that they copy all our legislation and that therefore we set their general standard, for better or for worse. In times like these, this standard means bankruptcy for a small community which is suffering terribly from unemployment.'

These remarks are of the utmost significance. They show that even the pre-Keynesian British Treasury of the 1930s was unwilling to force Northern Ireland to live on its own resources as was envisaged when the local Parliament was set up in 1921. There seems to be no other reason for this decision than a broadly humanitarian one and perhaps, it might be said, a small-u Unionist acceptance of the logic of Northern Ireland's continued membership of the United Kingdom. This decision by the Treasury has, however, a good case to be considered the most neglected significant development in twentieth-century Irish history. Even before the coming of the welfare state to Northern Ireland under the Attlee government of 1945–51 – which is the subject of this excellent book by Russell Rees – senior Northern Irish nationalist politicians like Cahir Healy were aware that the availability of British social welfare provisions had a significant impact on the nationalist zeal of the Catholic minority. Of course, the more radical and generous provisions of the Attlee era had an even more marked impact, especially in contrast to the dramatic failures of the Irish economy in the mid-1950s. In April 1956, the *Irish Times* editorialist in Dublin mused that if the present trend continued, 'Ireland will die – not in the remote unpredictable future, but quite soon.' There is another side to the story.

This financial dependence made Stormont vulnerable to political pressures from London – in particular, after the election of Harold Wilson's government in 1964 which contained a number of cabinet ministers, including Wilson himself, who were fundamentally unsympathetic to Ulster Unionism. Richard Crossman, for example, recorded in his Cabinet diaries: 'Neither Jack Diamond (Chief Secretary to the Treasury 1964-70) nor the Chancellor knew the formula by which Northern Ireland gets its money. In all these years it has never been revealed to the politicians and I am longing to see whether we shall get to the bottom of this very large and expensive secret.' It was resentment of this 'very large and expensive secret' which explains Harold Wilson's famous attack on the Ulster Unionists in 1974 in his 'spongers' speech.

Two points arise from this history. The Treasury's financial support for Northern Ireland has played a major role in keeping it in the United Kingdom, surviving even the intensity of the recent IRA campaign – in part, at least, because all Dublin governments have been determined not to foot the bill which Whitehall has been picking up. Secondly, why did British governments not use their economic power to force Stormont to adopt a more accommodating stance towards the nationalist minority? This is the 'missed opportunity' to which Dr Rees refers in the subtitle of this important book.

This work, which is based on the highest standard of original documentary research, provides a full answer to this question. Everyone with a serious interest in modern Irish history will have to engage with the scholarship on display here. The reader, however, will find himself or herself reflecting, along with the author, about what might have been. *Labour and the Northern Ireland Problem 1945–1951: The Missed Opportunity* has a particular resonance at a moment when economic pressures have increased the reliance of the regions of the United Kingdom upon the centre. Russell Rees' timely book deserves a wide and engaged readership.

PAUL BEW
November 2008

Introduction

The return of a Labour government, with an overall majority for the first time, at the British general election in July 1945 created a certain degree of apprehension among members of the cabinet in Belfast. Unionists had traditionally been suspicious of the British Labour party, and the problems that its surprise election victory created for the Stormont government can be divided into three categories. Firstly, it was widely known that Clement Attlee's new government was firmly committed to the establishment of the welfare state and was intent on ensuring considerable state intervention in the economy. This placed the Unionist government in an awkward position. While it had shown little enthusiasm for the proposals contained in the Beveridge report and desired the prompt removal of as many government wartime economic controls as possible, it was difficult to see how Stormont could pursue an independent line without risking serious damage to its relations with the Labour government. Secondly, it seemed possible that the new Labour administration might want to take a closer look at the treatment of the province's Catholic minority. Since the formation of the Northern Ireland state, Westminster had occasionally been made aware of particular grievances such as the alleged gerrymandering of both parliamentary and local government constituencies, the operation of the Civil Authorities (Special Powers) Act and the financial discrimination imposed on Catholic schools, but successive London governments had avoided intervening directly to ensure that the province's substantial minority was not disadvantaged by any law passed in the Northern Ireland parliament.[1] The Unionist party regarded this as a sensitive area, and its fears that a new Labour home secretary might be anxious to examine existing Stormont legislation were increased when news of the formation of a 'Friends of Ireland' group of MPs within the parliamentary Labour party, interested in highlighting the minority's grievances in the province, reached Belfast. Finally, there was some speculation that Labour's election victory might threaten the province's constitutional position, as Unionist leaders in Belfast were concerned by the presence of a significant number of backbench Labour MPs who were sympathetic to the idea of a united Ireland. At the same time, moreover, they could not have failed to notice the boost that Labour's election success had given to the province's nationalist community. After partition nationalists in the North had consistently looked towards Dublin for direction, but following the 1945 general election there seemed a possibility that they might also receive encouragement from the new government at Westminster.

It was the partitioning of Ireland by the 1920 Government of Ireland Act that effectively created the Northern Ireland problem. Yet, in spite of its shortcomings, the 1920 act allowed Westminster to disentangle itself from Irish affairs, and this provided a sharp contrast to the 1868–1921 period, when Ireland was frequently at the centre of British politics. Responding to Gladstone's Irish initiative, the Conservatives had expended huge energy, time and money on Ireland, much more than on any other part of the United Kingdom, in trying to make the union work. When this failed, they took steps to ensure that Irish landlordism was generously compensated, principally through the 1903 Wyndham Land Act, before taking advantage of the great Protestant crusade against Home Rule. The Conservatives used the successive Home Rule crises to weaken their Liberal opponents, as they fought desperately to ensure that they survived as the anti-socialist challenger to the emerging Labour party. Once that had been achieved, the story of Ireland after 1921 from the Tory perspective was no longer dominated by imperialism, but by disinterest in Northern Ireland, and this was largely shared by its new Labour rival. From 1921 onwards, therefore, the authorities in London were relieved to transfer responsibility for maintaining stability in the North to the new Unionist government in Belfast. Differences with the rest of Ireland were settled by the signing of the Anglo-Irish Treaty in December 1921. Although difficulties between London and Dublin later emerged, particularly when Éamon de Valera was in office, the Treaty did at least provide a starting point for the peaceful evolution of Anglo-Irish relations.

David Lloyd George's resignation in October 1922 marked the abandonment by Westminster of any intention to promote the unification of Ireland, and the aim of British policy thereafter was to preserve the status quo. De Valera's move towards greater sovereignty for the South during the 1930s ensured that such an objective could not be achieved, and one consequence of this development was that Neville Chamberlain's government was forced to re-examine its approach to relations with the government in Dublin. The 1938 Anglo-Irish Agreement, which brought the economic war to an end, and the period of negotiations preceding the Agreement, provided the clearest example of the links between London, Dublin and Belfast in the inter-war period.[2] The concessions made by Westminster under the terms of the Agreement, in an attempt to secure Irish goodwill before a further deterioration in the European situation, resulted in a dramatic improvement in London–Dublin relations following six years of political and economic confrontation. At the same time, the thaw in Anglo-Irish relations had a negative impact in Northern Ireland, as the Belfast government's distrust of Westminster, which had been apparent since its formation, was increased. The Unionists always doubted a Westminster government's commitment to defend partition when faced with intense pressure from Dublin, and this partly explains their fear of intervention by a hostile administration in London. It was somewhat ironic, therefore, that the Unionist leadership consistently underestimated Westminster's capacity for disinterest in Northern Ireland affairs, and cabinet ministers at Stormont constantly looked over their shoulders for unwelcome interference from the authorities in London. Not surprisingly, this concern increased when Labour was in power. For this reason the 1945–51 period must be viewed as a missed opportunity. Gentle prodding from a more attentive Labour government could have nudged the Unionist administration towards reform, particularly if this had been linked to the generous financial treatment enjoyed by Stormont in the immediate post-war years.

The first chapter traces the development of relations in the triangle of London, Dublin and Belfast from 1921. An attempt is made to examine London's views on Northern Ireland during the inter-war years and to explain how domestic political considerations were primarily responsible for determining Westminster policy on Northern Ireland. In the South domestic political considerations also dominated the thinking of the main political parties on the Northern Ireland problem. While Éamon de Valera, in particular, never hesitated to use the existence of the border as a lever in his handling of relations with Britain, he was equally adept at using the partition issue to gain advantage over his political rivals at home, and this accounts for much of his anti-partition rhetoric during the 1930s. Subsequently, the Second World War brought about a transformation in triangular relations. Éire's decision to remain neutral during the war damaged its relations with London. Neutrality also highlighted Northern Ireland's strategic importance, while the North's participation in the war raised the province's standing in the minds of ministers and officials in London. Consequently, Stormont–Westminster relations improved dramatically during the war. Hitherto, relations between London and Belfast had been dogged by serious financial wrangling, as the Treasury stuck rigidly to the financial provisions of the Government of Ireland Act and refused to share responsibility for maintaining public spending in the province at the British level. This created chronic economic difficulties for the devolved administration, particularly in the depression years of the 1930s. As a result of the war, however, the Unionist government was able to secure major financial concessions from Westminster and lay the foundations for continued Treasury assistance in the post-war period. Crucially, it galvanized the Unionist party into life and prepared it for the radical changes that were inevitable after the war.

NOTES

1. See especially PROL, DO 35/893/X11/123, 'U.K.–Ireland Political and Constitutional Relations: Treatment of the Catholic minority in N. Ireland', and DO 35/893/X11/251, 'U.K.–Éire Political and Constitutional Relations: Allegations made by the Éire Government as to the maltreatment of the minority in Northern Ireland, arising out of the Partition Question', which contain information of Westminster's investigations into the treatment of the minority. See also P.Canning, *British Policy towards Ireland 1921–1941* (Oxford, 1985), pp.221–38.
2. For the Unionist government's reaction to the 1938 negotiations, see P. Buckland, *The Factory of Grievances: Devolved Government in Northern Ireland 1921–39* (Dublin, 1979), pp.110–16. For the Westminster government's view of the negotiations, see Canning, *British Policy towards Ireland*, pp.198–220, and for the Dublin government's view, see J. Bowman, *De Valera and the Ulster Question 1917–1973* (Oxford, 1982), pp.160–82.

1

Triangular Relations and the Northern Ireland Problem, 1921–45

The formal constitutional relationship between London and Belfast was established by the Government of Ireland Act. This partitioned Northern Ireland from the remaining twenty-six counties and set up a regional government and parliament for the province. Under this scheme of devolution the new parliament was prevented from legislating on some of Northern Ireland's internal affairs by several provisions included in the act. A significant limitation was contained in section 5 of the 1920 act, which prohibited the local parliament from making laws interfering with religious liberty or equality. The intention here was to prevent a future Unionist government from enacting legislation that disadvantaged the Catholic minority. Westminster also retained certain powers to enable the mother parliament to legislate for both Great Britain and Northern Ireland on matters where uniformity was considered essential, and these 'excepted' services included matters of defence and trade agreements with foreign states. Other powers withheld by Westminster were known as 'reserved' services, the most important of which concerned the levying of income tax. Out of the province's revenue the regional government was required by section 23 of the act to pay a contribution towards imperial expenditure, and this was known as the imperial contribution. Finally, the 1920 act appeared to copper-fasten London's control, as section 75 decreed that in all cases the Northern Ireland parliament would be subordinate to the Westminster parliament. This meant, in theory, that any law passed by the regional parliament could be annulled by the imperial parliament instructing the governor to reserve the royal assent. Therefore, the Government of Ireland Act imposed formal restrictions on the powers of Northern Ireland's new parliament, and section 75 suggested that those powers which were transferred to the local parliament might be subject to close supervision by Westminster. In fact, such scrutiny of the new parliament and government did not take place, because successive Westminster governments were content to see responsibility for the administration of the province rest with the authorities in Belfast. By refusing to assert its authority, however, Westminster failed to ensure that the province's new government would act impartially. Such an outcome may have been impossible to achieve in the political climate of the early 1920s, but Westminster's reluctance to intervene in Northern Ireland affairs made the prospect of responsible, impartial government even more unlikely.

The 1920 act also failed to encourage the province's minority to participate in the new political process in Northern Ireland and, from the outset, it was clear that the nationalist community did not want to be part of the new state. This fundamental rejection of partition explains why Nationalist representatives refused to take their seats in the Northern Ireland parliament for prolonged spells during the inter-war period. Trapped in such a politically hostile environment where they would probably always be in a minority, it was natural for the nationalist population in the North to look towards Dublin, not only for leadership and direction, but also for protection. The Ulster Unionists, on the other hand, who had not requested the establishment of a regional parliament, quickly appreciated that it offered the greatest security against any attempt by either London or Dublin to remove partition. Under the leadership of Sir James Craig, who became the province's first prime minister in June 1921, the Unionist party lost little time in erecting the institutions necessary for governing the province. The entrenchment of longstanding religious divisions and the obvious lack of political consensus also made it difficult for a non-sectarian party such as the Northern Ireland Labour Party (NILP) to make political headway. When the very existence of the state was the major issue facing voters in all Northern Ireland elections, class issues struggled for attention. In the 1920s there was evidence that social problems were important within each sectarian bloc, but the abolition of PR for parliamentary elections in 1929 became another obstacle to the development of more normal politics in the province.

Perhaps, not surprisingly, the general view of the main political parties in the rest of Ireland was that the British government had created an artificial state in the North, and responsibility for abolishing partition rested with the administration in London. Yet within this context there was room for considerable flexibility in the parties' approaches to their relations with Westminster, and in their attitudes to the Unionist government in Belfast. Indeed, there was a marked contrast between the two main parties in the South for most of the inter-war period. The pro-treaty party, which for the period 1923–33 was known as Cumann na nGaedheal, and thereafter as Fine Gael, enjoyed relatively close relations with Britain, and the party's leader, W.T. Cosgrave, was regarded as a moderate on the partition issue. While they occasionally made the expected noises on the border question, Cumann na nGaedheal leaders soon realized that they did not have the means to alter the situation, and, consequently, the issue received little serious attention from the party. Fianna Fáil, on the other hand, took a more uncompromising line on the border and managed to exploit both the continuation of partition and the Irish Free State's membership of the Commonwealth for electoral gain in the twenty-six counties. Its leader, Éamon de Valera, was regarded as a hawk on the border question, and his more strident anti-partition rhetoric increased tension between Belfast and Dublin. The other main factor to influence the attitude of the two main parties towards Northern Ireland concerned the mistreatment of the Catholic minority by the Unionist government. While this may have led to a hardening of views on the partition issue at certain times, and resulted in representations being made to the authorities in London, both Fianna Fáil and Cumann na nGaedheal found that there was little either could do to offer real protection to the isolated nationalist community in the North.

The position of the province's Catholic minority received little attention in London, where the main political parties appeared to share the common objective of distancing themselves, as far as possible, from the Ulster question. Naturally, this suited Ulster Unionists who were concerned that a future Liberal or Labour government at Westminster might threaten the province's new constitutional position. A leading Unionist insider, Captain Charles Craig, the MP for the Westminster constituency of South Antrim, had expressed this fear as early as March 1920 during the debate on the Government of Ireland Bill: 'We profoundly distrust the Labour party and we profoundly distrust the right hon. gentleman for Paisley (Herbert Henry Asquith, the Liberal leader). We believe that if either of those parties, or the two in combination, were once more in power our chances of remaining a part of the United Kingdom would be very small indeed.'[1]

This distrust of parliamentary parties at Westminster did not extend to the Conservatives, who had long been regarded by the Unionists as their natural allies. This alliance, forged in the struggle against Home Rule, had guaranteed the Unionists favourable treatment in the Government of Ireland Act, though they recognized the lack of enthusiasm which the majority of Conservative MPs seemed to have for partition.[2] Consequently, throughout the inter-war period doubts existed among Unionists about the willingness of even the Conservative party to mount a rigorous defence of the province's constitutional position, if it were ever seriously challenged by one of the other major parties at Westminster. While the Government of Ireland Act had guaranteed Unionist control over the new state, there was concern that the Conservative-dominated coalition government viewed the new arrangement as a temporary measure pending the establishment of a united Ireland. The provision made in section 2 (1) of the 1920 act for the establishment of a Council of Ireland only added to Unionist fears about Westminster's ultimate intentions. This partly explains why the authorities in Belfast always viewed talks between London and Dublin with great suspicion, even when the Conservative party was in power, because if anything important was being negotiated, it was likely that Dublin would raise the partition issue.

POLITICAL RELATIONS IN THE TRIANGLE, 1921-39

The establishment of two new states in Ireland, one the result of the Government of Ireland Act of December 1920 and the other the result of the Anglo-Irish Treaty of December 1921, created a new framework for the development of relations between the London, Dublin and Belfast governments. Initially, London's relations with both the Dublin and Belfast governments were handled by the Colonial Office, but this did not satisfy the Unionist government, which pressed for a separate channel of communication with the administration at Westminster. By the end of January 1923, Craig persuaded the new Conservative government that a different group of officials should handle relations with Northern Ireland, and, consequently, the Home Office was made responsible for all formal communication with the Belfast government.[3] In fact, by June 1925 following the creation of a new department, responsibility for the handling of Westminster's relations with the Irish Free State was transferred to the Dominions Office. This division of Irish relations subsequently became a source of friction within the administration in London. While the Home Office was generally sympathetic to the authorities in Belfast, officials at the Dominions Office were sometimes critical of the Unionist government's treatment of the minority, as it made their task of developing harmonious relations with Dublin more difficult. This formal separation of Westminster's relations with Belfast and Dublin eased some of the Unionist administration's fears, though in these early years it frequently relied on Craig's personal contact and friendship with ministers at Westminster to protect Northern Ireland's interests in London.[4] It was significant that in December 1922, when Craig decided that he should have a month's holiday, Winston Churchill's cousin, Lord Londonderry, the minister for education and a member of the Northern Ireland Senate, was appointed to act as prime minister, because he was 'so much in touch with Ministers in Great Britain'.[5]

Previously, Craig's nerve had been tested during the negotiations leading up to the Anglo-Irish Treaty, when the Irish delegation pressed British ministers on partition. As a result, article 12 of the Treaty provided for the establishment of a Boundary Commission, and though its wording was ambiguous, the Irish delegates left London confident that it would establish the basis for reunification.[6] The Boundary Commission clause reinforced the view that British politicians could not be trusted or relied upon to defend Northern Ireland's constitutional position, and it made Ulster Unionists even more determined to have no contact whatsoever with Dublin.[7] Nevertheless, Craig felt justified in travelling to London on 21 January 1922 for a meeting with Michael Collins, the chairman of the Provisional Government, in order to discover his future intentions towards Ulster and to determine the North's approach to Belfast–Dublin relations.[8] An earlier clandestine meeting with de Valera in Dublin on 5 May 1921 had proved fruitless, and the cool reception given to Craig on his return alerted him to the potential pitfalls in any dealing with the South.[9] Yet the Unionist leader was prepared to take another political gamble by meeting Collins at the Colonial Office in the early part of 1922. While the two leaders each had problems that could have been resolved by direct dialogue – one wanted better treatment for Catholic workers in the shipyard and the other an end to the economic boycott of northern goods in the South – Craig had wider concerns. Part of his motivation for meeting Collins was his desire to open a channel of communication with the South which might pre-empt an unwelcome London–Dublin initiative on partition. Indeed, the main proposal of the first Craig–Collins pact concerned the alteration of the Boundary Commission agreement in favour of direct consultation between Belfast and Dublin to settle the question of the border. Craig's pragmatism on the partition issue indicated that he might even be prepared to consider the possibility of unity at some point in the future, if this was deemed to be in the North's interests.[10] Back in Belfast the Unionist premier briefed his cabinet colleagues on the discussions, highlighting Collins' domestic difficulties and, consequently, his desire for good relations with the new Northern Ireland state.[11]

Although the first Craig–Collins pact collapsed amid confusion over each government's expectations in relation to partition, the upsurge of violence in the North caused Churchill to renew his efforts to broker a more sustainable

North–South deal. Accordingly, both leaders returned to the Colonial Office on 29–30 March, and their deliberations led to the conclusion of a second pact.[12] Again, reference was made to a resolution of the border issue through direct Belfast–Dublin talks, but the real purpose of the agreement was to end the fighting in the North. Collins had offered to halt IRA attacks in return for a Craig promise to provide protection for the province's Catholic minority, but the escalation of sectarian violence in April–May rendered the agreement irrelevant.[13] Indeed, any prospect of a further Craig–Collins deal was shattered by the outbreak of civil war in the South at the end of June 1922. The Irish Civil War undoubtedly eased the pressure on Ulster Unionists and ultimately forced the authorities in Dublin to reconsider their northern strategy. Although Collins had engaged in bilateral talks with Craig, it was apparent that the leader of the Provisional Government favoured a policy of non-recognition of the northern state and was committed to lobbying Westminster for an end to partition. Clear evidence of this non-recognition policy had occurred in February 1922, when the Provisional Government agreed to pay the salaries of all northern teachers who refused to recognize the Belfast Ministry of Education.[14] By the end of October 1922, however, the Provisional Government had decided to end these payments as part of a wider, more conciliatory northern policy. The onset of the Civil War in the South had helped to convince some members of the Provisional Government, notably Ernest Blythe, that, as there was no immediate prospect of unity, the only practical approach for Dublin to take in its relations with the North was to recognize the Belfast government and encourage the nationalist minority to co-operate with the Unionist administration.[15] Collins' death on 22 August 1922 had been the decisive factor in the abandonment of the Provisional Government's non-recognition policy. Had he lived, there is little doubt that the Belfast government would have faced serious pressure on the minority question.[16]

Of course, both the Civil War and the enormous problems of reconstruction facing the Cumann na nGaedheal government after the conflict had delayed the operation of the Boundary Commission. While Ulster Unionists remained nervous of the threat posed by the commission, particularly after Labour came to power in January 1924, the Cosgrave government only pressed for its establishment in the summer of 1924, once it became clear that the border issue could not be settled through direct dialogue with Belfast. Moreover, by the time the commission finally convened in October 1924, it was apparent that the authorities in Dublin did not expect a radical alteration of the new frontier. In the end, events conspired to cause serious embarrassment to the Cumann na nGaedheal administration. After almost a year's deliberation, during which evidence was taken from the population in the border area, the commission's report, recommending only minor changes of territory, was leaked to the press.[17] The 1925 agreement was a disaster for northern nationalists who had pinned their hopes on the Boundary Commission. The formal recognition of the border had signalled a shift in the Dublin government's northern strategy, a move that had undoubtedly been facilitated by Collins' death.

At the same time, the Belfast government's absolute refusal to consider any alteration of the new frontier appeared to have been vindicated by the conclusion of the Boundary Commission saga. Clearly, Unionist intransigence had paid off, and this success was to influence the Belfast administration in its future dealings with both Dublin and London. For their part the authorities at Westminster were evidently relieved that the 1925 agreement had closed an uncertain opening chapter in Anglo-Irish relations following the signing of the Treaty.

The years 1925–31 have been described as a period of 'relative quiescence' on the border question following an initial phase from 1921–25 when the very existence of the border was under threat.[18] During this period of calm the Irish Free State chose, by skilful and usually harmonious negotiation, to develop as a self-governing dominion independent of Westminster, rather than dwell on the partition issue.[19] This was to change in 1932, however, when Fianna Fáil came to power. In reopening the border question, de Valera also highlighted the Northern Ireland government's treatment of the minority, and this was to have an impact on Dublin–Westminster relations. Of course, both Dublin's hosting of the 1932 Eucharistic Congress and de Valera's brief entry into northern politics, when he won the South Down seat in the 1933 Northern Ireland election, added to the tension between Dublin and Belfast, though this merely clarified the issues for Ulster Unionists. This feeling was expressed by Lord Londonderry, who in 1933 reflected on de Valera's return to power: 'We are now faced by the more or less open opposition of a de Valera government instead of the somewhat doubtful friendship of a Cosgrave government, whose very existence and good will would probably depend entirely upon the concessions they could get from us.'[20]

Yet de Valera's real target was London, not Belfast, and his quest to dismantle the Treaty brought him into direct conflict with the authorities at Westminster. In the 1932 general election Fianna Fáil's manifesto had concentrated on just two issues: the abolition of the oath of allegiance and the withholding of land annuity payments which were due to the Treasury in London. Certainly, the prospect of a Fianna Fáil election victory had caused alarm at Westminster, where a decision was taken in March 1933 to establish an Irish Situation Committee, chaired by Ramsay MacDonald, the prime minister, which would oversee contact with Dublin.[21] Difficulties were anticipated, as a number of British ministers continued to regard de Valera as the renegade who had rejected the Treaty and plunged Ireland into civil war.[22]

The following years witnessed a deterioration in Anglo-Irish relations, as de Valera's decision to withhold the land annuity payments led to an economic war between the two countries. At the same time, Fianna Fáil efforts to dismantle the Treaty and seek greater independence for the Irish Free State revealed that the real source of the conflict was political, not economic. Of course, de Valera's uncompromising attitude brought electoral advantages at home, but the public image of an intransigent negotiator obscured the fact that he had adopted a gradualist, pragmatic approach in steering the Free State towards a republic. He was also an opportunist. The abdication crisis in 1936 allowed the Dáil to rush through the External Relations Act, and this together with the new Constitution in 1937 enabled Éire, as it was now called, to become a virtual republic with only a tenuous link to the Commonwealth.[23] De Valera's Constitution also caused great controversy in the North. While Article 2 claimed sovereignty over all thirty-two counties of Ireland, Article 3 recognized the de facto position of Northern Ireland by specifying that until Ireland was united, sovereignty would only apply to Éire. Prompted by Craigavon (Sir James had become Viscount Craigavon in 1927), Chamberlain publicly repudiated Éire's claims over the North, but the Westminster government refused Craigavon's demand for an assurance that London fully recognized 'Northern Ireland's constitutional right to remain part of the United Kingdom' and that it would, 'should occasion arise, give us any necessary assistance'.[24] Craigavon's government was also furious at the special position accorded to the Catholic Church in Article 44 of the new Constitution, and this was seized upon by Unionist propaganda to highlight the influence exerted by the Church on the state in Éire.

While the 1937 Constitution must have stiffened Unionist opposition to partition, it also presented the Belfast administration with the opportunity to divert attention from its economic troubles in the late 1930s and focus on the border issue. The Anglo-Irish economic war had seriously damaged the Northern Ireland economy, and Unionists knew that any attempt to resolve the outstanding issues would see the authorities in Dublin raise the partition issue. Initially, Craigavon had adopted a moderate stance, advising Westminster to avoid any action that might drive the South out of the Commonwealth.[25] Yet Unionists knew that when the time came to settle the dispute, the border issue would be on the negotiating table and they could never quite rely on Westminster's determination to resist southern pressure on partition. Still, Unionists frequently exaggerated their predicament. When Fianna Fáil took office in 1932, de Valera recognized that there was no short-term solution to the border question, and he publicly stated that his government was powerless to take effective action that might lead to an ending of partition. While the Belfast government took little notice of such statements, the Dominions Office in London quickly appreciated that de Valera viewed unity as a distant prospect.[26]

Although his strident anti-partition rhetoric was principally aimed at a home audience, de Valera was quick to use the existence of the border as a bargaining chip in negotiations with London, a strategy that had been unsuccessfully deployed by Sinn Féin during the Treaty negotiations in 1921. During the 1938 negotiations, which lasted from January until April and finally led to a settlement of the economic war, de Valera had set out four outstanding issues to be resolved. The Éire government had been satisfied with the outcome of the negotiations on the last three points, namely the settlement of the land annuities problem, the new trade agreement that ended the tariff war and, thirdly, the return of the ports, but no progress had been made on the question of partition, which de Valera had placed at the top of the agenda for discussion.[27] In fact, partition had strengthened de Valera's hand in the negotiations, as it allowed him to reject more unpalatable British suggestions on the grounds that London had failed to include any initiative to end partition. Although the dominions secretary at Westminster, Malcolm MacDonald, and many of his officials in the department believed that the long-term solution to the Anglo-Irish problem would rest on the removal of the border, he had stated as early as 1936 that unification could not be established 'without the consent of Northern as well as Southern

Ireland'.[28] While this principle was maintained during the 1938 negotiations, the prominence given to Northern Ireland's constitutional position naturally caused some unease among Unionist supporters in the province. Independent Unionist MPs, Tommy Henderson and John Nixon, criticized the Unionist government's complacency, claiming that the province's position was under threat,[29] but Craigavon had declined an invitation to the negotiations, much to Westminster's relief, and was content to rely on regular briefings by MacDonald.[30]

Elsewhere, the border played a significant role in southern politics. While de Valera could exploit partition in his dealings with Britain, he also had to consider Fianna Fáil's powerful republican flank. Undoubtedly, this accounted for de Valera's uncompromising public stance on the border question, but the ending of partition was never his primary concern. Indeed, civil servants in Dublin's Department of External Affairs could confirm that there had been no dramatic break in 1932, as the Fianna Fáil government merely carried on the work begun by the Cosgrave administration in developing Anglo-Irish relations to their logical conclusion.[31] The one recurring theme during this period was that de Valera made unity subordinate to his quest for sovereignty. Hence, little consideration was given to the impact that measures such as the 1936 External Relations Act and the 1937 Constitution would have in the North, or on the prospects for eventual unification. Furthermore, his decision to maintain Irish neutrality during the war confirmed that de Valera's priority would always be sovereignty, not unity.

FINANCIAL RELATIONS IN THE TRIANGLE, 1921–39

For much of the inter-war period financial relations in the London, Dublin, Belfast triangle created tension which complicated political relations. In particular, the new Northern Ireland government was frequently unable to persuade the Treasury in London to support the province through difficult economic periods. Constrained by the provisions of the Government of Ireland Act, which had originally been designed to apply to the South where more resistance to continued British rule was anticipated, the Unionist government found itself in serious trouble, especially during the early 1930s when unemployment rose sharply. Its firm adherence to the 'step-by-step' policy, which committed the Unionist administration to keeping pace with Britain in the provision of major cash social services, principally unemployment insurance, proved financially disastrous for the Belfast government.[32] The step-by-step policy was deemed a political necessity by a Unionist administration desperate to retain Protestant working-class support. An early indication of the government's nervousness on the social services issue occurred in 1922, when the minister of labour, J.M. Andrews, claimed that 'the "White Cross" Funds had been used to put Roman Catholic workers in a better position than their fellows of the Protestant faith'.[33] While this was highly unlikely, the decision to keep in step with unemployment benefit rates in Britain led Hugh McDowell Pollock, Northern Ireland's first minister for finance, to conclude at the end of 1923 that the province's Unemployment Fund was insolvent. A confident Craig reacted by informing his cabinet team that he expected Westminster to acknowledge the new state's difficulties and offer 'financial assistance in accordance with our requirements'.[34] The Unionist premier's optimism soon evaporated, as the Treasury consistently rebuffed his proposals for a complete revision of Northern Ireland's financial relations with Westminster.

Instead, two piecemeal solutions were brokered to overcome the Unionist government's short-term difficulties. In 1926 Westminster agreed to Northern Ireland's demand for a partial amalgamation of the two Unemployment Funds, but the agreement did not provide for any shortfall if the unemployment rate in Northern Ireland was higher than in Great Britain.[35] More significantly, the Colwyn Award of 1925 had enabled Northern Ireland to place expenditure on necessary services as the first charge on her revenue, leaving the imperial contribution to be based on the difference between revenue and actual expenditure.[36] As unemployment declined in the 1926–30 period, the financial pressure on the Northern Ireland exchequer eased, but problems subsequently arose as Belfast and London clashed on Colwyn's definition of the province's basic needs and how these should be met. Andrews was adamant that not only should the first charge on the province's revenue be the provision of services in step with Britain, leaving the balance to be forwarded as an imperial contribution, but also that Westminster should make a payment to meet the cost of these 'local needs' in difficult years.[37] In a letter to Craigavon in September 1931 Andrews supplemented his demand for what was, in effect, a 'minus' imperial contribution by proposing the full transfer of Northern Ireland's social services 'back to Westminster as reserved services ... lock, stock and barrel'. Indeed, as he explained to Craigavon, Andrews was experiencing major political difficulties in administering social services on a step-by-step basis with Westminster:

> ... my position is becoming so embarrassing as to be almost impossible, as equality means simply following Great Britain as regards legislation and administration no matter what Government is in power. It has meant that I have fathered the policy of two Unionist Governments, two Labour Governments, a Coalition Government, and now, if things continue as they are, a National Government ... To stand up and defend the policy of each in turn, especially very frequently holding different views one's [sic] self is, to put it mildly difficult, and yet to depart from equality would not only be unjust but would, in my opinion, lead to disaster.[38]

From 1931 both Craigavon and Andrews were to stress the importance of finding a permanent solution to Northern Ireland's financial woes, while they had 'friends' at Westminster in the form of a Conservative-dominated National government.[39] Both men were convinced that the 1929–31 Labour government had been hostile to Northern Ireland, with the chancellor, Philip Snowden, singled out by Craigavon as a bitter opponent of partition. His advice to his ministers was, therefore, to wait until the Conservatives had returned to power before presenting the province's case for an overhaul of the financial provisions in the 1920 act.[40] Professor Buckland has argued persuasively that such a view was misplaced, as Westminster's financial relationship with Northern Ireland was dominated by Treasury officials whose advice was rarely challenged by chancellors in the inter-war period, irrespective of their party label.[41]

The other obstacle facing Craigavon in negotiating a new financial settlement with Westminster was division within his own cabinet. While both he and Andrews wanted a new financial agreement with Westminster that would include provision for a minus imperial contribution in difficult years, Pollock and the influential Sir Wilfrid Spender, who in addition to his role as head of the civil service was also the permanent secretary to the Ministry of Finance, argued that a full amalgamation of the two Unemployment Funds would be sufficient to ease the financial pressure on the province. Moreover, as minister of finance, Pollock's chief concern during the 1930s was to balance his budget, and this required what Andrews described as begging expeditions to the Treasury.[42] Without reaching agreement on one line of policy, the Unionist government approached the Treasury early in 1934 for assistance to balance the previous year's budget. Andrews' demand for a comprehensive overhaul of financial relations was firmly rejected by the chancellor, Neville Chamberlain, forcing the Unionists to follow the Pollock–Spender piecemeal policy. In May 1935 the Treasury finally agreed to amalgamate the two funds, but would only pay for 75 per cent of the province's excess expenditure.[43] The new agreement meant that the Treasury was paying considerably more into the Northern Ireland exchequer, but Westminster refused to sanction the minus imperial contribution that Andrews still sought. Indeed, the Treasury's concession on the Unemployment Fund was only made after Pollock had given an undertaking that the school-leaving age in Northern Ireland would not be raised in line with Britain's, as it would prove too costly.[44] In the end, a combination of the 1936 Unemployment Reinsurance Agreement and an improving economy, which led to a small drop in the province's unemployment total, enabled Stormont to escape the embarrassment of financial insolvency, though the fear of bankruptcy in difficult years continued to haunt at least one wing of an ageing Unionist cabinet. While the Treasury recognized, on occasion, that the province's difficulties were not a result of excessive expenditure,[45] it was not prepared to alter the financial clauses of the 1920 act, which had failed to guarantee the province sufficient revenue to develop its social services in line with the rest of the United Kingdom. In such circumstances, Stormont's dogged commitment to the step-by-step policy, the school-leaving age apart, both exacerbated Northern Ireland's financial difficulties and stifled debate within the Unionist party on a wide range of social and economic issues.

Further damage to the Northern Ireland economy was caused by the Anglo-Irish economic war that had broken out following Fianna Fáil's election victory. Pollock had informed the Treasury in January 1934 that the Free State's retaliatory duties were hitting the province's trade with the South, but he had refused to press for special treatment from the Treasury as this might embarrass the chancellor in his conflict with Dublin.[46] Such goodwill was seldom reciprocated by a Westminster government that frequently ignored Northern Ireland's interests in its attempts to find a solution to the economic war. During the negotiations in 1938 the Stormont authorities highlighted the fall in trade during the economic war, claiming that in 1924 the province's exports and re-exports to the South were valued at £7,853,000, but by 1936 the comparable figure was down to £1,636,000.[47] In the previous month, when it emerged that de Valera was unwilling to accept free trade between Éire and the United Kingdom, Stormont had continued to press for free trade between the North and South. De Valera's subsequent rejection of free trade within Ireland presented the Unionist government with a dilemma. While Craigavon was anxious to help Chamberlain, the new prime minister, bring the trade war with Dublin to a conclusion, both Andrews, who had succeeded Pollock as minister of finance, and Sir Basil Brooke, the minister of agriculture, had threatened to resign if Westminster failed to secure more favourable trade terms for the province. Accordingly, the Stormont cabinet informed Westminster that it objected to the whole character of the proposed Anglo-Éire trade agreement. While Éire would be given free entry to the United Kingdom market for most of her goods, she would retain the power to impose protective tariffs against competition from United Kingdom-manufactured goods. Naturally, this would prolong the province's trade difficulties with the South and, as the Stormont memorandum suggested, would give the Fianna Fáil government 'the means of bringing further economic pressure on Northern Ireland'. Although the phrase, 'to throw in her lot with Éire', was deleted from the original draft, it was clear that the Unionist government felt a sense of betrayal, and its position was further undermined by Craigavon's personal assurance to the authorities at Westminster that Stormont would support a new trade agreement, provided the province received adequate economic compensation in other areas.[48]

Craigavon's move had forced his government's hand on the trade negotiations, and an indication of Unionist unhappiness at Northern Ireland's treatment in the Anglo-Irish Agreement, signed on 25 April 1938, came when Craigavon, in a speech at Stormont, outlined the concessions won by the province.[49] As prime minister, Craigavon was more exposed than his ministers to Westminster pressure for Stormont to take a less parochial view and consider the wider United Kingdom interest when assessing the detail of the trade agreement. In return for his support the Unionist government was promised a greater share of defence spending, though there was no mention of specific contracts. Previously, the Stormont administration had expressed its frustration at the province's poor share of rearmament work, particularly when the potential of the shipyard was considered.[50] A second concession, Craigavon told the local parliament, was that Westminster would assume responsibility for the payment of agricultural subsidies to Northern Ireland farmers.[51] Thirdly, the Northern Ireland premier reported that he had secured an improvement to the 1936 Unemployment Reinsurance Agreement. Under its terms the Treasury had agreed to cover any debt up to £1 million, but in 1938 it agreed to meet any debt, no matter how large. This appeared to be a significant concession, because by 1938 the prospective unemployment deficit was £1.7 million, though the Treasury probably realized that it would have to pay the deficit in any case.[52] Obviously, the Anglo-Irish negotiations in the early months of 1938 had given Stormont the opportunity to renew its demand for increased assistance from the Treasury, and Craigavon sought a formal guarantee that London would meet any Stormont budget deficit that was not the result of a higher standard of social services or a lower level of taxation.[53] This was, of course, precisely what the Treasury had refused at critical points during the 1930s, but by agreeing to the Simon Declaration, named after Sir John Simon, then serving as chancellor of the exchequer in the National Government, Westminster had finally removed Stormont's fear of bankruptcy during some future economic crisis. Craigavon tried to use the Simon Declaration to sell the Anglo-Irish Agreement to his supporters, but the Treasury did not regard it as a significant concession in the changed circumstances of 1938. In fact, the Treasury readily agreed to the terms of the Simon Declaration. With taxation at such a high level to fund the rearmament programme, which was not charged to the Northern Ireland exchequer, the Treasury could confidently predict that 'Northern Ireland is likely to have a handsome surplus for as long as we can foresee.'[54]

In his Stormont speech, however, Craigavon indicated that he took a much wider view of the Simon Declaration. Looking ahead to the possibility of a reduction in United Kingdom taxation rates or to the expansion of social services on the mainland, either of which would seriously reduce any surplus for the province's exchequer, Craigavon insisted that Westminster now recognized this difficulty and had agreed to 'make good this deficit' so that Northern Ireland would 'enjoy the same social services and have the same standards as Great Britain'.[55] For the Unionist government this meant that the province could now follow a 'parity' policy, keeping social services exactly equal to Britain's, in the knowledge that Westminster would provide the finance necessary to sustain such a policy.[56] By extension, the Unionist government assumed that the Simon Declaration would enable it to close the gap, where it existed, between social service provision in Great Britain and Northern Ireland. Yet any such move would require Treasury approval, and as the authorities in London refused to accept that the province had any leeway to make up, Craigavon's optimism was clearly misplaced. In fact, the real impact of the Simon Declaration was only felt after the war, when it became a useful bargaining chip in the Unionist administration's campaign to share in the enormous increases in social services expenditure introduced by the Labour government. This was not foreseen in 1938, however, and the concessions gained by Craigavon in return for Northern Ireland's support of the Anglo-Irish Agreement were of little significance. Indeed, the trade settlement had a detrimental effect on the province's economy, because in the seven months after April 1938 Éire's exports northwards increased by 28 per cent, whereas Northern Ireland's exports southwards actually decreased by 6 per cent.[57] Disgruntled Unionists accused Craigavon of failing to defend the province's interests, and the Unionist premier's position was further undermined by the favourable treatment given to Dublin. The headline news from the Anglo-Irish Agreement was the return of the Treaty ports, but the British also accepted Éire's recommendation on the land annuity payments, and it had been Dublin's decision to withhold these payments that had started the trade war in 1932. Not surprisingly, Chamberlain's decision to offer such concessions to an intransigent de Valera in the hope of putting Anglo-Irish relations on a new footing has been viewed as a development of Chamberlain's general policy of appeasement.[58]

STORMONT, WESTMINSTER AND THE NORTHERN MINORITY, 1921–39

This desire to improve relations with Dublin meant that the authorities at Westminster frequently ignored Stormont's claims for special treatment. Spender had previously warned his political masters that this was likely to happen, as the Treasury informed him that it would not be responsible for protecting Northern Ireland's interests in any forthcoming negotiations with Dublin.[59] Indeed, a number of key officials at Westminster were openly hostile to the Unionist administration. In December 1937, just before negotiations had commenced, Sir Harry Batterbee, an assistant under-secretary at the Dominions Office, suggested that the abolition of the border should be included in the forthcoming settlement. Although his minister, Malcolm MacDonald, did not pursue this policy during the negotiations, he was determined that Stormont would not be an obstacle to any agreement between London and Dublin. The Treasury was equally unsympathetic. The permanent secretary, Sir Warren Fisher, who had clashed repeatedly with the Unionist administration when it sought financial assistance, was adamant that the answer to Northern Ireland's economic problems lay in the ending of partition. While Chamberlain and MacDonald rejected de Valera's demand for the removal of the border during the 1938 talks, the Unionist government was correct in thinking that support for the province at Westminster was less than enthusiastic. The Anglo-Irish Agreement highlighted Stormont's weakness and demonstrated that Northern Ireland's interests would always be subordinate to Westminster's.[60] Meanwhile, de Valera's natural desire to make political capital out of Éire's victory in 1938 brought further embarrassment to the Unionist administration. His subsequent, and unconnected, release of a number of IRA prisoners drew an untypical response from Spender, who was clearly dismayed at British concessions to Éire: 'Mr. De Valera has decided to celebrate the new Treaty by granting an amnesty to murderers and other political offenders of the first degree. This is not an unsuitable method of emphasising the surrender of the British Government.'[61] Spender's frustration with Westminster highlighted the problems facing Stormont in 1938. Any attempt by the government in London to improve relations with Dublin, something which Chamberlain was keen to foster before the political situation in Europe became even more unstable, presented the Éire government with an opportunity to attack Stormont and undermine partition. De Valera was particularly skilful at exploiting such an opportunity.

Outright opposition to partition, which frequently manifested itself in militant anti-partition rhetoric, was, of course, a central tenet of Fianna Fáil ideology. In terms of practical policy the clearest expression of Fianna Fáil's attitude to the North had appeared in the 1937 Constitution. While the Constitution may only have eased the party's conscience on the border issue, it lifted the spirits of the province's Catholic minority which was always grateful to learn that its plight remained a serious issue for the authorities in Dublin. Yet de Valera enjoyed a curious relationship with the nationalist community in the North. Once in power he made no attempt to forge closer links with the minority, and in 1933 he flatly rejected a request from Joe Devlin and Cahir Healy, the two leading northern Nationalist MPs, for admission to Dáil Éireann.[62] Although he kept them at arm's length, northern Nationalists continued to look towards de Valera for political leadership, and he recognized that the 1938 negotiations with Chamberlain gave Dublin its best opportunity since the Boundary Commission shambles to make representations on behalf of the nationalist minority. Previously, such representations made little impact in London, but the situation was very different in 1938 with Westminster actively seeking to open a new chapter in Anglo-Irish relations. In London, meanwhile, the Dominions Office showed most concern at de Valera's attack on the Unionist government's record, as it believed that Stormont's treatment of the minority weakened Westminster's negotiating position in its dealings with Dublin. Some officials at the Dominions Office, notably Batterbee, were forthright in their condemnation of the Unionist government's handling of the minority question. Moreover, Craigavon's decision to call a Northern Ireland general election in February 1938 was regarded by the Dominions Office as an unwelcome attempt to put pressure on the Westminster authorities at a critical stage of the negotiations.[63] In spite of the concerns expressed by the Dominions Office, other key Whitehall departments were reluctant to become directly involved in the province's affairs.

Craigavon's early promises of impartiality were soon broken, as the Unionist premier failed to carry the more extreme members of his cabinet who viewed all nationalists as disloyal. In particular, the new government's draconian security policy discriminated against the Catholic minority. The reliance on the Ulster Special Constabulary, particularly the 'B' Specials, and the application of the Civil Authorities (Special Powers) Act, which was used almost exclusively against Catholics, outraged the nationalist minority in the North. As early as July 1922 Sir Stephen Tallents, who had been appointed as the imperial government's representative in Northern Ireland, ominously observed that feeling against the Specials was more bitter than it had been against the Black and Tans.[64] In spite of such warnings, little attempt was made by the authorities in London to intervene on behalf of the minority in Northern Ireland. While they had some reservations about the conduct of the Unionist government, most observers at Westminster assumed that Craigavon was a moderate who acted as a bulwark against his more extreme followers.[65] Indeed, their one attempt to intervene on behalf of the minority had proved embarrassingly unsuccessful and served as a warning to future Westminster administrations about the pitfalls of meddling in Northern Ireland affairs. In 1922 the Lloyd George government attempted to thwart the Unionist administration's decision to abolish PR in local government elections by withholding the royal assent to the 1922 Local Government Bill. An impasse followed, with the Belfast government refusing to withdraw its proposals and threatening to resign if the bill did not become law. As the obvious alternative would have been for Westminster to impose direct rule, something which the authorities in London were desperate to avoid, the controversial measure was waved through as Westminster backed down.[66]

Of course, some distinction must be made between the political and legal constraints on the Northern Ireland government. Politically, Westminster could only persuade, threaten or bribe the regional government, but legally, if a

Northern Ireland bill was thought to contravene the 1920 act, the authorities in London could determine its validity by reference to the Judicial Committee of the Privy Council. In the inter-war period the Home Office had considered referring both the 1925 and the 1930 Education Bills to the Judicial Committee, because it was felt that they contravened section 5 of the 1920 act which dealt with the protection of minorities. Yet, in spite of the very real doubts surrounding the legal validity of the province's education legislation, the Home Office decided to steer clear of such a contentious issue, and neither the 1925 nor the 1930 Education Bill was referred. Accordingly, by the 1930s the province's education system was clearly discriminating in favour of Protestants.[67] Similarly, although both the use of the 'B' Specials and the operation of the Special Powers Act were unpopular with successive Westminster governments, little serious effort was made to restrain the Unionist administration in its policy towards the minority. An obvious reason for Westminster's acquiescence in the mistreatment of the minority was the absence of effective opposition in Britain to the government's non-intervention policy. Only the Liberal and Labour press voiced any criticism, but this was insufficient to influence government policy. Instead, the key influence on the government's Irish policy in the inter-war years came from the right in the form of the Die Hards, a recalcitrant group of reactionaries who, having been infuriated by what they regarded as the surrender to Sinn Féin leaders during the Treaty negotiations in 1921, were determined to safeguard Ulster's interests at Westminster.[68] In the critical formative years, when the continued existence of Northern Ireland was still open to considerable doubt, the activities of this powerful right-wing pressure group proved to be of valuable assistance to the Unionist government.[69] In short, domestic political considerations at Westminster, in the shape of Die Hard influence, ensured that the Belfast government would be forced neither to accept some form of unification nor to moderate its policy towards the Catholic minority.

Thus, the Northern Ireland policies of both the Conservative and Labour governments during the inter-war period were indistinguishable. Both MacDonald and Stanley Baldwin, the Conservative leader from 1923–37, shared a mutual interest in keeping such a potentially divisive issue out of British politics.[70] Crucially, the activities of the Die Hards also influenced the government's larger Irish policy. When the economic war broke out following Fianna Fáil's election success in 1932, Churchill and the Die Hards ensured that a firm line was taken with de Valera. It was not until Chamberlain had become prime minister in 1937 that the British made a determined effort to break the deadlock in London–Dublin relations and secure some sort of agreement with de Valera. Growing instability in Europe had rendered the settlement of difficulties with Éire more urgent, and, in his eagerness to remove one sphere of difficulty for Britain, Chamberlain was prepared to make generous concessions to the Dublin government. When negotiations opened, de Valera's concentration on the issue of partition aroused real interest in Northern Ireland affairs. A number of leading newspapers carried investigative articles on the province, and most were forthright in their condemnation of the Northern Ireland government.[71] Although the British emphasized from the outset that there could be no question of any form of coercion against Northern Ireland, de Valera's persistent allegations against the Unionist government's mistreatment of the Catholic minority raised fears among the British that he might use the issue as an excuse for breaking off the talks.[72]

Still, the Irish leader's persistence did have some effect at Westminster, because in March 1938, while the negotiations were still in progress, the authorities in London decided to examine the claims made against the Unionist government.[73] This involved an investigation by both the Home Office and the Dominions Office, focusing primarily on allegations about the gerrymandering of both local and parliamentary constituencies in Northern Ireland. The Home Office had previously examined such claims in 1924. Although it concluded that the Unionists had secured obvious advantages following the 1922 Local Government Act, it had defended the Belfast government by arguing that the minority had brought this upon itself by its refusal to participate in the redrawing of the new electoral areas.[74] In 1938 the Home Office could only offer the same defence for the action taken by the Unionist government. C.G. Markbreiter, an assistant secretary, justified the action taken by arguing: 'It is of course obvious that Northern Ireland is, and must be, a Protestant "state", otherwise it would not have come into being and would certainly not continue to exist.' Similarly, Markbreiter dismissed the claim that nationalists suffered from discrimination in public employment. While he recognized that discrimination against Catholics did occur in private employment, Markbreiter stressed that the Stormont government did its best to protect the minority from this, though in some instances it was powerless.[75] Not surprisingly, the Dominions Office took a different line, and both Batterbee and J.E. Stephenson, an assistant secretary, prepared minutes for the Dominions Office. Stephenson generally adopted the Home Office line, believing that ministers at Westminster had been unduly impressed by de Valera's allegations about the gerrymandering of constituencies and the treatment of the minority.[76] The more senior Batterbee, on the other hand, was critical of the Unionist government. In assessing the allegations of gerrymandering, Batterbee dismissed the argument that the nationalist boycott of the commission established to redraw local government boundaries absolved the Unionist government of responsibility for the end result. He was also frustrated by the lack of information being provided by the Home Office.[77]

Further evidence of the Dominions Office's uneasiness emerged when the department's parliamentary secretary, Lord Hartington, concluded that while many of the charges made against the Stormont government were exaggerated, de Valera's allegations had not been without justification. Despite his obvious reservations, and despite Batterbee's promptings, Hartington decided against 'pressing the Home Office further at the moment', but, significantly, he added: 'I think that they are beginning to wake up to the fact that the situation wants careful watching!'[78]

Though its impact was clearly limited, de Valera's criticism of Stormont's treatment of the minority had aroused some concern at Westminster. Evidence of this emerged in November 1938, when a more detailed investigation into de Valera's allegations was undertaken. On this occasion the Home Office was to provide the Dominions Office with minutes on four subjects: the question of whether the province was being maintained by Westminster subsidies; gerrymandering; discrimination against the minority in public employment; and, finally, discrimination against the minority in education.[79] In general, the Dominions Office accepted Home Office arguments on education, finance and discrimination, though, on the last issue, Batterbee noted that in the area of local government employment Unionist-controlled councils rarely employed Catholics.[80] However, it was on the gerrymandering issue that serious concerns were raised. Here, even the Home Office conceded that in the establishment of local government constituencies, 'there may be a grievance'.[81]

The Home Office memorandum included a note by Adrian Robinson, an assistant secretary in the Northern Ireland Ministry of Home Affairs, who admitted that political considerations had governed decisions on local government areas taken by the Belfast authorities. Again, Robinson justified these actions by pointing to the nationalist boycott of the Leech Commission. Indeed, the Dominions Office gained a further insight into Stormont thinking when Robinson added a one-line postscript, which was later deleted, saying: 'When they (the Roman Catholics) do behave like reasonable human beings they get a fair crack of the whip.'[82] Naturally, Batterbee registered his disapproval of this gerrymandering and claimed that on this point 'Dev has justice on his side.'[83]

In his concluding remarks Batterbee attempted to highlight what he saw as a major problem for the Craigavon government:

> To sum up – except as regards gerrymandering the Home Office put up a fairly good case. There is no reason to suppose that there is deliberate injustice to the Catholics on the part of the Government. But as Stephenson points out in his minute, the bias of the Northern Irish authorities is bound to be in favour of those who are supporters of the present regime; it is everywhere inimical to good and impartial administration where Government and Party are so closely united as in Northern Ireland. In the South, Mr. de Valera was at one time largely dependent on the I.R.A. for support, but he has been able to throw off his dependence on that body – in a way in which the Government of Northern Ireland have not been able to throw off their dependence on the Orange Lodges.

Perhaps even more significantly, he sounded the following warning:

> If the Government of Northern Ireland wish partition to continue, they must make greater efforts than they have made at present to win over the Catholic minority, just as on his side Mr. de Valera, if he wishes to end partition, can only do so by winning over the Northern Protestants. At present both sides are showing a lamentable lack of statesmanship and foresight.[84]

Nevertheless, in spite of these reservations, the authorities in London refused to press the Unionist government on its treatment of the Catholic minority. Batterbee himself offered one explanation for such caution, when he stressed that intervention by Westminster could only follow a detailed impartial enquiry which, he conceded, was 'impracticable'. To improve the situation he hoped that the forthcoming appointment of a United Kingdom representative in Dublin would provide the Dominions Office with an independent assessment of the Belfast government's actions.[85] Although there was an obvious reluctance on Westminster's part to intervene directly in the province, the events of 1938 suggested that the Stormont administration could expect, thereafter, to come under greater scrutiny, particularly in relation to its treatment of the minority. Much of the credit for this apparent change of emphasis must go to de Valera, who skilfully exploited the maltreatment of the Catholic minority in his handling of Anglo-Irish relations. By the end of 1938 even the Home Office was alive to the need for closer supervision of the Unionist government, as Westminster sought to build on the progress made in its relations with Dublin. It was also true, of course, that the Stormont government felt that its position had been undermined both by the recent Anglo-Irish Agreement and by the general improvement in London–Dublin relations. Certainly, by the end of 1938, the outlook for Northern Ireland could only be described as bleak. The prospect of a deterioration in Stormont–Westminster relations seemed likely, and some form of intervention in the province's internal affairs could not be ruled out.

By focusing on Stormont's treatment of the minority during the 1938 negotiations de Valera had demonstrated to the administration in London that it could no longer afford to ignore the predicament of nationalists in Northern Ireland. Clearly, de Valera had established a good working relationship with Chamberlain, though the Irish leader was keen to stress that there could be 'no real reconciliation between Ireland and Britain while the unity of Ireland was being prevented'.[86] Naturally, de Valera's success in highlighting the plight of the northern minority had raised expectations of an end to partition among that community. Yet, as one historian of northern nationalism has noted, the province's Nationalist leaders were left frustrated by de Valera's performance in 1938.[87] While the Fianna Fáil leader had proved very effective in exploiting the maltreatment of the northern minority, he made no progress on the central issue of partition. Moreover, the taoiseach's attitude in 1938 identified him as the archetypal 'scientific republican'. For de Valera the removal of the border was inevitable. Unity was Ireland's destiny, and the laws of history meant that Irishmen only had to wait for Britain to right the wrong done to their country in 1921. Such a view encouraged the negative spirit of intellectual and political complacency evident in Dublin and allowed de Valera and other party leaders in the South to ignore the need for a more constructive northern policy, which might have seen the Dublin government working with Westminster to reach an accommodation with Unionism.

THE IMPACT OF THE WAR ON TRIANGULAR RELATIONS

Any trends that had been established by the end of 1938 proved to be short-lived, as the war fundamentally altered the balance of relations in the London–Dublin–Belfast triangle. The Fianna Fáil government's determination to stay neutral in the conflict meant that the Royal Navy was denied access to the three Treaty ports that had been returned to Dublin under the terms of the 1938 Anglo-Irish Agreement. Each attempt by the British government to entice or pressurize de Valera into conceding the use of these naval bases met with failure. Initial frustration at Éire's stand turned to anger when Churchill became prime minister and British shipping losses in the north Atlantic mounted. Even after the war Churchill continued to criticize the decision to relinquish control of the ports, claiming that many lives were 'lost as a result of this improvident example of appeasement'.[88] At certain points, particularly in the 1940–1 period, when British pressure for the use of the bases intensified, relations between Britain and Éire became very strained. However, Churchill's bullying impetuosity was partially offset by the diplomatic skills of Sir John Loader Maffey, later Lord Rugby, who was appointed United Kingdom representative to Éire in September 1939. He had the necessary qualities of understanding, discretion and patience which did much to ease the tension in London–Dublin relations. In the summer of 1940 Westminster dispatched Malcolm MacDonald, the minister of health, who had established an excellent relationship with the Irish leader when he was at the Dominions Office, to conduct new negotiations with de Valera on the use of the ports. When de Valera countered with the argument that the continuation of partition made closer co-operation with Britain impossible, MacDonald was instructed to offer a United Ireland as bait for Dublin's release of the bases. To Churchill's frustration, however, de Valera refused to be drawn by such an uncertain prospect of eventual reunification which failed to specify precisely how inevitable Ulster opposition would be overcome.[89] Nevertheless, sufficient evidence exists to conclude that even a cast-iron guarantee on the removal of the border would have failed to move de Valera on neutrality. Éire's neutrality was not the result of partition. Instead, de Valera's priority was to use the 'Emergency', as the period of the Second World War was known in the South, to establish the undisputed independence of the twenty-six counties, and he steadfastly refused to risk Éire's sovereignty by abandoning neutrality in search of unity. Not surprisingly, de Valera's repeated rejections of Westminster's advances enraged Churchill and placed a further strain on London–Dublin relations. The British prime minister subsequently challenged the Éire government's resolve in December 1941, when the United States entered the war. This was the occasion of Churchill's dramatic telegram to de Valera: 'Now is your chance. Now or Never. A Nation once again. Am very ready to meet you at any time'. Such a vague and impulsive offer of unification, if it even was that, failed, once again, to dent de Valera's intransigence.[90] Yet the American entry into the war increased the pressure on the Dublin government. When large numbers of American troops began to arrive in Northern Ireland in 1942, the taoiseach expressed his outrage at the American occupation, claiming that it represented 'an official sanction by the United States of the partition of Ireland'.[91] De Valera's prickly approach infuriated the new American minister to Ireland, David Gray, who adopted an increasingly anti-Éire stance as the war progressed. Within two months of his appointment in April 1940 a hostile Gray had become convinced that de Valera would not sacrifice neutrality, even in return for the ending of partition.[92] For the remainder of the war the notoriously indiscreet American diplomat participated in a series of initiatives, each designed to embarrass the Fianna Fáil government and swing public opinion in the United States against Éire. He was equally anxious, moreover, to ensure that there was little sympathy in America for any post-war anti-partition campaign led by de Valera.[93] In the end, Gray's efforts failed to destabilize the Dublin government, and the Emergency marked a resounding personal triumph for de Valera, who showed real political skill in resisting British and American pressure to end Éire's neutrality.

The Allied invasion of Europe eased much of the pressure on the Fianna Fáil government, but when the war did end, the angry verbal exchange between Churchill and de Valera brought Anglo-Irish relations, at least on the surface, to a new low.[94] Churchill had been unable to contain his anger following the taoiseach's action in paying a visit of condolence to the German legation in Dublin on the announcement of Hitler's death. In spite of de Valera's scrupulous devotion to neutrality, however, the truth was that Éire's neutrality favoured the Allies. There was a high degree of co-operation between the authorities in London and Dublin, most of which went unnoticed. In military terms there was close collaboration on intelligence matters, while joint preparations for the repulsion of a possible German invasion had resulted in the formulation of the secret 'W' Plan, whereby British soldiers could be rushed into Éire to assist the Irish armed forces.[95] More practically, RAF pilots were permitted to fly over the 'Donegal corridor' in their missions to protect convoys in the north Atlantic, and pilots who came down in neutral Éire could expect to be slipped secretly back across the border.[96] Éire also made a significant contribution to Britain's wartime economy. The export of food to Britain rose sharply, and the Fianna Fáil government took a number of steps to provide a flow of war workers, all with travel permits issued by officials in Dublin, to fill vacancies in British factories.[97] This was, of course, in addition to the large numbers who joined the British armed forces. To ensure that this benevolent neutrality was not compromised the Fianna Fáil government ruthlessly suppressed all IRA activity in the South. Large numbers of suspects were interned at the Curragh, and six volunteers were executed, while a further three died on hunger strike.[98] Meanwhile, every effort was made to frustrate IRA attempts at collusion with the Nazis, and German spies, who had been dropped by parachute into Ireland, were quickly hunted down.[99] Yet the impression conveyed to the Irish public was that Éire was scrupulously neutral during the Emergency. This had been the objective of the rigorous censorship operation, presided over by Frank Aiken, the minister for defence in the Fianna Fáil government. The assistance given to Britain received little publicity, as de Valera successfully concealed his pro-British sympathies. Any other course would have created deep political divisions in the South, but it is also possible to argue that friendly neutrality was more beneficial to Britain than Éire's participation in the war, which would have given the British extra coastline to defend.

The successful policy of neutrality had demonstrated Éire's independence, but one consequence of this had been to make partition more entrenched. This offered the Stormont government an opportunity to recover some of the ground lost in 1938. With no access to the Treaty ports Northern Ireland assumed great strategic importance in the struggle to keep open the shipping lanes between Britain and North America. As the most westerly port in the British Isles, Derry became vitally important during the Battle of the Atlantic, when it was used as a base for convoy escorts. Not surprisingly, Unionist leaders emphasized how essential it was for Britain to maintain her presence in Northern Ireland.[100] Stormont also saw the war as an opportunity to boost the province's ailing economy by supplying Britain with many of its war needs. In time, industry in Belfast was diverted to the manufacture of naval vessels, bombers, tanks, guns and ammunition, while the province's agricultural capacity was fully utilized to supply Britain with food. Yet the ineptitude of the Unionist government and its lethargic approach during the early years of the war meant that the initial effect of the province's participation in the conflict was minimal. In addition, the slow pace of voluntary recruitment in Northern Ireland, in spite of frantic appeals by Unionist ministers, left the Stormont authorities open to ridicule, particularly when evidence of higher recruiting figures from Éire was presented. Moreover, their failure to persuade Westminster to extend conscription to Northern Ireland caused considerable embarrassment, as the province was clearly unable to claim that it was making the same sacrifices as the rest of the United Kingdom. By the end of the war, however, Churchill was happy to heap praise on Northern Ireland's war effort, extolling the province's 'loyalty and friendship' in the struggle against Germany.[101]

At the outbreak of hostilities the Unionist leadership solemnly declared that Northern Ireland would share the burden of war with the rest of the United Kingdom. Craigavon informed Stormont MPs: 'There is no slackening in our loyalty. There is no falling off in our determination to place the whole of our resources at the command of the Government in Britain.'[102] These resources included the Harland and Wolff shipyard, which launched 150 vessels during the course of the war, and the Short Brothers and Harland factory, which built over 1,500 bombers.[103]

Northern Ireland's agricultural industry also made a major contribution.[104] Westminster's decision to introduce a uniform price system throughout the United Kingdom encouraged the North's farmers to increase their production in the knowledge that they had a guaranteed market for their produce, and that they would earn a reasonable profit. The province could also claim that it suffered along with the rest of the United Kingdom from German bombing. Four air raids were mounted against Belfast in April–May 1941, and these had devastating consequences for a city that was inadequately defended against air attack and did not have a proper procedure for evacuation. In total, just over 1,000 people died and almost 100,000 were temporarily homeless, while more than 56,000 houses were damaged, many close to the shipyard and aircraft factory.[105] The Belfast blitz had brutally exposed the shocking inadequacies of a bewildered Stormont government, which faced a barrage of criticism for its lack of civil defence planning and general complacency. It was during the first raid that the Stormont minister of public security, John MacDermott, took the momentous decision to ask the Éire government to send fire appliances across the border.[106]

In a belated response to these events the Stormont authorities took the unprecedented step of seeking the Fianna Fáil government's assistance in the organization of a new evacuation programme. The Ministry of Home Affairs had furnished Éire's Department of Justice with the names of people who were prepared to be evacuated to County Donegal, and the administration in Dublin organized hosts who would receive a billeting allowance from Belfast.[107]

While German bombing had placed Northern Ireland in the front line, the absence of conscription meant that the province did not fully share in the wartime experience. When conscription was introduced in Britain in April 1939, Craigavon had pleaded for the measure to be extended to Northern Ireland, but vehement protests from both the de Valera government and the Catholic minority in the North persuaded the authorities at Westminster to reject Unionist demands.[108] While northern nationalists were influenced by the South's decision to remain neutral, it was also true that on the outbreak of the war many of them hoped for a German victory, confident that Nazi rule would be preferable to living under a Unionist government.[109] Indeed, opinion only shifted following the Belfast blitz and the American entry into the war, but considerable opposition to conscription remained.[110] A further request by Craigavon for the extension of conscription was rejected in May 1940, but the situation was transformed twelve months later as Britain found herself desperately short of manpower. By this stage ministers at Westminster were prepared to apply conscription in the province, but they sought the Stormont cabinet's view before making a final decision.[111] Predictably, the Unionist government's reply was unequivocal in its support for the extension of conscription, arguing that its advantages would outweigh any problems caused by nationalist opposition.[112] Yet the cabinet's response concealed serious Unionist misgivings. Dawson Bates, the premier's closest colleague, expressed his concern that conscription would result in an influx of workers from Éire eager to fill vacancies left by the province's new conscripts. This prompted Andrews, Craig's successor as prime minister, to insist on the establishment of a cabinet sub-committee to examine the full implications of conscription for Northern Ireland.[113]

It was in May 1941 that the Churchill government came to realize that Unionist rhetoric on the application of conscription did not match the real position on the ground. On the previous occasions when the extension of conscription was considered, the authorities at Stormont had been fairly certain that Westminster would not press the case for compulsory military service. In May 1941, however, it was the British government that first raised the issue, and the expectation that it would be implemented led the Unionist government to take a more cautious approach. The main advocate of extending conscription to Northern Ireland was Ernest Bevin who, as minister of labour and national service, was most concerned by the shortage of manpower. Bevin had not been impressed by the frequent declarations of loyalty issued by the government in Belfast, and he told his cabinet colleagues: 'It had been hoped that substantial numbers of recruits from Ulster would have been obtained by voluntary methods. Up to March, however, these methods had produced only about 25,000 recruits of whom an unknown but, it is thought, a substantial proportion came from Éire.'[114] Such was the need for additional manpower that Westminster was prepared to face down intense opposition from a variety of sources, and a new bill extending conscription to the province was drafted. Yet, at the last moment, Westminster abandoned its plans to proceed with conscription, as Unionist reservations became apparent. Charles Wickham, the inspector-general of the Royal Ulster Constabulary, warned the government in London that support for conscription among the Protestant community in Northern Ireland was luke-warm, adding that Protestants would not co-operate in any new scheme unless Catholics agreed to participate.[115] The Westminster authorities gained a further insight into the Unionist leadership's thinking on the issue, when Andrews and three of his ministerial colleagues visited Chequers on 24 May 1941 to finalize details for the introduction of conscription. By 27 May the Westminster admin-istration abandoned its plans to extend conscription to Northern Ireland follow-ing further contact with a nervous Andrews who admitted that opposition to the measure had been underestimated.[116] An angry Bevin subsequently recalled that the Belfast government had taken 'cold feet' on this issue.[117] In the end, the Unionist government was relieved to see the matter dropped, but Bevin responded furiously to the Unionist assertion that responsibility for the failure to extend conscription lay solely with the government in London, as he told Andrews:

> The impression I gained when the final decision was taken was that after your return (from the 24 May meeting) to Ireland the difficulties loomed much bigger than was thought at our meeting over here and therefore the decision not to proceed was mutual. Of course, I acknowledge that the responsibility for the final decision was with the War Cabinet here. I did say, as far as I personally was concerned, I was prepared to go through with it.[118]

The war had presented the Stormont government with the opportunity to reopen its case for greater financial assistance from the Treasury. By 1942 the adminis-tration in Belfast was taking a lead from Westminster, as it began to consider the question of post-war reconstruction in Northern Ireland. At the time the Andrews government believed that it would be in a powerful negotiating posi-tion, because the Imperial Contribution paid from the Northern Ireland excheq-uer had soared during the early years of the war, when the province's Ministry of Finance became more closely integrated with the Treasury.[119] Both the minister of finance, James Milne Barbour, and his number two, John Maynard Sinclair, were strongly in favour of the continuation of this arrangement, because it guar-anteed the province's financial stability.[120] Within the Unionist cabinet, howev-er, both Andrews and Bates raised concerns about the political impact of increasing Treasury control over local expenditure. Bates, who only became aware of these financial arrangements in the summer of 1941, claimed that the Unionist cabinet had been reduced to the status of an 'Advisory Committee',[121] while the equally incompetent Andrews later astonished Spender, when he asked for a copy of the arrangements for Stormont's financial relations with the Treasury, because he had forgotten them.[122] Both of these ageing ministers, who had served in cabinet since 1921, had been shaken by recent electoral setbacks which reflected the growing unpopularity of the Unionist government. In March 1941, North Down, Craigavon's old seat, was lost in a straight fight with an Independent Unionist, and in December a by-election in Willowfield produced a win for Harry Midgley of the NILP in what had previously been a safe Unionist seat. Spender described the Willowfield result as a 'bombshell' for the government.[123]

With the Unionist electorate passing judgement on his government's lacklustre performance, Andrews felt under real pressure to produce some kind of advanced post-war reconstruction plan which would, at least, hold out the promise of improved living standards for the Unionist party's working-class supporters. Such a task would have required delicate negotiations with the Treasury, and this was evidently beyond Andrews. In his increasingly desperate attempts to shore up support for his party, the Unionist premier made a series of pledges, promising substantial improvements in social services after the war. Andrews' generous promises, which had certainly not been costed, angered Treasury officials who expressed concern at both the 'text' and the 'tone' of the Unionist leader's pronouncements.[124] Nevertheless, Andrews pressed on with his post-war agenda, and it became necessary for Westminster to apply ministerial pressure in an effort to bring the Stormont premier under control. In correspondence exchanged between the chancellor of the exchequer, Sir Kingsley Wood, and Andrews in August and September 1942, the Treasury warned against the introduction of higher standards of social services than those available in Britain and stressed that there had to be prior agreement between Belfast and London before specific guarantees were given by Unionist ministers. While Wood also acknowledged that Northern Ireland has some 'leeway' to make up, he would only promise that the Treasury would give a sympathetic hearing to any plans put forward by Stormont to narrow the gap.[125] Still, a beleaguered Andrews persisted in trying to organize an extensive post-war reconstruction programme, and a serious clash with the Treasury would have resulted had the Unionist cabinet been fully behind its leader.[126]

In his attempts to restore his government's popularity Andrews had embarked on a reckless course which would, ultimately, have split the Unionist government. Good sense was only restored when Brooke replaced him in May 1943. Andrews' dithering over conscription in May 1941 and, more particularly, his disagreements with the Treasury over Northern Ireland's post-war reconstruction programme had seriously strained Stormont–Westminster relations, but Brooke's accession to power instilled new confidence in the Unionist government at Westminster. Even before Craigavon's death there had been rumblings within the Unionist party. Edmund Warnock, who had just resigned from his post as parliamentary secretary to the Ministry of Home Affairs, claimed that the Unionist administration was practically in a 'state of coma' and later expressed his frustration at the government's failure to seize the opportunity presented by the war to strengthen Northern Ireland's position within the United Kingdom: 'The political position of Northern Ireland has always been one of some difficulty, and here was a heaven-sent opportunity to put us on top of the wave, to put us absolutely 100 per cent right with Great Britain.'[127] Andrews might have been able to deflect some of the criticism from the backbenches by dismissing the unpopular and ineffective Bates, but he would still have found it difficult to carry on as prime minister. Warnock was even more forthright in his condemnation of the Andrews government, and Brooke warned the prime minister that such criticism reflected 'views expressed in wider circles and views for which there is some foundation'.[128] Yet, in spite of the obvious discontent within the Unionist party, there was a great reluctance to force the issue. In January 1943 a parliamentary party meeting heard a call for radical changes in the cabinet, but the resolution lacked the necessary support, and all references to this discussion were excluded from press reports.[129] In the end it took a palace revolution to dislodge Andrews. Sources close to the party organization at the time maintain that Brooke did not actively participate in the move to overthrow Andrews, but it is clear that he was well aware of the manoeuvrings within the party to oust the prime minister, and that he was not prepared to come to Andrews' defence.[130] On his accession Brooke made a decisive break with the past by replacing the old guard with younger, more able ministers such as Sinclair and with working-class leaders such as Harry Midgley and William Grant. These men were more attuned to the detail of a post-war reconstruction programme and better understood the demands of an extensive programme of social services that was likely in the wake of the Beveridge report. Brooke's appointment also reassured the authorities at Westminster, particularly officials at the Treasury, as it was understood that he saw progress for the province resting on greater co-operation and consultation with Westminster. With Brooke at the helm, Stormont–Westminster relations improved, leaving Northern Ireland in a stronger position to take advantage of the radical changes in social services promised in the post-war period.

NOTES

1. House of Commons Debates (hereafter cited as HC Debates), 5th series, vol. 127, cols 989–90, 29 March 1920: cited in P. Buckland, *James Craig* (Dublin, 1980), p.41.
2. Buckland, *James Craig*, p.40.
3. PRONI, CAB4/69/19, Cabinet Conclusions (hereafter cited as Cab. Conclus.), 29 January 1923.
4. Buckland, *The Factory of Grievances*, p.45. The author describes Craig as Northern Ireland's ambassador in London.
5. PRONI, CAB4/59/24, Cab. Conclus., 7 December 1922.
6. For an extensive account of the negotiations leading up to the Treaty, see F. Pakenham (Lord Longford), *Peace by Ordeal* (London, 1962). See also R. Fanning, *Independent Ireland* (Dublin, 1983), pp.23–4.
7. D.W. Harkness, *Northern Ireland since 1920* (Dublin, 1983), pp.10–11. See also Canning, *British Policy towards Ireland*, pp.55–6.
8. Buckland, *The Factory of Grievances*, p.202.
9. Ibid., p.70. For de Valera's version of the event, see Bowman, *De Valera and the Ulster Question*, pp.47–8.
10. P. Bew, 'The political history of Northern Ireland since partition: The prospects for North–South co-operation', in A.F. Heath, R. Breen and C.T. Whelan (eds), *Ireland North and South: Perspectives from Social Science* (Oxford, 1999), pp.404–7. Professor Bew argues that Craig's thinking on North–South relations during these formative years was influenced by his concern for Protestants in the South, but the rapid decline in the southern Protestant population, which was evident by the end

of the 1920s, released him from any obligation to that community.

11. PRONI, CAB4/30/9, Cab. Conclus., 26 January 1922.

12. For the terms of the second Craig–Collins pact, see A.C. Hepburn, *Ireland 1900–25, Volume 2: Documents and Analysis* (Newtownards, 1998), pp.214–16.

13. É. Phoenix, *Northern Nationalism: Nationalist Politics, Partition and the Catholic Minority in Northern Ireland 1890–1940* (Belfast, 1994), p.227.

14. Ibid., pp.189–91. This cost the Dublin exchequer £18,000 per month.

15. Fanning, *Independent Ireland*, pp.34–6.

16. N. Mansergh, *The Unresolved Question: The Anglo-Irish Settlement and its Undoing 1912–72* (London, 1991), p.225. Mansergh concurs with Dr Laffan's assessment on what would have happened if Collins had lived: see M. Laffan, *The Partition of Ireland 1911–25* (Dublin, 1983), pp.95–8. On the other hand, Bew has argued more recently that Craig's sincere attempts to reach a settlement with Collins greatly impressed the authorities at Westminster, and this would have strengthened London's determination to defend the new state against attacks from the South: see Bew, 'The political history of Northern Ireland since partition', pp.413–14.

17. A. Jackson, *Ireland 1798–1998: Politics and War* (Oxford, 1999), pp.210–14.

18. Buckland, *The Factory of Grievances*, pp.68–9.

19. The best account of the development of the Irish Free State as a dominion is D.W. Harkness, *The Restless Dominion* (Dublin, 1969).

20. Buckland, *The Factory of Grievances*, pp.70–1. Lord Londonderry had previously served as minister of education in the Northern Ireland government from 1921–6, and he became minister of air in Ramsay MacDonald's National government.

21. Bowman, *De Valera and the Ulster Question, 1917–1973*, pp.110–12.

22. See D. McMahon, 'A transient apparition: British policy towards the de Valera government 1932–5', *Irish Historical Studies*, 22, 88 (September 1981), pp.331–51.

23. F.S.L. Lyons, *Ireland since the Famine* (London, 1973), pp.517–23 provide an introduction to the 1936 External Relations Act and the 1937 Constitution.

24. Buckland, *The Factory of Grievances*, p.71.

25. See D.S. Johnson, 'Northern Ireland as a problem in the Economic War 1932–38', *Irish Historical Studies*, 22, 86 (September 1980), pp.144–61.

26. Bowman, *De Valera and the Ulster Question*, pp.109–16.

27. Ibid., pp.163–4 and p.174. More recently, Professor Girvin has argued that de Valera was prepared to reject the financial deal on offer from the British in 1938, and it was only when his objectives were 'overridden by the more moderate majority in the cabinet' that the Agreement was signed: see B. Girvin, *The Emergency: Neutral Ireland 1939–45* (London, 2006), p.52.

28. See D.W. Harkness, 'Mr de Valera's dominion: Irish relations with Britain and the Commonwealth, 1932–1938', *Journal of Commonwealth Political Studies*, 8, 3 (November 1970), p.213. MacDonald had established this as being one of the two fundamental principles that would have to be adhered to if unity was to be achieved. The other was that de Valera would have to maintain the Commonwealth link. For a full discussion of MacDonald's impact on Anglo-Irish relations, see D. McMahon, *Republicans and Imperialists: Anglo-Irish Relations in the 1930s* (New Haven and London, 1984).

29. NIHC Debates, vol. 21, cols 706–26 and 868–9, 28 April 1938.

30. Buckland, *The Factory of Grievances*, pp.111–12.

31. Harkness, *The Restless Dominion*, p.253.

32. Buckland, *The Factory of Grievances*, p.85.

33. PRONI, CAB4/30/9, Cab. Conclus., 26 January 1922. White Cross funds were the proceeds from Catholic charities collected to give financial aid to unemployed Catholic workers in Belfast.

34. PRONI, CAB4/88/6, Cab. Conclus., 2 October 1923.

35. R.J. Lawrence, *The Government of Northern Ireland: Public Finance and Public Services 1921–1964* (Oxford, 1965), pp.51–2.

36. Buckland, *The Factory of Grievances*, p.92. Previously, a stipulated imperial contribution of approximately £8 million was the first charge on Northern Ireland's revenue.

37. PRONI, CAB9A/3/5, 'Financial position January 1933–November 1937', memo by Andrews on financial relations with Great Britain, 9 April 1931.

38. PRONI, CAB9C/1/7, 'Unemployment Insurance Agreement January 1928–1948', Andrews to Craigavon, 26 September 1931.

39. PRONI, CAB9A/3/5, notes on conference at Stormont on financial relations with Great Britain, 12 and 15 December 1933.

40. PRONI, CAB4/273B/25, Cab. Conclus., 19 November 1930.

41. Buckland, *The Factory of Grievances*, p.90.

42. PRONI, CAB9A/3/5, notes on conference at the Treasury, 3 March 1934. For a discussion of this

internal cabinet division, see P. Bew, P. Gibbon and H. Patterson, *Northern Ireland 1921–1996: Political Forces and Social Classes* (London, 1996 edition), pp.60–3.

43. PRONI, CAB9A/3/5, Chamberlain to Pollock, 13 February 1934, and notes on Treasury meetings between Hopkins and Pollock and his officials, 3 January 1934, and between Baldwin and Chamberlain and Craigavon, Pollock and Andrews, 22 January 1934. See also CAB4/321/37, Cab. Conclus. on the 1934 budget, 25 April 1934, and CAB9A/3/5, S.D. Waley, a principal assistant secretary at the Treasury, to Pollock, 7 May 1935. This became law in the 1936 Unemployment Reinsurance Agreement. The main change was that the calculation for the percentage, which Northern Ireland could freely draw from the fund, was based on the insured rather than the total population, and the new agreement was extended to cover unemployment assistance as well as insurance: see Lawrence, *The Government of Northern Ireland*, pp.58–9.

44. PRONI, CAB9A/3/5, notes on meeting at the Treasury, 16 April 1935, and Spender to Sir Charles Blackmore, the Stormont cabinet secretary, 22 February 1937. Spender estimated that the new agreement was worth £1 million to Northern Ireland for the 1936–7 financial year.

45. Buckland, *The Factory of Grievances*, p.91.

46. PRONI, CAB9A/3/5, notes on conference at the Treasury, 3 January 1934. Pollock claimed that the drop in trade with the South and the decrease of the Irish Free State's exports, particularly cattle, to Britain had significantly increased unemployment in both Londonderry and Newry.

47. PRONI, CAB4/397/2, cabinet memo sent to the home secretary, 25 March 1938.

48. Ibid. See also Buckland, *The Factory of Grievances*, pp.111–15.

49. NIHC Debates, vol. 21, cols 706–26, 26 April 1938. See also Johnson, 'Northern Ireland as a problem in the Economic War', p.159. The term 'bribe' was used frequently by Westminster officials to describe Northern Ireland's compensation.

50. NIHC Debates, vol. 21, col. 663, 26 April 1938.

51. Ibid., cols 661–2, 26 April 1938. This meant that when agricultural subsidies were paid to farmers in Great Britain, and circumstances justified the payment of similar subsidies to Northern Ireland farmers, the money required would be obtained from Westminster.

52. Johnson, 'Northern Ireland as a problem in the Economic War', p.157.

53. PRONI, CAB4/397/3, Craigavon to Sir Samuel Hoare, the home secretary, 25 March 1938.

54. Johnson, 'Northern Ireland as a problem in the Economic War', pp.157–8. This was Waley's opinion.

55. NIHC Debates, vol. 21, cols 662–3, 26 April 1938.

56. Ibid., col. 1131, 17 May 1938. In his budget Andrews stated that the Simon Declaration gave the government 'complete security against periods of depression in our finances'.

57. Johnson, 'Northern Ireland as a problem in the Economic War', p.161.

58. Canning, *British Policy towards Ireland*, pp.177–8.

59. PRONI, D715/9, Sir Wilfrid Spender, Financial Diary (hereafter cited as Fin. Diary), 23 January 1937.

60. Buckland, *The Factory of Grievances*, pp.113–16.

61. PRONI, D715/10, Fin. Diary, not dated.

62. C. O'Halloran, *Partition and the Limits of Irish Nationalism* (Dublin, 1987), p.152.

63. Buckland, *The Factory of Grievances*, p.68. Indeed, Craigavon emphasized the fact that he was calling the election in response to Éire's claims on partition, but a more significant reason was his anxiety to crush W.J. Stewart's Progressive Unionist Party before it became properly established. There is also evidence that the 1935 Belfast riots and the injudicious public utterances of a number of leading Unionists during the 1930s alerted a number of officials in London to embarrassing developments in the province.

64. Canning, *British Policy towards Ireland*, p.64.

65. Ibid., p.54.

66. For a full explanation of Westminster's handling of the episode, see Buckland, *The Factory of Grievances*, pp.267–75.

67. For a discussion of the 1925 and 1930 Education Acts, see S. Farren, *The Politics of Irish Education 1920–65* (Belfast, 1995), pp.86–105.

68. M. Cowling, *The Impact of Labour* (Cambridge, 1971), p.139. Winston Churchill was another influential figure who was keen to defend Ulster's interests; see pp.166–8.

69. Canning, *British Policy towards Ireland*, pp.59–60.

70. Ibid., p.100.

71. Ibid., p.199.

72. Ibid., p.222.

73. The results of the investigation are contained in a Dominions Office file, PROL, DO 35/893/X11/123, 'U.K.– Ireland Political and Constitutional Relations: Treatment of the Catholic minority in N. Ireland'.

74. Ibid., memo by Alexander Maxwell (later Sir Alexander Maxwell), a principal secretary at the Home Office, 22 April 1924. In fact, the only hint of criticism raised by the Home Office was a reference to the occasional 'injudicious public utterances' made by Unionist ministers.

75. Ibid., note prepared by Markbreiter for the home secretary, March 1938. See also Canning, *British Policy towards Ireland*, p.223.
76. PROL, DO 35/893/X11/123, minute by Stephenson, 10 March 1938.
77. Ibid., minute by Batterbee, 7 March 1938. At the time there was no Home Office official dealing specifically with Northern Ireland affairs.
78. Ibid., minute by Lord Hartington, 9 March 1938.
79. See PROL, DO 35/893/X11/251, 'U.K.– Éire Political and Constitutional Relations: Allegations made by the Éire Government as to the maltreatment of the minority in Northern Ireland, arising out of the Partition Question'.
80. Ibid., minute by Batterbee, 18 November 1938.
81. Ibid., Home Office summary, 'Allegations made in connection with Partition', November 1938.
82. Ibid., Robinson's note was included in the Home Office minute, 'Gerrymandering Constituencies'. The sentence was probably deleted by a Home Office official.
83. Ibid., minute by Batterbee, 18 November 1938.
84. Ibid. See also M. Elliott, *The Catholics of Ulster: A History* (London, 2000), p.386.
85. Ibid., minute by Batterbee, 18 November 1938.
86. PROL, DO 35/893/X11/123, press reports for week ending, 4 March 1938.
87. Phoenix, *Northern Nationalism: Nationalist Politics, Partition and the Catholic Minority in Northern Ireland 1890–1940*, p.386.
88. W.S. Churchill, *The Second World War (Vol. 1): The Gathering Storm* (London, 1948), p.248. At the same time, Churchill was fully aware of the political complexities surrounding any plans for the reoccupation of the ports, and he adopted a more cautious line in cabinet than his predecessor, Chamberlain: see Girvin, *The Emergency*, pp.105–8.
89. R. Fisk, *In Time of War: Ireland, Ulster and The Price of Neutrality, 1939–45* (Dublin, 1983), pp.190–207.
90. Ibid., pp.323–4.
91. Girvin, *The Emergency*, pp.215–17. Gray was particularly incensed by de Valera's use of the war for his own political ends and by his refusal to acknowledge that Britain was doing what it could to protect the whole island of Ireland.
92. Ibid.
93. Bowman, *De Valera and the Ulster Question*, pp.250–2.
94. Ibid., pp.255–6. See also Fisk, *In Time of War*, pp.538–41, and Girvin, *The Emergency*, p.10.
95. Fisk, *In Time of War*, pp.236–44.
96. J.T. Carroll, *Ireland in the War Years 1939–1945* (Newton Abbot, 1975), p.30.
97. SPOI, S11582a, 'Irish Labour: Emigration to G.B. and N.I., 1940–44'. The file contains several letters from Fianna Fáil supporters who were worried that the existing arrangements were 'pro-British'. See, for example, Michael Kilroy, a district leader of the LDF to de Valera, 24 March 1941. One estimate puts the number of Irish men and women working in war industries in Britain close to 200,000: see Girvin, *The Emergency*, p.179.
98. Carroll, *Ireland in the War Years*, p.279.
99. T.P. Coogan, *The IRA* (London, 1980), pp.26–75. Only one of the spies, Hermann Goertz, remained at large for any length of time.
100. Fisk, *In Time of War*, pp.281–2.
101. For the full text of Churchill's Victory Broadcast, see W.S. Churchill, *The Second World War (Vol.12): Triumph and Tragedy*, pp.341–8.
102. NIHC Debates, vol. 22, col. 1902, 4 September 1939.
103. Lyons, *Ireland since the Famine*, pp.731–3.
104. Among Stormont departments, it was the Ministry of Agriculture that responded most effectively to the demands of war: see B. Barton, *Brookeborough: The Making of a Prime Minister* (Belfast, 1988), pp.132–4 and p.155.
105. For a full discussion of the impact of German bombing, see B. Barton, *The Blitz: Belfast in the War Years* (Belfast, 1989).
106. Fisk, *In Time of War*, pp.487–9.
107. SPOI, see file S12939, 'Reception of Evacuees from N.I.'. The absence of further German air raids meant that these evacuation arrangements never had to be put into action.
108. Fisk, *In Time of War*, pp.95–7.
109. See PROI, MacDermot papers, 1065/15/2, MacDermot speech to Council on Foreign Relations, 30 September 1941, and interview with James Doherty, the former Nationalist party chairman.
110. M. Farrell, *The Orange State*, (London, 1976), pp.156–7.
111. PRONI, CAB4/475/16, Morrison to Andrews, 20 May 1941.
112. PRONI, CAB4/475/15, cabinet memo sent to Morrison, 21 May 1941. See also Barton, *Brookeborough: The Making of a Prime Minister*, pp.198–9.

113. PRONI, CAB4/475/17, Cab. Conclus., 21 May 1941.
114. PROL, CAB66/16, W.P. (41) 107, 21 May 1941.
115. PROL, CAB66.16, W.P. (41) 111, 21 May 1941.
116. Barton, *Brookeborough: The Making of a Prime Minister*, pp.198–9.
117. PRONI, CAB9C/13/3, 'Unemployment relief schemes and grants 1939–43', Andrews to Bevin, 24 March 1942. The letter repeated some of the charges made by Bevin. Political leaders in the South had been convinced that conscription would be extended to the North: see UCD Arch. Dept., Patrick McGilligan papers, P 35c/182, notes on meeting on 'Northern Conscription', 23 May 1941.
118. PRONI, CAB9C/13/3, Bevin to Andrews, 1 April 1942.
119. The increase in the Imperial Contribution was partly due to accounting anomalies, as certain items previously financed by the local exchequer were now paid by the Treasury: see PROL, T160/1194/F14464/043/03, 'Northern Ireland: Memoranda on financial relations with Great Britain', memo by Milne Barbour, March 1942.
120. PRONI, CAB9A/30/4, 'Miscellaneous financial matters 1937–43', memo by Milne Barbour on financial relations with the Treasury, 28 July 1941, and PROL, T160/1194/F14464/043/03, memo by Sinclair, 'The Financial Relationship Between the Exchequers of Great Britain and Northern Ireland under the Government of Ireland Act, 1920', August 1942.
121. PRONI, CAB9A/30/4, Bates to Andrews, 29 July 1941.
122. PRONI, D715/18, Fin. Diary, 25 March 1942.
123. Ibid., December 1941.
124. PRONI, COM7/2, 'Post War Planning Committee Correspondence 1942–43', Compton to Spender, 31 July 1942, and Spender to Brooke, 4 September 1942.
125. PRONI, CAB9C/1/7, Kingsley Wood to Andrews, 14 September 1942. The term 'leeway' appears in all discussion of Northern Ireland's post-war social services. See also Bew et al, *Northern Ireland 1921–1996*, pp. 83–6.
126. For a flavour of Unionist dissension, see PRONI, CAB9C/1/7, Andrews to Milne Barbour, 22 September 1942, and Milne Barbour's reply, 24 September 1942.
127. NIHC Debates, vol. 23, col. 1272, 28 May 1940, and cols 2156–7, 25 September 1940.
128. PRONI, COM 7/2, Brooke to Andrews, 19 September 1942.
129. PRONI, D715/20, Fin. Diary, 8 January 1943.
130. Information from Unionist source. See also Barton, *Brookeborough: The Making of a Prime Minister*, pp.215–28.

2

Stormont and the Labour Government

On the surface Northern Ireland was in a much better position by the end of the war. Agriculture and manufacturing industry had been revitalized, and relations between Belfast and London had improved immeasurably from the low point of 1938, despite the Andrews hiccup. On the other hand, however, partly as a result of the impact made by American servicemen stationed in the province, expectations of social and economic progress had risen sharply by the end of the war. The Unionist government was aware of the need for change, but, while a new generation of leaders more in tune with the party's rank-and-file supporters had emerged under Brooke, there had been no real shift in policy. Certainly, a closer working relationship had been established between the Treasury and the Ministry of Finance, though the experience of the war years had demonstrated that increased financial assistance from Westminster inevitably meant tighter Treasury control over the province's expenditure. This had been acceptable during the war years, but Labour's shock election win created a dilemma for the Brooke administration. Previously, the Unionist leadership had been deliberately vague in its attitude to the Beveridge proposals, but Labour's rapid introduction of welfare legislation forced the government in Belfast to make a decision on the implementation of the welfare state. Furthermore, Labour's commitment to increased state intervention in the economy raised more serious difficulties for the Unionist government. Brooke and his colleagues had to decide if the financial advantages to be gained from working closely with Westminster in the field of economic policy would outweigh the political disadvantage of accepting and adopting socialist legislation. Of equal concern to the Unionist leadership was the need to counter the threat posed by the NILP, a task that was made more delicate by the success of the Labour government at Westminster. The 1945 Northern Ireland general election had confirmed that Unionism was losing ground to the NILP in Belfast, and Brooke and his colleagues were anxious to reverse this trend.

THE 1945 ELECTION

The results of the 1945 general election, which were announced on 26 July, shocked the authorities in Belfast. For the first time Stormont would have to deal with a Labour government that had a clear majority in the House of Commons. The two previous Labour governments had been minority administrations, and, while they had created a number of problems for the Unionist government, particularly in the area of finance, there had never been any serious likelihood of a major confrontation developing between London and Belfast. With Conservative Central Office predicting a Tory majority of eighty in the general election, the local Unionist press expressed astonishment at the amazing swing in public opinion.[1] Some 3,000,000 personnel in the forces were eligible to vote in 1945, and they were kept well informed of the campaign by newspaper and radio. The fact that so many serving members of the forces were standing as candidates clearly added to the interest and excitement among the troops.[2] Even during the three-week gap from polling day on 5 July to the count, a delay to allow the service vote to be returned, there had been no hint of a Labour victory. Labour's election manifesto was essentially a blueprint for the welfare state, and it chimed with an electorate that was looking to the future, not to Churchill and past glory. Yet shortly before polling day, the *Belfast Newsletter* preferred to concentrate on the province's constitutional position, reminding voters that while Churchill's support was not in doubt, a major question mark existed over the Labour party's commitment to Northern Ireland's future.[3] Following the announcement of Labour's shock victory, however, Brooke and his colleagues must have consoled themselves with the knowledge that several key members of the Labour front bench had held important positions in Churchill's wartime government and would, therefore, have been fully aware of Northern Ireland's useful contribution to the war effort. Moreover, Bevin's appointment as foreign secretary, where he would be fully engaged in the complex field of post-war international relations, was a relief to Unionist leaders, because he had been Northern Ireland's most consistent critic in the Churchill government. Still, the Stormont administration could not be entirely confident about Labour's stance on the border, and the new government's commitment to welfare spending and its promise of much greater state intervention in the economy further increased the Unionist cabinet's concerns. While the Unionist press chose to ignore these potential problems, an *Irish News* editorial highlighted the dilemma now facing the devolved administration: 'Thus in the relationship between Whitehall and Stormont problems and anomalies will appear at every turn. "Ulster" may boast of remaining firm for Unionism while Britain swung Labour. But how far can it remain firm for Unionism while carrying out the orders of a Labour Administration the next few years will tell.'[4]

Unionist difficulties had been exacerbated by the overlap of the Stormont and Westminster general election campaigns. The results of the Northern Ireland election were announced on 10 July, only two weeks before the announcement of the Westminster results, and in their efforts to combat the threat posed by the NILP during the Stormont campaign the Unionist leaders adopted an uncompromising anti-socialist line, particularly in Belfast. In a speech delivered in Oldpark, Brooke had attacked Labour's commitment to nationalization and economic planning, claiming that socialism would abolish the liberty of the individual subject: 'Once they started nibbling at the biscuit of Socialism before they knew where they were their children would be tied hand and foot.'[5] Naturally, Labour's subsequent landslide victory caused considerable embarrassment to the Unionist leaders, as they prepared to work closely with their ideological rivals on the major issues of post-war reconstruction. Meanwhile, the NILP's performance in the 1945 Stormont election confirmed that there was significant support in the province for the introduction of advanced welfare legislation. The party had raised its profile following the publication of the Beveridge report, and in 1945 it had campaigned enthusiastically on welfare issues such as education, housing, health and unemployment. To meet this challenge the Unionist party, particularly in Belfast's working-class constituencies, had to look beyond its traditional focus on the province's constitutional position by campaigning vigorously on social issues. In his Cromac constituency the minister of finance, John Maynard Sinclair, was careful to emphasize that the Unionist party was composed of people 'in all walks of life', while in St Anne's the minister of home affairs, Edmund Warnock, claimed that his only objective in public life was to further the welfare of the working class.[6]

In the end the Unionists recorded a convincing election success, giving them a majority of thirteen in the Northern Ireland House of Commons, but a careful examination of the results revealed that the electorate had moved noticeably leftwards. The two seats won by the NILP in 1945 failed to give a true reflection of advances made by the party. Hugh Downey captured Dock from the sitting Unionist, and Robert Getgood triumphed over the government chief whip, Sir Wilson Hungerford, in Oldpark; both had comfortable majorities. Elsewhere in the city, William Grant, a prominent cabinet minister, fought a tough battle with his NILP opponent in Duncairn before emerging with a majority of just over 1,000. In St Anne's the NILP candidate polled more than 7,600 votes, which represented 43.1 per cent of the total votes cast in a straight fight with Warnock, while the Communist candidate in Cromac, Betty Sinclair, won 33 per cent of the total votes cast in her contest with the minister of finance. The other Communist candidate standing in Belfast, W.H. McCullough, also polled well, gaining 36.7 per cent of the poll in his contest with Lord Glentoran in the Bloomfield division. Altogether, the NILP fielded fifteen candidates and gained 66,053 votes, which represented 18.6 per cent of the total poll. Considering the fragmentation of the working-class vote caused by the participation of other left of centre parties, the NILP had made significant inroads into Unionist support, and it could look forward with genuine optimism to consolidating its position in future Stormont elections. In addition, the NILP leaders were given an added boost by Labour's victory at Westminster, as they believed that the presence of a Labour administration in London, committed to major welfare reforms and to a full employment policy, would reflect favourably on the NILP.

In the 1945 Northern Ireland election the party had battled with the pro-union Commonwealth Labour Party (CWLP) to secure Protestant working-class votes. Formed in December 1942 by the NILP veteran, Harry Midgley, the CWLP adopted a much clearer position on the border question, stressing that by maintaining the union with Great Britain, Northern Ireland workers would enjoy a much higher standard of living than they ever possibly could in any all-Ireland state.[7] By 1945 Midgley had become a leading and influential personality in Ulster politics, having previously held cabinet rank, first as minister of public security and then as minister of labour, in Brooke's recently formed administration. From 1933 until 1938, when he represented the Dock constituency for the

NILP, Midgley had actively sought support from both sides of the sectarian divide, but his support for the republican government in the Spanish Civil War thrust him into conflict with the Catholic Church and this was to cost him his Stormont seat.[8] In the 1945 election his new party fielded six candidates, three of whom stood against NILP candidates in Belfast, and appealed directly to the Protestant section of the working-class community. Although only Midgley was successful, the six candidates managed to poll over 28,000 votes, which represented almost 8 per cent of the total poll, and this was sufficient to prevent the NILP adding to its two Stormont seats. In the Ballynafeigh constituency of Belfast the combination of the NILP and CWLP votes would have been sufficient to see the defeat of Frederick Thompson, the Unionist candidate. Further fragmentation of the working-class vote was caused by the participation of two Federation of Labour candidates, one of whom, Jack Beattie, was again returned for Pottinger.[9] Unlike Midgely, his former colleague, Beattie had gradually adopted an anti-partition stance which led to his expulsion from the NILP in October 1944.[10] Yet, in spite of these challenges on both sides of the working-class divide, the NILP had polled impressively in many areas of Belfast, though further electoral progress would depend on the party's success in promoting bread-and-butter politics above traditional sectarian concerns. Of course, during the election campaign in 1945 Unionists had made every effort to highlight the threat to the border, but, worryingly for Brooke and his colleagues, the results had demonstrated that the NILP had achieved some degree of success in switching the electorate's attention to social and economic issues.

While the national swing to the left had not been mirrored in the Northern Ireland election, there had been sufficient movement to cause apprehension among Unionist leaders at Stormont. Meanwhile, the upheaval in British politics had also given new impetus to the ailing Nationalist party in the North. Following the Northern Ireland election the ten successful Nationalist MPs decided to take their seats at Stormont, hoping that the new government in London would be more sympathetic to their demands. In addition, the presence of a Labour government persuaded Anthony Mulvey and Patrick Cunningham, the two Nationalists who had been returned at the general election for the two-member Westminster constituency of Fermanagh and Tyrone, to take their seats in the House of Commons.[11] It was equally apparent, however, that these Nationalists, most of whom were rural, conservative figures, would share some of the Unionist party's anxiety over the introduction of socialist legislation. Still, Nationalists saw an opportunity to embarrass their opponents, and the *Irish News* was quick to highlight some of the problems facing the Unionist party: 'Ulster Unionism at Westminster will form part of the opposition to the new regime. As such they will often vote against measures which when they become law will be accepted and defended and passed by the Unionist government in the Six Counties, more fearful than ever of falling out of step with Britain.'[12]

Indeed, the historical alliance between the Conservative and Unionist parties, initially forged in the struggle against Home Rule, meant that the Ulster Unionists accepted the Conservative whip and followed the Tory party line on all major policy issues. The party's historian has described the Ulster Unionists at Westminster as socially and educationally more conservative than the Conservatives, stressing that the Unionist party had not sent a working-class representative to Westminster since 1922.[13] With Labour in office, however, continued support for the Conservatives would create problems, because Unionist MPs at Westminster would be voting against welfare proposals that the Brooke administration would later introduce at Stormont. In an effort to minimize differences between Unionists in Belfast and London a new 'inner cabinet' was established by the Unionist MPs at Westminster. The first such group was formed in 1944, as a result of Brooke's concern that Northern Ireland's position might be overlooked when the House of Commons came to consider major post-war reforms.[14] The procedure laid down was that A.J. Kelly, the Northern Ireland liaison officer at the Home Office, would examine the Imperial Order Papers so that any issues affecting Northern Ireland could immediately be brought to the notice of the relevant Stormont departments. The onus was then on the minister concerned to advise his counterpart in the inner cabinet of Westminster MPs on the appropriate action. The 1945 arrangement gave seven of the Westminster MPs responsibility for a Northern Ireland department, and it was intended that they should work closely with the corresponding ministers at Stormont.[15] The presence of a Labour administration at Westminster made the effective working of this arrangement even more important to the Stormont government, and Brooke drew attention to this when the cabinet discussed the liaison arrangement shortly after the opening of the new session of parliament. The prime minister also noted that while the idea of an inner cabinet of Ulster Unionists was satisfactory in theory, it had not thus far worked successfully in practice, and increased consultation would now be required under more difficult circumstances.[16] No explanation was offered for the ineffectiveness of the arrangement, but it was likely that the irregular attendance by some of the Ulster Unionists had created obvious practical difficulties.

While Brooke and his ministers were clearly disappointed by the performance of their Unionist colleagues at Westminster, they knew that the key decisions would be taken at Stormont. In his first post-war budget speech Sinclair, the minister of finance, was careful to explain that Northern Ireland's intention to follow Westminster's lead in social services did not mean that Stormont would act as a rubber stamp parliament for Westminster's welfare legislation: 'I am not prepared to accept the theory ... that we should slavishly follow the whole pattern of life in Great Britain ... but rather that we should preserve in the administration of our services here the greatest possible degree of flexibility.' Sinclair also attacked the use of the phrase 'step-by-step' in his statement, claiming that the expression was only originally intended to refer to the cash social services and was never intended to have a wide interpretation.[17] Originally, 'step-by-step' referred to keeping pace with British welfare benefits, but Sinclair regarded the term as politically embarrassing with Labour in power and preferred to refer to parity when discussing Northern Ireland's social services.[18]

This subtle change enabled the Unionist government to defend its introduction of welfare measures by arguing that parity of taxation with the rest of the United Kingdom meant that Northern Ireland citizens should enjoy parity in social services. Moreover, the use of the term 'parity' obscured the impression that Stormont was merely following the lead of a socialist government at Westminster, thereby allowing the Brooke administration to rebuff charges made by its Labour and Nationalist opponents, while simultaneously mollifying the concerns of Unionist backbenchers, many of whom believed that the welfare proposals contained traces of socialism which they disliked.

THE IMPLEMENTATION OF THE WELFARE STATE

The relative success of various Labour candidates in the 1945 Stormont general election had provided clear evidence that there was significant support for welfare legislation among the Protestant working class. Earlier, Brooke had issued a guarded response to the Beveridge proposals, arguing that post-war social service provision would depend on available funding. In the same Stormont speech Brooke implied that Andrews' 1942 leeway agreement with the chancellor was worthless, as he stressed that the Treasury had only promised to consider Northern Ireland's leeway claims sympathetically.[19] The obvious implication was that the Northern Ireland government could not guarantee that the Treasury would agree to provide the necessary finances to allow Northern Ireland to close the gap in those social services where the province lagged behind. Nevertheless, the growing popularity of the NILP, the Ulster people's anticipation of radical social and economic changes after the war, and, perhaps equally significantly, the presence in the Unionist cabinet of two new ministers, William Grant and Harry Midgley, who were genuinely interested in improving the province's social services, made it almost inevitable that the administration at Stormont would commit itself to follow the British lead in welfare legislation in the postwar period. Before the 1945 elections Brooke had announced that his government would definitely maintain social services on an equal footing with those in Great Britain, but he was careful, as always, not to commit the Unionist administration to any specific undertakings other than those which had already been introduced at Westminster.[20] The logic of Brooke's position, based on the commitment to parity in social services, ensured that Stormont would have to delay formulating its own legislation until it saw the exact line being taken by Westminster. This left his government open to the charge, as former premier Andrews was quick to point out, that it was failing to introduce schemes to make up the leeway existing in certain social services.[21]

The leeway issue was something which Brooke and his colleagues chose to ignore in parliament, but, behind the scenes, Sinclair and his Ministry of Finance officials were busily engaged in important negotiations with the Treasury on this matter. After the fall of Andrews, the Ministry of Finance sought to prepare the ground for a radical restructuring of financial relations between the two governments. In a memorandum sent to the Treasury, J.I. Cook, an assistant secretary at the Ministry of Finance, expressed the Unionist government's wish that financial relations should reflect improved political relations between Stormont and Westminster. Whereas the Government of Ireland Act had 'envisaged a floating off of (Northern) Ireland', he claimed that the province now sought closer integration with the rest of the United Kingdom, particularly in financial matters. Cook also took this opportunity to reiterate Stormont's general views on the gap which existed between Great Britain and Northern Ireland in certain social services: 'The principle of equal standards of social service ... should be outside the realm of any controversy ... Above the provision for such equal services there should be a provision for the acknowledged arrears of expenditure required to bring Northern Ireland up to the British standard!'[22]

A preliminary investigation by the authorities at Westminster had revealed that the implementation of some of the Beveridge proposals in Northern Ireland would be relatively more expensive than in Great Britain, because of the higher incidence of sickness and unemployment prevailing in the province.[23] It was not surprising, therefore, that the Treasury initially refused to be drawn into giving the Northern Ireland government a firm commitment on the leeway question. However, vague promises no longer satisfied the Ministry of Finance, and the Treasury was informed that Sinclair required definite information on how the leeway in certain social services would be closed. In fact, the Northern Ireland department had included a definite proposal of its own. It suggested withholding a sum of £6 million from the imperial contribution to set up a fund, which the Northern Ireland government could draw upon to finance schemes intended to reduce the leeway.[24] The Treasury was obviously alarmed by this proposal, probably fearing that it would create a dangerous precedent and lead to further deductions from the imperial contribution, whenever the Northern Ireland government produced any proposals to reduce the leeway. On this occasion the Treasury persuaded Sinclair to drop his proposal by promising Northern Ireland a sum of £6 million, which was to be spent by the local authorities on health and other services that lagged behind.[25] News of this £6 million grant was given in Sinclair's 1944 budget speech.[26] Most of this money was spent on water and sewage schemes, providing some defence for the Brooke administration from backbench criticism of its reluctance to tackle the leeway issue. Yet the Northern Ireland government realized that it would require much larger grants from the Treasury before it could hope to achieve parity with Great Britain in all of the social services. As the Treasury had still not given any firm guarantee on the provision of finance for leeway purposes, it seemed likely that the issue would be raised repeatedly in the post-war period.

Sinclair also used his 1944 budget speech to elaborate on the Unionist government's attitude to the Beveridge report. Although he was unable to make any specific guarantees until Westminster's overall policy on the social services had been determined, he did promise that 'the adoption of any of the services popularly associated with the name of Beveridge will extend to Northern Ireland in accordance with the declared policy of your Government to ensure to our people the same social service amenities as exist in the rest of the United Kingdom'.[27]

Therefore, although the Stormont government was unable to give specific undertakings on post-war measures designed to improve the province's social services, it was clear that the Unionist administration had committed itself to following Westminster's lead. While this obviously curtailed Stormont's freedom of action, it was a sacrifice that the Unionist government was prepared to make in order to improve the province's social services and retain Protestant working-class support. Brooke and his ministers assumed that by binding themselves to Westminster in this way they would be more likely to receive the necessary financial assistance from the Treasury. Labour's unexpected victory did not alter Brooke's resolve, even though it caused considerable unease among the more conservative-minded MPs on the Unionist backbenches. Moreover, the relative success of the NILP convinced the leadership that Stormont would have to follow Westminster's lead in welfare legislation if Protestant working-class support was to be retained. Outside welfare services, however, it was clear that the Unionist government would make every effort to exert full control over other areas of economic policy.

One of the first problems to confront the Unionist government following Brooke's emergence as leader was housing. In the inter-war period Northern Ireland had fallen well behind England and Wales in the construction of new dwellings. The main reason for the province's poor record was the reluctance of both the Unionist government and the local authorities, most of which were Unionist controlled, to accept responsibility for the provision of new houses. Instead, the Belfast administration relied on private enterprise, supported by government subsidies, to cater for the province's housing needs.[28] As in other areas of social and economic policy in the inter-war years, the Unionist government's housing policy reflected its general laissez faire approach, but the housing shortage was suddenly exacerbated by the impact of German air raids on Belfast in 1941. This focused attention on the province's shortage of dwellings and highlighted the government's earlier neglect of Northern Ireland's housing needs. Demands from Unionist backbenchers for urgent action fell on deaf ears, as Andrews and Bates refused to sanction the creation of a new ministry, which would take responsibility for the construction and repair of dwellings, claiming that any change should await a decision on post-war priorities.[29] It was precisely this kind of confused inaction that contributed to the growing disquiet within the Unionist party, which ultimately led to Andrews' downfall in May 1943.

While the Brooke government demonstrated greater urgency, its initial contribution to the housing shortage was insignificant. Facing the old problem of binding the Treasury to a major financial commitment, Lowry, the new minister of home affairs, argued that something positive should be done immediately to reassure the government's supporters that action was being taken, 'even if the number of houses … provided would be almost negligible'. He wanted Stormont to open negotiations with the Treasury on the approximate number of houses that Northern Ireland was entitled to build in order to make up the leeway, but recognized that, as building on the mainland was confined to the replacement of homes damaged during air raids, there would be little likelihood of success.[30] After further consideration, however, Lowry agreed to a request for financial assistance for 2,000 new homes to replace houses destroyed in the blitz, but the authorities in Belfast were informed that the Treasury would only agree to the construction of 250 new houses.[31] These negotiations with the

Treasury on housing provision for the province demonstrated the worthlessness of Andrews' 1942 leeway agreement. Only a 'vague promise' to consider further grants was forthcoming from the Treasury,[32] and the Unionist government was forced to concede that independent action by the Stormont authorities to tackle the province's housing needs was impracticable.[33]

Yet the Brooke government remained under pressure to make some gesture on housing. A survey undertaken by the Ministry of Home Affairs, which was published in 1944, highlighted the seriousness of the situation in the province. It estimated that 100,000 new houses were required to meet immediate needs, and that of the existing stock of 323,000 dwellings, 229,500 needed repairs.[34] With the NILP attacking government inaction, Brooke responded by creating a Ministry of Health and Local Government, which took up its duties on 1 June 1944 and was given housing as one of its responsibilities. Furthermore, his choice of the trade unionist and former shipyard worker, William Grant, to head the ministry deflected some of the criticism, because it was widely known that Grant was genuinely committed to the improvement of Northern Ireland's social services. From the outset, the new minister argued that the state would have to share the housing burden with local authorities.[35] Grant also urged immediate action, and he proposed the establishment of a Housing Trust, similar to the Scottish Special Housing Association, that would work alongside the local authorities on house building.[36] Significantly, Midgley had previously argued the case for such a body in cabinet, but his proposal was rejected by Lowry, the minister responsible for housing, who thought there would be considerable opposition from both the people and the local authorities to such widespread state interference in housing.[37] Over the course of the next twelve months, however, a growing awareness of the Ulster people's post-war expectations and the sheer size of the province's housing requirements forced the cabinet to accept the need for urgent action, and this led to the adoption of Grant's proposal. Finance for the Trust was to be provided by loans from the Stormont government, which had secured Treasury approval, as the new arrangement would not go beyond the financial provisions involved in the funding of the Scottish Special Housing Association.[38] Notwithstanding the need for an energetic government response and Grant's obvious enthusiasm for the project, some Unionist ministers remained sceptical about state interference in housing, particularly in relation to the Trust's power to obtain building land by compulsory purchase.[39] Crucially, Brooke was steadfast in his support for Grant, and he recognized that only radical changes in housing policy would enable his government to retain public confidence. The prime minister was also aware that his government's plans would be hampered by a shortage of skilled labour and materials after the war, and he was adamant that the state should take control of all building activity and introduce a scale of priorities.[40]

The Housing (No. 2) Bill, which included the proposal to set up a Northern Ireland Housing Trust, was given a stormy second reading when it was introduced at Stormont in November 1944. Several Unionist backbenchers, including the former prime minister, Andrews, now a constant critic of the Brooke government, attacked the Housing Trust, claiming that it represented the nationalization of housing in the province.[41] Opposition to nationalization had always been one of the Unionist party's fundamental principles, and, as Westminster had no plans for a similar measure, some backbenchers attributed the establishment of the Trust to Midgley's influence.[42] Sinclair attempted to restore calm on the back-benches by emphasizing that the Trust would provide only 25 per cent of the houses required in the post-war period.[43] In addition, the cabinet had ensured that legislation for the Housing Trust was consistent with its general attitude towards immigration from Éire. It specified that a tenant had either to have been born in Northern Ireland or to have lived in the United Kingdom for the previous seven years in order to be eligible for a Trust house.[44] Although the housing measures passed in 1945 had departed from the British pattern by providing subsidies for private builders, Grant continued to be bitterly criticized by local builders' organizations and by right wingers within the Unionist party. At the Ulster Unionist Council in February 1946 he was attacked as an opponent of private enterprise, and a resolution demanding more concessions to private builders was adopted.[45] Yet the 1945 act, which had established the Northern Ireland Housing Trust, did not interfere with the generous subsidies offered to the local authorities. In fact, Grant had been forced to reverse his earlier decision to withdraw subsidies to private builders, following pressure both from the backbenches and within the cabinet. While he claimed that even this U-turn would fail to satisfy the building lobby, Grant was keen to remind his cabinet colleagues that the money was being provided by a Labour government, which offered no parallel financial assistance to private enterprise building in Great Britain.[46]

Despite his frustration, Grant recognized, as did Brooke, that the new Labour government was more inclined to acknowledge and act on Northern Ireland's case in the leeway argument than any of its predecessors. On the introduction of the 1946 Housing and Local Government Bill, which incorporated the private enterprise subsidies, he praised the Labour government for its sympathy and practical assistance in dealing with this contentious issue.[47] In preparing the new legislation Grant had sought to eliminate speculative building. He insisted that an Excessive Rents Tribunal control the rents of the new subsidized houses and wanted an embargo on the sale of these houses for at least ten years after their completion. Following further criticism, however, the government was forced to accept a Senate amendment rejecting the no sale clause.[48] Accordingly, while Grant had been greatly encouraged by the Labour government's response to the province's housing shortage, he faced increasing opposition from within his own party to the government's housing programme, particularly in relation to the activities of the Housing Trust. Nevertheless, he was determined that the government should become increasingly involved in the provision of new houses in the province. In March 1946, in conjunction with the Rev. Robert Moore, the minister of agriculture, Grant prepared new proposals for rural housing which would have offered substantial government aid to the poorest farmers for the erection of new dwellings and the improvement of existing ones.[49] On closer examination Grant realized that the rural district councils, some of which had built no houses for over twenty years, urgently required the assistance of the

Housing Trust, but there was considerable opposition from the councils to this proposed extension of the Trust's responsibilities. When legislation did appear in 1946 to give the Trust responsibility for some rural housing, it also included concessions to private enterprise housing.[50]

As early as 1946, therefore, it was clear that the Unionist government, which Grant had boasted was 'miles ahead of the housing legislation passed at Westminster',[51] had begun to waver in the face of pressure from the party's right wing. The post-war social awareness displayed by the Unionist government, coupled with Grant's enthusiasm for increased state participation in the provision of houses, had enabled Stormont to embark on a comprehensive housing policy. In this it was given considerable assistance and encouragement by the post-war Labour government, which appeared to have a good understanding of the social problems facing the Northern Ireland authorities. Grant had shown that finance for the provision of new houses was available, when specific proposals were put to the Labour government, but, faced with opposition from within the party, the Unionist government failed to take full advantage of a benevolent administration at Westminster and build on its initial achievements. Opposition to the government's housing programme centred on the activities of the Northern Ireland Housing Trust. The efforts of a genuine social reformer such as Grant could not outweigh his party's natural conservatism. Although a more radical response to Northern Ireland's housing requirements had been deemed a political necessity, support for state involvement in the housing programme, through the medium of the Housing Trust, was always lukewarm. The actions of Unionist-dominated local authorities were a constant source of frustration to the Trust, which was unable to rely on the resolute support of the Stormont government. Subsequently, the Housing Trust faced considerable opposition from the Ministry of Finance, a development that appeared to gather momentum with Grant's death in 1949. The Treasury's attention was drawn to this in 1950, and the Ministry of Finance was informed of its concern. As it had been unable to obtain money from the Northern Ireland government, the Housing Trust had to borrow money from the finance houses in London, but this alarmed officials at the Treasury who feared that these institutions would quickly withdraw their capital, if they saw something more profitable.[52] Clearly, the Unionist administration lacked the necessary conviction to implement a comprehensive state housing scheme, even though generous financial backing from the Labour government could have been anticipated. Instead, the Unionist government bowed to backbench pressure for the promotion of private enterprise housing and refused to challenge local authorities, which remained in control of most of the province's public housing. Of course, in later years, local government control of housing became one of the minority's main grievances, because it was alleged that local politicians used the allocation of houses for both political patronage and the careful control of local government electoral areas. Successive Unionist governments defended themselves by claiming that they issued no such directives, but this did not absolve the Brooke administration from responsibility for its neglect and inaction, despite Grant's repeated warnings about local government inefficiency in relation to housing.

NORTHERN IRELAND AND LABOUR'S ECONOMIC POLICY

Labour's shock election victory also had major implications for the Northern Ireland economy, as a much greater level of state interference was now anticipated. In the inter-war period a laissez faire approach had characterized the Craigavon government's economic strategy, and the Belfast administration found itself unable to respond effectively to the economic turmoil of the early 1930s. The recession had been particularly damaging to the province's old staple industries of textiles and shipbuilding, and unemployment rose sharply. The Unionist government's limited attempts to create employment through measures such as the 1932 and 1937 New Industries (Development) Acts had little impact, and, instead, most attention was concentrated on ensuring that unemployment benefits were maintained at the same level as those provided in Great Britain. In fact, the province's unemployment total only fell significantly during the Second World War, and, even then, progress was painfully slow. In 1942, when war contracts were stimulating the local economy and there was a labour shortage on the mainland, the province's unemployment rate was still running at 5 per cent.[53] The Brooke government's more vigorous prosecution of the war effort boosted both agriculture and industry, but the new Unionist administration quickly appreciated that the state would have to assume increased responsibility for the creation of employment in the post-war period. This was deemed a political necessity if the Unionist party was to retain Protestant working-class support. Of course, the key question in the provision of employment for Northern Ireland would be the division of responsibility between the Stormont and Westminster governments.[54]

Under the terms of the 1920 act the provision of employment was a transferred matter, but, by the end of the war, the Brooke government was pressing the authorities in London for assistance in cutting unemployment. Sinclair, in particular, was adamant that Westminster had to share the burden, as Stormont did not have the capacity to pursue an independent full employment policy.[55] Such a demand, however, drew a sharp response from Ernest Bevin, still seething at the absence of conscription in Northern Ireland, which he argued was the main reason for the province's continuing unemployment problems. In his role as chairman of the Distribution of Industry Committee, Bevin warned the Unionist cabinet that further assistance for industry in the province would undoubtedly generate ill feeling on the part of employers in Great Britain.[56] A more sympathetic voice came from Sir Stafford Cripps, the president of the Board of Trade, who offered to absorb the province's redundant aircraft labour in England. Yet the Unionist leader was in no position to accept such an offer. While Brooke acknowledged that a transfer of labour might ultimately prove inevitable, he insisted that 'on political grounds such a step should only be contemplated as a last resort'.[57] For the Unionist administration, therefore, agreement with Westminster on a full employment strategy had become a crucial issue. With the NILP taking a keen interest, Brooke felt under pressure to issue an upbeat statement in the spring of 1945, outlining his government's plans for tackling future unemployment. As the authorities in Belfast wanted to place on record their view that the major responsibility for the provision of post-war employment in Northern Ireland would rest with Westminster, the Home Office was informed that the Brooke statement would highlight the fact that in pursuit of a full employment policy ministers in London were 'taking all possible steps, in conjunction with the Northern Ireland Government, to encourage the establishment of industrial enterprises here which will absorb the available labour capacity'.[58] Not surprisingly, officials in Bevin's department objected to Brooke's choice of words, and a Home Office reply suggested that the statement should confine itself to stating that the Unionist government would have the 'full co-operation' of the Westminster authorities in promoting industry in Northern Ireland.[59]

The Westminster government's refusal to commit itself to specific guarantees concerning the provision of employment in Northern Ireland in the post-war period increased apprehension among Unionist ministers, and an angry Sinclair urged Brooke to stand firm on what he described as a matter of principle:

> The whole basis of the relations between the two Governments rests on this, that as citizens of the United Kingdom our people, who pay the same taxation and are subject to the same controls and regulations, should receive the same treatment. Between the wars we seem to have been content to make a song and dance about parity of social services in which unemployment benefit has loomed large, and to allow the British Government to rather escape its responsibility for the far more important aspect of parity in the employment field, namely employment itself.

Failure to reach a favourable agreement, Sinclair argued, would fatally damage the Unionist government, because new plans to report unemployment statistics by region would expose Stormont's failings. In concluding, Sinclair emphasized that Stormont's responsibility for providing full employment could only be 'a minor one', whereas the government at Westminster would have to 'shoulder the lion's share'. It was absolutely essential, he stressed, to convince the authorities in London that Northern Ireland was 'as much entitled to a high level of employment' as any other part of the United Kingdom.[60] In the end the failure to reach agreement on the terms of Brooke's speech on post-war employment policy meant that the Stormont government was forced to postpone the statement. This only added to Stormont's embarrassment, because, towards the end of March, the Unionist government had to announce that the province's unemployment total had passed the 23,000 mark.[61] With the prospect of a steady increase in this figure after the war, the government became even more anxious to reassure its supporters. Consequently, a new draft statement with less emphasis on Westminster's role was presented to the Home Office for approval. The authorities at Stormont now wanted to include a sentence which referred not only to what the Unionist government could do to provide employment, but also highlighted the extent to which it would have to rely on Westminster 'for co-operation and assistance'.[62] Although this proposal omitted any reference to Westminster bearing the major responsibility for the provision of employment in Northern Ireland, officials at the Ministry of Labour and National Service continued to object: 'We feel that the statement overstresses the effect on conditions in Northern Ireland of action by the Imperial Government to stimulate prosperity in the United Kingdom generally.'[63] A further amendment, which stated that Westminster was 'taking all possible steps' in conjunction with Stormont to utilize Northern Ireland's resources, seemed, at last, to have satisfied all the Westminster departments concerned. As the civil servants at Stormont were making their final preparations for Brooke's statement, however, Gransden, the cabinet secretary, received a telephone message from London informing him that Bevin, in his capacity as chairman of the Distribution of Industry Committee, had objected to the expression 'the British Government were taking all possible steps' to utilize the province's resources.[64] Therefore, two months of frantic discussion had failed to produce a satisfactory solution for the Belfast government, which was desperate for Westminster to assume more responsibility for the provision of new jobs in post-war Northern Ireland. This left the Brooke government in a difficult position, as the local parliament debated post-war economic and employment policy in May 1945. At Stormont the NILP was pressing the Unionist administration for specific guarantees on employment policy in the knowledge that the post-war government at Westminster, whether Labour or Conservative, would be committed to full employment. In its response an embarrassed Unionist front bench could not hide its pessimism, as it played down expectations of full employment in the province.

Better news for the local economy at the end of the war came with the preparation of the Northern Ireland Industries Development Bill, which was designed to attract new industry to the province. Although not covered by Westminster's 1945 Distribution of Industry Act, which created a number of Development Areas to promote industrial activity in depressed regions that had suffered from high unemployment in the inter-war period, Northern Ireland intended to have more wide-ranging powers under its own legislation. This would allow the Ministry of Commerce at Stormont to offer more generous financial inducements to new firms than would be available in the Development Areas on the mainland.[65] While the Unionist government gave guarantees that it would not engage in direct competition with the Development Areas, serious differences soon emerged between the Ministry of Commerce in Belfast and the Board of Trade in London. In spite of these teething problems with the operation of the 1945 Industries Development Act, the measure was partially successful. One aim of the legislation had been to widen the province's industrial base in order to reduce the impact of future economic recessions. By January 1946 ten new factories, including Courtaulds and Metal Box, had been established, and it was anticipated that they would create some 4,700 new jobs.[66] Earlier, however, Sir Roland Nugent, the minister of commerce, had sounded a note of caution when he informed the cabinet that in its eagerness to attract new industry the Unionist government was incurring the wrath of existing industrialists, many of whom were, of course, influential in the party.[67] Although the Brooke administration pressed on with the new strategy, it later made a significant contribution to the older manufacturers with the passage of the 1951 and 1953 Re-equipment of

Industry Acts. Under this legislation grants were provided to meet one third of re-equipment and modernization costs, but, unlike the Development Areas on the mainland, neither of the two acts required the established industries to create new employment.[68]

Further problems in the immediate post-war period arose over the allocation of scarce resources such as coal and steel. The new Labour government introduced a new system to give priority in the distribution of these resources to the Development Areas. As Northern Ireland suffered more acutely from these shortages, Westminster agreed to treat the province as a Development Area, but, in spite of this understanding, industrial progress in the province was delayed because the necessary materials were frequently not made available. As a Treasury official explained, Northern Ireland's difficulty in obtaining materials was 'due to the fact that the authorities responsible for allocating materials periodically forget that Northern Ireland should be treated as a development area'. Indeed, John Wilmot, the minister of supply in the Attlee administration, confessed to Sinclair that 'Northern Ireland had been forgotten' in the allocations of structural steel, while Hugh Gaitskell, the chairman of the Materials Committee, informed the Treasury that he had not even received instructions to treat the province as a Development Area in distributing scarce resources.[69] As a consequence of this oversight, Hugh Dalton, the chancellor of the exchequer, urged Cripps to give more assistance to the promotion of industrial activity in the province. While he recognized that Northern Ireland had to look after its own interests, the chancellor emphasized that a prosperous regional economy meant a higher imperial contribution to the United Kingdom exchequer, and that some of the province's exports, particularly linen, were good earners of United States currency, something which was very important for the British economy in 1947.[70] This support for the Stormont administration led to the establishment of harmonious relations between the Treasury and the Ministry of Finance in Belfast. Moreover, the Attlee government's willingness to inject cash into the province contrasted sharply with the actions of its predecessors. Towards the end of the war the Churchill government had stubbornly refused to commit itself on a range of post-war measures that would have necessitated increased support for the province, and, during the 1930s, when Conservative-dominated coalition governments were in power, the Treasury was constantly in dispute with the Ministry of Finance, often over trivial amounts of cash.

More serious problems in Stormont–Westminster relations were anticipated when the Unionist government began to study the legislative programme of Attlee's new Labour administration. Neither the proposed introduction of the welfare state, which the Unionist government could turn to its advantage, nor the nationalization programme, which had little relevance to Northern Ireland, would present difficulties, but Brooke and his colleagues were wary of Labour's intention to retain, and possibly extend, wartime economic controls. This problem first arose with the Supplies and Services (Transitional Powers) Bill which was designed to centralize control of the distribution of raw materials and finished products. When the Unionist cabinet discussed the measure, Nugent, the minister of commerce, emphasized the increasing difficulties since Labour took office. Brooke himself expressed concern at Westminster's intentions. While it might have been convenient in this instance to allow the authorities at Westminster to exercise such control, the Unionist premier warned that it would be a mistake 'to allow them to take over our legislative powers'.[71] On the other hand, three of his ministers urged caution, fearing that there might be an inclination on the part of the Unionist government to overreact to economic measures proposed by the new Labour government. As Grant explained: 'The fact that the present Government of the United Kingdom has a different political complexion to our own should ... be regarded as a passing phase and should not make us lose sight of the vital necessity for keeping our Northern Ireland economy linked as closely as possible to the United Kingdom.'[72]

Grant's view received strong support from Sinclair and Moore, the minister of agriculture. Sinclair argued that contentious measures such as the Supplies and Services Bill would prove less embarrassing to the Unionist government if left to Westminster, while Moore reminded his colleagues that the proposed legislation was really an extension of a system that had worked to the province's benefit during the war.[73] Eventually, the cabinet decided that the bill did not represent a threat to Stormont's powers, and no opposition to the measure was offered.

A similar dilemma occurred only a few weeks later, when the Stormont cabinet considered the Investment (Control and Guarantees) Bill. One clause in the bill, which covered the general control of investments within the United Kingdom, infringed on a transferred service. While Sinclair conceded that this made economic sense, he expressed personal reservations on the broader implications of Stormont's acceptance of the bill, arguing that it would be dangerous to establish a precedent allowing Westminster to legislate on any transferred service.[74] In the cabinet discussion that followed, Brooke considered the prospects of deteriorating relations between Belfast and London, if Labour sought to introduce 'more extreme socialistic measures' which would have to be followed at Stormont:

> The Government might have to face a situation in which a measure which they considered they had no alternative but to introduce ... would be unacceptable to members of the Unionist party, and if the Government could not rely on their support chaotic conditions would result ... he was extremely uneasy on this score and had been considering whether any changes could be made to avert such a situation. The possibilities were Dominion status or a return to Westminster.[75]

Similar concerns over the erosion of Stormont's powers were again raised in December 1945, when the cabinet discussed a Brooke memorandum on a proposal by the BBC to broadcast a series of talks, entitled 'The Week in Stormont'. The Unionist leader thought the series 'highly undesirable', as it would give Nationalist MPs a platform to promote their anti-partition campaign. Of even more significance, however, was his view that the programmes could convey the impression that the Belfast parliament was 'of little importance'. Although the Northern Ireland director-general of the BBC guaranteed that guests would be carefully selected for the three programmes, and that their scripts would be scrutinized 'to ensure that nothing objectionable was said', Brooke continued to oppose the series.[76] In spite of Brooke's opposition, the BBC decided to press ahead, only to drop the series when it realized that individual Unionist MPs would not participate. Clearly, Brooke had used his influence on the backbenches to force the cancellation of the series.[77] This rather trivial episode illustrated the Unionist government's determination to emphasize the prestige of the Stormont parliament at a critical period when it believed itself to be under close scrutiny by the new administration at Westminster.

In highlighting the importance of the local parliament the Unionist government was naturally anxious to defend its control over transferred powers. This had become a problem because Labour's plans to increase state control of the economy meant that it frequently wanted to legislate on a United Kingdom basis and, therefore, override some of the transferred powers delegated to Stormont. Yet any insistence on strict constitutional procedure might prove detrimental to the Northern Ireland economy. When the cabinet considered the Defence (Services for Industry) Regulations, which gave some of Stormont's transferred powers to the Board of Trade, Brooke outlined the problems facing his government:

> ... it had been the consistent view of the Cabinet that services clearly within our powers should be left to be dealt with by the Parliament of Northern Ireland ... however ... if we adhered strictly to this policy in the present instance Northern Ireland industry might be deprived of certain benefits which would otherwise accrue to it by inclusion in the regulations on a United Kingdom basis.[78]

Once again, despite its reservations, the cabinet decided not to object to the Defence Regulations. While it was clear that the Board of Trade was taking control of some of Stormont's powers, Brooke and his team satisfied themselves with a request that the authorities in Belfast be consulted before any regulations affecting the province were made.[79]

Still, anxiety about the future prospects for devolution in Northern Ireland, with Labour in power, continued to trouble the Unionist government during 1946. This led to a serious debate in the cabinet about the advantages of dominion status. The two leading proponents on each side of the dominion status argument were Nugent and Moore, and both had their supporters within the cabinet. In January 1946 Nugent circulated a document in which he advocated seeking additional powers for Stormont, though this might stop short of full dominion status.[80] His argument was based on the view that it was the Labour government's intention to 'control the entire economic life of the United Kingdom'. Soon, Nugent warned, Labour could introduce legislation which would be unacceptable to Stormont, or, worse, it might unintentionally whittle away Stormont's independence through a series of orders and regulations designed to develop its own policies. For the minister of commerce, this would present a greater problem, because each separate piece of legislation would seem harmless and 'scarcely worth fighting', but repetition of the process would lead to the province 'being run from Westminster'. In these circumstances, Nugent advocated an extension of Stormont's existing powers, a development that he thought would find favour with the 'Ulster electorate', which had 'the typical mentality of a society based on small farms and small businesses'. In return for such an extension of devolution, Nugent suggested that Northern Ireland could give up its representation at Westminster. This was not a knee-jerk response to the experience of a socialist government in London, because Nugent was convinced that Stormont would face difficulties in its future relationship with Westminster, even if a Conservative government was in office: 'Britain seemed to have shifted significantly leftwards, and governments, Labour or Conservative, would hereafter assume much tighter planning and control, irksome to Ulstermen used to semi-independence.'[81] In the following month Nugent's recommendations received tentative support from Brian Maginess. He claimed that Stormont was moving towards a situation where it could become a Westminster department, while, simultaneously, the Unionist party would 'commit suicide by carrying out socialist legislation'. Nevertheless, Maginess issued a cautious note in his memorandum, warning that any move towards dominion status might have grave economic consequences. In his concluding remarks Maginess stated that the present Unionist government had three alternatives. It could maintain the status quo and try to overcome the difficulties that would arise with Labour in office. Alternatively, he suggested that Stormont could request more powers, while continuing to receive financial assistance. Finally, he made the tentative suggestion that Stormont could press for much greater independence and 'live within its own resources', though he acknowledged that there were potential pitfalls with this proposal, as it could limit social service provision in the province, and this 'would weaken one of our most telling arguments' against unification with Éire. While he noted that firm conclusions could not yet be reached, it was clear that Maginess favoured dominion status, if sufficient support for agriculture and social services could be negotiated with Westminster. If these safeguards could be obtained, Maginess claimed:

> We would be masters of our own house, having actual as well as nominal power and responsibility. We would no longer be able to confess our inability to control our own destinies and we would be relieved of the constant anxiety as to what an unfriendly British Government might be tempted to do in the way of pressing us to end partition.

The crucial arguments, which persuaded the Unionist cabinet to reject any move towards dominion status, were advanced by Moore in two memoranda in April and June 1946.[82] The minister of agriculture had undertaken an investigation into the likely impact of dominion status on the province's agricultural industry. On financial grounds alone, he argued that dominion status did not make sense. Current British subsidies were worth £13 million per year to Northern Ireland farmers, and this sum simply could not be met from the province's resources. Furthermore, he warned that any attempt by the Unionist government to modify the existing constitutional position could lead to serious difficulties:

We would certainly not be able to look for any financial assistance from Westminster and might well find ourselves in the position of having higher taxation, lower social services, and lower agricultural prices than in Great Britain. We might well be sacrificing the substance of economic security on the British level for a shadowy independence which might carry the seeds of its own destruction through a deterioration in our economic prosperity.

Moore's argument convinced his colleagues that they should not be tempted by dominion status. While he had been primarily concerned about the prospects for the province's farmers, his analysis of the potential consequences of dominion status had raised major doubts about Northern Ireland's economic future. Nugent, the leading advocate of increased devolution, remained sceptical, but, as minister of commerce, he headed the department most likely to be affected by the Labour government's policy of tighter economic planning and control. This effectively reduced his capacity for independent action. However, other members of the cabinet had their own concerns. As minister of health, Grant was opposed to any move towards dominion status, as he knew that the Northern Ireland exchequer could not finance the level of expenditure on social services envisaged under the welfare state. This view was endorsed by a majority of Unionist ministers, who realized that any move towards dominion status threatened the adoption of welfare measures that were deemed essential if the Stormont government was to retain Protestant working-class support and halt the NILP's advance.

Nevertheless, Labour's commitment to increased state intervention in the economy proved to be a recurring problem for the Unionist government. At Stormont's request Northern Ireland was omitted from the scope of Labour's Borrowing (Control and Guarantee) Bill on the condition that a similar measure would be introduced in the devolved parliament. When the Unionist cabinet discussed the measure, it was agreed that the Stormont bill should include a five-year limiting clause, but the initiative was rejected by the chancellor. News of Westminster's intervention caused Nugent to warn that the introduction of the Northern Ireland Loans Guarantee and Borrowing Bill, which would be a permanent feature, was 'tantamount to acceptance of socialist doctrine'.[83] Although both Nugent and Sinclair expressed their dissatisfaction, the measure was passed without a time limit. The Brooke government's repeated acceptance of Labour's economic legislation, however, was beginning to cause misgivings both on the Unionist backbenches and within the wider party. These doubts increased substantially, when the controversy over the Statistics of Trade Bill emerged in the final months of 1946. Nugent had argued that Northern Ireland should be omitted from the Westminster bill, though he acknowledged that a similar measure would have to be introduced at Stormont, because these statistics were necessary to formulate the full employment policy to which the Unionist government was committed.[84] Yet the release of this information would be regarded as a burden by the province's business community and a further sign of unwelcome government interference in the economy. Previously, Nugent had pressed the case for dominion status, but he now no longer found it necessary to confine his views to the secrecy of cabinet meetings. In a speech to the Oxford University Conservative Association he informed his audience that Northern Ireland needed 'a greater degree of self government so as to ease the administrative difficulties which arise from our form of subordinate constitution in a time when Governments regulate the lives and activities of their citizens in far greater detail than they did when that Constitution was drafted'.[85]

It was the controversy over the Northern Ireland Statistics of Trade Bill, which was eventually introduced in October 1947, that led to a wider debate on dominion status within the Unionist party. Indeed, the threat of a major backbench revolt forced the postponement of the second reading, as the government attempted to appease angry Unionist backbenchers with the promise of the establishment of an independent committee of businessmen to recommend changes to the existing bill.[86] The leading backbench advocate of dominion status was W.F. McCoy, the MP for South Tyrone, who consistently argued that while Stormont continued as a subordinate parliament, 'Socialist legislation could be forced upon Ulster.' In return for full dominion status McCoy suggested that Stormont should give up territorial rights to Britain for all time, concede the right to declare war and 'at all times give unswerving loyalty and attachment to the Crown and Protestant establishment of the throne and Constitution'.[87] In their response to McCoy, leading Unionists were anxious to stress that the Labour leadership fully supported Northern Ireland's constitutional position, and Brooke pointed out that as Stormont was a subordinate parliament, it had no alternative but to pass legislation that was vital to the United Kingdom economic interest: 'We must play the game with the Imperial Government, no matter what that Government is.' Yet, at the same time, Warnock sought to reassure Unionist supporters by declaring that 'there is no member of the Ulster Government who has the slightest sympathy with socialism, in any shape or form'.[88]

While most backbenchers did not share McCoy's enthusiasm for full dominion status, there was considerable dissatisfaction with Stormont's tame acceptance of Labour's economic legislation. This prompted the cabinet to review the government's relations with the administration in London, allowing Nugent to return to the problems that Stormont experienced with a Labour government in power at Westminster. He was concerned that the present Labour government had immense executive powers, much greater than any pre-war government, which included 'the increasing use of taxation for social and political, rather than purely financial purposes'. In effect, Nugent claimed that the Labour administration possessed sufficient powers 'to turn us into a Socialist State', and though Labour ministers had used these powers with moderation thus far, they were 'after all Socialists', who were conditioned to believe 'the State more important than the individual and autocratic action natural and laudable in the interests of the State'. Strict wartime controls had been acceptable under Churchill's leadership during the war, but 'even more drastic action in peace under a Government which you distrust, and indeed, suspect of using the crisis to rivet a socialist system round your neck' could not be tolerated. Nugent's memorandum then highlighted the Unionist government's dilemma, as refusal to accept these measures would disrupt Stormont–Westminster relations and would eventually lead to the province being 'kicked into Éire'. He did not believe, moreover, that a Conservative victory at the next election would resolve the problem: 'Even if a Conservative majority is returned, Labour will still be the only alternative government and will sooner or later be in power again, and whatever Government is in power in England, it is bound to adopt measures which are either unnecessary or actually harmful here.'

In his conclusion Nugent offered three alternatives for his colleagues to consider in cabinet. His first suggestion, not surprisingly, was a thorough investigation of the implications of dominion status for the province. As a second option, he asked the cabinet to consider the proposal made by Major J.B. Perceval-Maxwell, the parliamentary secretary to the Ministry of Commerce, that the Unionist government should seek a one-clause amendment to the Government of Ireland Act, which would make Stormont sovereign in so far as legislation on transferred matters was concerned. This would not offer the same protection as dominion status, but it would make Northern Ireland 'constitutionally safe from having Socialist legislation passed over our heads'. Finally, Nugent proposed that Brooke should meet Attlee to discuss the Unionist government's problems in the hope that the Labour leader would consider implementing changes to ease these difficulties.[89]

Although Nugent had put forward three options, it was clear from the tone of his memorandum that he still favoured full dominion status. Brooke took the opposite view. The prime minister was clearly angered by the growing criticism of 'the allegedly Socialistic leanings' of his government, but he was astute enough to recognize that the demand for dominion status from some of his backbenchers and certain sections of the business community was partly due to the ill feeling generated by petrol rationing and the row over the Statistics of Trade Bill. While these 'restrictions, controls and shortages' had irritated many Unionist supporters, Brooke emphasized that there was no indication that his government's adoption of welfare proposals had contributed to the growing demand for dominion status. For Brooke, the need to maintain parity in social services with Britain was vital for the Unionist government, and it was a compelling argument against tampering with the present constitutional position. Although he acknowledged that there had been some problems in dealing with the Labour government, Stormont 'had been able to surmount them ad hoc as they arose'. If a major difficulty did emerge in the near future, Brooke thought it wise to concede Westminster's supremacy. In his concluding remarks Brooke made a tentative proposal that he thought would ease the difficulties for his administration in working with the Labour government. He suggested that Ulster Unionists at Westminster should not 'go into the Lobby against the Government on every occasion'.[90] The radical suggestion that Ulster Unionist MPs at Westminster should occasionally support the Labour government had originally been made by Herbert Morrison, the lord president of the council, during an informal meeting with Brooke, while on a visit to Northern Ireland in September 1946.[91] Morrison was, of course, a key figure in the Attlee government, and he had established a close relationship with Brooke during the latter stages of the war.[92] Yet, while Brooke had included the Morrison proposal in his memorandum, his closing remarks indicated the tentative nature of the proposal:

> It must be recognised that the electorate who sent them to Westminster and who maintain our Party in power at Stormont regard Unionism and Conservatism as almost synonymous: the Ulster members have in the main been elected on an anti-socialist platform and it would be wrong to expect them to subordinate their duties to their constituents to compliance with the policy of co-operation which ... must continue to be our course of action.[93]

When the cabinet discussed these issues, Maginess also queried the wisdom of Westminster Unionists working so closely with the Conservative opposition: 'The Government of Northern Ireland was not a Tory Government; it was a Unionist Government.' Nevertheless, the majority of the cabinet did not approve of a realignment of the party's Westminster MPs. Warnock led the opposition, claiming that any inconsistency caused by the fact that 'Ulster Members were in active opposition to the Labour Government while the Government of Northern Ireland were co-operating with them was of relatively minor importance.'[94] Warnock's casual dismissal of such potential embarrassment ignored the criticism faced by the authorities at Stormont over measures such as the Statistics of Trade Bill. Probably, Warnock's observations were coloured by his own experience as minister of home affairs. Controversial issues, such as the Special Powers Act, the control of immigrant labour from Éire and the limited local government franchise, remained under Stormont control with little interference from the Labour administration in London. Outside cabinet, meanwhile, Brooke was anxious to highlight the policy differences between his government and the Attlee government at Westminster. In a speech to the Antrim Unionist Association in November 1947 Brooke declared that his government had not adopted any of Labour's nationalization features. Instead, in an era when all governments were expected to assume more responsibility for the welfare of their citizens, his Unionist administration was determined 'to steer a middle course between the extreme philosophy of laissez faire on the one hand and the fetish of Socialisation on the other'.[95] Still, Brooke's adherence to a 'third way' did not limit the desire for change in some Unionist quarters. Within a fortnight a *Belfast Newsletter* editorial pronounced that the call for dominion status was tending to become insistent.[96] At the end of the month Brooke responded with his fiercest attack to date on the dominion status lobby. Warning that any attempt to adjust the province's constitutional position would reopen the partition question in a dangerous way, Brooke added that increased devolution would seriously threaten his government's ability to maintain welfare services at the current level, and this would cost the party Protestant working-class votes. The Unionist premier, ever wary of the threat posed by the NILP, argued: 'The backbone of Unionism is the Unionist Labour Party. Are these men going to be satisfied if we reject the social services and other benefits we have had by going step-by-step with Britain?'[97]

In spite of these warnings, rumblings over dominion status continued into 1948, as a small group of backbenchers, led by McCoy, maintained the pressure on the Brooke government. Consequently, the party hierarchy took the decision to bar McCoy from addressing the annual Unionist conference in February 1948. Although a resolution, declaring that the advocacy of dominion status was contrary to the interests of the party, was passed unanimously by conference, it was very clear to a nervous Unionist leadership that there was considerable discontent among many delegates with recent party policy. A subsequent motion, stating that the introduction of 'undigested Socialist legislation' was not in the province's best interests, reminded party leaders of the uneasiness stemming from Stormont's collaboration with the Labour government. Underlying some of McCoy's criticism was the belief that existing constitutional arrangements could result in the province being voted into a united Ireland by a hostile Westminster parliament which had ignored Stormont's wishes.[98] While such arguments could be easily brushed aside, it was more difficult to refute the charge that Stormont had deferred to Westminster on too many issues. A further conference motion, criticizing the government's tendency to introduce legislation without a clear mandate from the electorate, served to highlight this, sometimes embarrassing, recent development.[99] In the end, Brooke and his colleagues emerged relatively unscathed from the 1948 party conference, but they realized that an immediate effort would be required to arrest the growing dissatisfaction among Unionist supporters over the government's economic strategy. Accordingly, the prime minister asked his cabinet colleagues to examine the possibility of removing some of the regulations governing the allocation of scarce resources. Otherwise, the Unionist premier warned, attacks on the government's 'so-called socialistic policy' would continue.[100] While individual ministers were considering a way forward, the cabinet had to reach a decision on the application of the Labour government's Monopoly (Enquiry and Control) Bill to Northern Ireland. Although this particular measure could have been construed as an attack on capitalism, the cabinet decided that it had to stay in line with general United Kingdom economic policy and agreed to Northern Ireland's inclusion in the Westminster bill.[101]

Therefore, while Labour's economic policies caused occasional frustration for the authorities at Stormont, there was a clear understanding of the advantages of maintaining uniformity across the United Kingdom. By 1948, moreover, many of their problems had begun to disappear. After three years of Labour rule the Unionist government knew that it had weathered the storm. Most of Labour's election manifesto had been implemented, leaving the nationalization of the iron and steel industry, which did not affect Northern Ireland, as the only controversial issue still to be tackled.[102] The other factor, which had come to the Unionist government's rescue during the closing months of 1948, was the concentration on the border question following the Dublin government's announcement of its intention to declare a republic. For Brooke, this presented Stormont with an opportunity to call for Unionist unity by rallying party supporters to face the new threat presented by Dublin. Once again, however, Nugent took a different view. He saw Éire's decision to leave the Commonwealth as an opportunity to reshape Stormont–Westminster relations. Nugent argued that the province was now in 'an exceptionally favourable position' to demand increased devolution for Northern Ireland. Fearing the extension of socialism under a future Labour government, the minister of commerce claimed that the principal reason for seeking further devolution was the need for the province to have control over its own taxation. He stressed that 'the very high taxation' imposed by the Attlee government was not suited to the province's poorer, basically agricultural economy. If the present high level of taxation continued, Nugent warned that this alone, 'may well drive us in spite of ourselves … into a Socialist economy'.[103] By this stage, however, Nugent was an isolated figure in the cabinet, as Brooke took the lead in expressing a new measure of confidence in the Labour government. Referring to the Unionist government's strategy while a Labour government was in office at Westminster, Brooke stressed that 'as a matter of common sense and practical politics' Stormont has had 'to attune many of its actions to the policy of the United Kingdom Government in power for the time being irrespective of that body's political colour'.[104] In 1948 a correspondent of *The Round Table* noted the changes which had taken place in the province since Labour's return to power:

> One result of the last three years has been a certain realignment of the Unionists themselves. The lessening of the threat of constitutional change which so long strengthened the right wing has enabled the party to regain more of [a] liberal tradition. The prime minister has not deferred to the older and more diehard element in going ahead with social reforms.[105]

Of course, this 'realignment' was primarily due to the presence of a Labour administration at Westminster and not to any diminution of the threat of constitutional change. While Brooke's strategy had attracted criticism from a group of right-wing Unionists, it also resulted in major achievements that consolidated the party's position. The introduction of the welfare state undermined the appeal of the NILP, which had appeared as a major threat to the Unionist party's hold on the Protestant working class after the 1945 elections.

The strength of the Northern Ireland economy in the post-war period also increased popular support for the Brooke government. There had been a decline in the province's unemployment total in both 1947 and 1948, but an increase in the following year prompted the government to seek further assistance from Westminster in the creation of new jobs. A.J. Kelly, the Northern Ireland liaison officer at Westminster, suggested that Stormont officials prepare the groundwork, leaving Unionist ministers free to enter discussions at an advanced stage 'to drive the nails home'. Such a strategy had worked successfully in the preparation of the Ireland Bill, and it was clearly preferable to the system deployed in the inter-war period, when the starting point for negotiations was an appeal by the Ministry of Finance to the Treasury. Moreover, Kelly's correspondence highlighted the benefits of a Labour government at Westminster, as he welcomed the prospect of a second term, because this represented the province's best chance of securing assistance to boost Northern Ireland's industry and provide new jobs.[106] Indeed, Attlee himself had taken a particular interest in Northern Ireland's economic prospects at the beginning of 1950. He was concerned about rising unemployment, noting that: 'It is of course of considerable political importance that we should do all we can to ensure full employment in Northern Ireland.' The Labour premier was keen to broaden the province's industrial base, and he urged the relevant Westminster departments to ensure that there was 'the utmost co-operation' with Stormont to secure this end.[107] In his assessment that a strong economy was of 'political' significance, Attlee clearly wanted to see a stable Northern Ireland, in which support for the British connection remained strong. Since Labour had come to power, the prime minister's opinion of the Unionist government, and Brooke in particular, had risen steadily. Yet his cabinet colleagues did not share Attlee's enthusiasm for helping Stormont to overcome its economic problems. Harold Wilson, the president of the Board of Trade, declared that the province's unemployment was no worse than in depressed areas in Britain. Consequently, Wilson firmly rejected Stormont's case for assistance in the provision of new employment, arguing that the administration had its own powers for attracting new industry, and this was more comprehensive and flexible than Westminster legislation.[108] With no support forthcoming from Westminster, the Unionist government was forced to announce at the end of 1950 that, in spite of its efforts, there were 17,500 unemployed males in the province.[109]

There was further frustration for the Stormont administration following the 1950 general election, when it emerged that Labour was intent on extending its economic powers. On Sinclair's suggestion, the Unionist cabinet reconsidered the 1946 and 1947 memoranda on dominion status and made arrangements to collate McCoy's proposals on increased devolution, which might be used, if future circumstances warranted.[110] All such debate ended, however, with Labour's defeat at the general election of October 1951, and the incoming Conservative government scrapped plans for regulating production and controlling prices. It had been the Attlee administration's economic policy that had angered the province's business community and generated the demand for dominion status among a small section of Unionist backbenchers. This desire for increased devolution also found regular expression in cabinet, where Nugent, who as minister of commerce was most restricted by Labour's economic policy, frequently pressed his colleagues to seek greater independence. Dissatisfaction with the Unionist government had increased in late 1947 and early 1948, but Brooke recognized that much of this disquiet was caused by opposition to the application of controls and the extension of rationing. He also realized that all of these restrictions were necessary, as the United Kingdom found herself facing serious food and fuel shortages following the financial crisis of 1947.[111] Earlier, Brooke had been vociferous in his condemnation of the dominion status campaign. While he accepted that increased state intervention in the economy under Labour had significantly limited Stormont's capacity for independent action, Brooke was willing both to introduce Labour-inspired economic measures at Stormont and to allow Westminster to legislate on certain transferred services. There were obvious political problems with such a course of action, but the Unionist leader judged that these were more than outweighed by the financial benefits. Of course, the willingness to accept so much of Labour's economic programme made it essential for the Belfast administration to emphasize the importance of the local parliament, and to highlight those areas where Stormont differed from Westminster's legislation.

Although the Unionist government was severely criticized for its acceptance of socialist economic measures, particularly between 1945 and 1948, it pursued an independent line in other areas of economic policy. The best example of this was its refusal to follow Westminster's lead in repealing the 1927 Trade Disputes Act. This legislation had been introduced by Baldwin's Conservative government following the 1926 General Strike, and its aim was to curb trade union powers. Its repeal had been a key point in Labour's manifesto, and this was duly implemented in 1946. When the repeal bill was before parliament, Maginess, the minister of labour at Stormont, warned his colleagues that they could expect to come under pressure to repeal Northern Ireland's corresponding legislation. In reviewing the act, Maginess explained that it contained four main provisions, two of which might easily be repealed. However, repeal of the remaining provisions would, in his opinion, create problems and should not be contemplated. One of these dealt with the principle of 'contracting in'. The 1927 legislation required a trade unionist to 'contract in' in order to contribute to the union's political fund, whereas repeal would make it mandatory for the individual to pay into the fund, unless he 'contracted out'. Maginess objected to such a change, as it would provide a financial boost for the Unionist party's political opponents. In his assessment of the Labour government's decision to repeal the 1927 act, the minister of labour stressed that Stormont should not 'blindly' follow Westminster's lead, as the measure had nothing to do with social service provision. Accordingly, he urged his colleagues to resist pressure for repeal of the province's parallel legislation: 'If pressure is brought from any source to make us go the whole length in repeal, I think we should resist.'[112] Stormont's refusal to follow the Labour government's lead on this issue attracted some attention at Westminster. In February 1947, John Edwards, the parliamentary secretary at the Department of Health, considered Stormont's retention of the Trade Disputes Act and asked the Home Office if anything could be done 'to prod the Northern Ireland Government into activity'.[113] Although the Home Office had also received representations from individual British-based trade unions, it was content to issue the standard response that the Westminster government could not interfere with Stormont's decisions on such matters.[114] Yet this did not mean that the Unionist government could escape scrutiny in its handling of labour relations. When an English newspaper carried a report in April 1946 of the RUC baton-charging 300 strikers in Gilford, the Home Office demanded a full account of the incident.[115] While such intervention by the Home Office was unusual, it served as a reminder to the Unionist leadership that the Westminster administration was not totally blind to the indiscretions of the Northern Ireland authorities.

Stormont's decision to retain the Trade Disputes Act enabled Unionist ministers to refute the argument that they slavishly followed the Westminster line on all issues. A token attempt to force the repeal of the 1927 act was subsequently made by Jack Beattie, when he introduced a private member's bill at Stormont. Rejecting Beattie's proposition, that the government should go 'step-by-step' with the Labour administration, Maginess explained to MPs: 'The step-by-step policy only refers to the social services. We are in no way bound to follow …

British legislation. If an Act of Parliament is passed there which we think is a good Act we can follow it. If an Act of Parliament is passed there which we think is a bad Act we will not.'[116]

On occasion, the Unionist government was also able to adapt Westminster policy to suit local conditions. The best example of this flexibility occurred in the development of the province's agricultural policy in the late 1940s. When the authorities at Stormont first considered the long-term direction of agricultural policy, the Westminster government was in the process of framing its own wide-ranging Agriculture Bill. It intended to introduce a system of assured markets and guaranteed prices, while imposing new efficiency regulations to ensure that agricultural land was properly managed. Moore wanted the province's farmers to benefit from the assured markets and guaranteed prices, but he knew that they would oppose any attempt to impose efficiency standards under threat of land dispossession, as advocated by the Labour government. Although the minister of agriculture favoured the inclusion of Northern Ireland in the Labour government's measure, with slight modifications made to suit conditions in the province, his cabinet colleagues rejected this. They were concerned at the constitutional implications of Northern Ireland farmers receiving subsidies under Westminster legislation, as this was a transferred service. Consequently, the cabinet decided that Stormont should have its own bill.[117] Yet this was only a partial solution to the problem, because the difficulty of imposing efficiency standards remained. Moore had insisted that Northern Ireland had to ensure that agricultural land was properly managed, if the province's farmers were to have access to the benefits of assured markets and guaranteed prices. This prompted a serious debate in cabinet, as Nugent argued that the different system of land tenure in Northern Ireland, where the majority of farmers cultivated their own land, necessitated a different approach to disciplinary measures under consideration:

> I hope that we can convince the English Ministers that our circumstances are so different that we can and should seek efficiency by a different road to the one which they intend to take. But if we fail, I think rather than surrender the most important of all the transferred powers, the control of our own agricultural policy, to English direction, we should ... ask to be left out of the Bill altogether, and take our chance on the basis of world prices.[118]

Although Nugent urged his colleagues to reject 'any element of dictation', they backed Moore's proposal, and the authorities at Westminster were informed that the Unionist government would include provisions in its own Agriculture Bill that would secure efficiency standards comparable to those required under the British legislation.[119] However, when it emerged that Unionist backbenchers were unhappy at the extent of the disciplinary measures being proposed, the cabinet hesitated in introducing the Agriculture Bill, and Brooke warned Moore of the political dangers in proceeding with the measure.[120] Yet Moore remained concerned that a Stormont bill which failed to guarantee the highest standards of efficiency would be unacceptable to Westminster. At the very least, he wanted powers to compel an inefficient farmer to let his land to an approved tenant, but he was unable to persuade his cabinet colleagues that this was necessary.[121] When his Agriculture Bill finally came before the Northern Ireland parliament in December 1948, it included a number of alternative clauses designed to promote greater efficiency in Ulster farming, but most of these were substantially amended during the bill's committee stage. In the end, Stormont's legislation differed significantly from Westminster's 1947 Agriculture Act, as Moore's fears of interference by the Labour government proved unfounded. This was, indeed, fortunate for the Unionist administration. Such was the scale of opposition among both backbenchers and farmers to the introduction of these new regulations in agriculture that any attempt by the Labour government to impose its will would, most likely, have led to a serious confrontation between Stormont and Westminster. On the other hand, of course, intervention in the province's affairs was something that the Attlee administration was keen to avoid. As a result, the Northern Ireland Agriculture Act imposed few restrictions on the province's farmers, while providing access to assured markets and guaranteed prices. Moreover, agriculture was one area of the economy where the Unionist government was able to retain a significant level of local control, and this proved useful in countering demands for increased devolution.

NOTES

1. See the *Belfast Telegraph*, 27 July 1945, and the *Northern Whig*, 27 July 1945. Labour had been 5/1 with bookmakers on the mainland.
2. Interview with Mr Jack Rees, a sergeant serving in Germany with the 51st Highland division in 1945.
3. *Belfast Newsletter*, 26 June 1945.
4. *Irish News*, 28 July 1945.
5. *Belfast Newsletter*, 6 June 1945.
6. *Belfast Newsletter*, 7 June 1945.
7. J.F. Harbinson, 'A History of the Northern Ireland Labour Party 1891–1949' (Unpublished MSc. thesis, Queen's University, Belfast, 1966), p.121 and p.130.
8. Midgley's views on the Spanish question were published as a booklet entitled *Spain: The Press, The Pulpit And The Truth*. For a detailed study of Midgley's career, see G. Walker, *The Politics of Frustration: Harry Midgley and the Failure of Labour in Northern Ireland* (Manchester, 1985).
9. Beattie's colleague, J.H. Collins, lost to Harry Diamond, who stood as a Socialist Republican in Falls.
10. Harbinson, *A History of the Northern Ireland Labour Party*, p.171. The new party was formed by Beattie in December 1944.
11. Farrell, *The Orange State*, p.145. Both Mulvey and Cunningham had held their seats since 1935, but had never attended Westminster.
12. *Irish News*, 28 July 1945.
13. J.F. Harbinson, *The Ulster Unionist Party 1882–1973: Its Development and Organisation* (Belfast, 1973), p.106.
14. PRONI, CAB4/571/4, Cab. Conclus., 28 January 1944.
15. PRONI, CAB4/634/4, inner cabinet, 13 September 1945.

Sir Hugh O'Neill (Antrim)	–	Prime Minister
Major S.G. Haughton (Antrim)	–	Finance
Sir William Allen (Armagh)	–	Home Affairs
Lt. Col. C.H. Gage (South Belfast)	–	Labour
Prof. D.L. Savory (Queen's Uni.)	–	Education
Sir Ronald Ross (Londonderry)	–	Agriculture
Sir Walter Smiles (Down)	–	Commerce

16. PRONI, CAB4/634/13, Cab. Conclus., 13 September 1945.

17. NIHC Debates, vol. 29, col. 1307, 21 November 1945.
18. The term 'parity' used by Sinclair referred to a general principle and it has been subject to various interpretations. An official definition of the principle of parity was not developed until 1955: see W.D. Birrell and A.S. Murie, *Policy and Government in Northern Ireland: Lessons of Devolution* (Dublin, 1980), pp.280–3. Harkness has described 'step-by-step' as 'keeping pace with British welfare benefits': see Harkness, *Northern Ireland since 1920*, p.32.
19. NIHC Debates, vol. 26, col. 2412, 3 November 1943.
20. NIHC Debates, vol. 28, cols 27–8, 20 February 1945. In this debate the only specific proposal made by Brooke referred to a Disabled Persons (Employment) Bill which had already been introduced at Westminster.
21. Ibid., col. 79, 21 February 1945.
22. PROL, T160/1277/F18624, 'Postwar Financial Relations with the Government of Northern Ireland', memo by Cook, 7 December 1943.
23. Ibid., memo by R.R. Bowman, permanent secretary to the Ministry of Labour, not dated.
24. Ibid., C.H. Petherick, second secretary at the Ministry of Finance, to E.A. Shillito, a principal secretary at the Treasury, 5 April 1944.
25. Ibid., see note by Sinclair, 28 April 1944.
26. NIHC Debates, vol. 27, col. 1259, 23 May 1944.
27. Ibid., col. 1252, 23 May 1944.
28. W.D. Birrell, P.A.R. Hillyard, A.S. Murie and D.J.D. Roche, *Housing in Northern Ireland* (London, 1971), p.80. The authors have described this as 'a determined reliance on private enterprise and a rejection of public responsibility'.
29. PRONI, see file CAB9B/258, 'Proposed Ministry of Health and Reconstruction'.
30. PRONI, CAB4/556/3, memo by Lowry, 24 September 1943.
31. PRONI, CAB4/557/16, memo by Lowry, 6 October 1943, and CAB4/558/14, Cab. Conclus., 14 October 1943.
32. PRONI, CAB4/560/17, memo by Lowry, 26 October 1943.
33. NIHC Debates, vol. 26, cols 2090–2, 16 November 1943.
34. Lawrence, *The Government of Northern Ireland*, p.152. The survey also looked at long-term housing requirements and estimated that at least 200,000 new houses would be needed to eliminate overcrowding and slums.
35. PRONI, CAB4/595/3, memo by Grant, 4 August 1944.
36. Birrell and Murie, *Policy and Government in Northern Ireland*, p.213.
37. PRONI, CAB4/560/14, memo by Midgley, 25 October 1943, and CAB4/560/22, Cab. Conclus., 26 October 1943.
38. PROL, T233/442/9/332/01, 'Northern Ireland Housing Trust: formation and financing', note by Shillito, 25 October 1944.
39. PRONI, CAB4/595/6, Cab. Conclus., 10 August 1944.
40. PRONI, CAB4/599/10, Cab. Conclus., 28 September 1944.
41. See a speech by Andrews, NIHC Debates, vol. 27, col. 2108, 1 November 1944.
42. See, for example, a speech by Dr W. Lyle (Queen's University), NIHC Debates, vol.27, col. 2193, 8 November 1944.
43. NIHC Debates, vol.27, col. 2283, 21 November 1944.
44. PRONI, CAB4/602/3, memo by Grant, 13 October 1944.
45. Bew et al., *Northern Ireland 1921–1996*, p.100.
46. PRONI, CAB4/636/3, memo by Grant, 2 October 1945.
47. NIHC Debates, vol. 29, col. 1657, 8 January 1946.
48. NI Sen. Debates, vol. 29, cols 443–58, 6 February 1946.
49. PRONI, CAB9N/4/11, 'Rural Housing 1945–50', memo by Grant and Moore, 2 March 1946.
50. PRONI, CAB4/669/6, memo by Grant, 17 May 1946, and CAB4/671/7, Cab. Conclus., 30 May 1946. See also Birrell and Murie, *Policy and Government in Northern Ireland*, p.214.
51. NIHC Debates, vol. 30, col. 1714, 10 July 1946.
52. PROL, T233/442/9/332/01, A.T.K. Grant, an assistant secretary at the Treasury, to Cook, 30 October 1950.
53. Lawrence, *The Government of Northern Ireland*, p.64.
54. PRONI, CAB9C/1/7, Sinclair to Brooke, 24 May 1943.
55. PRONI, COM7/44, 'Disposal of premises: "Admiralty" 1944–47', Sinclair to Brooke, 16 March 1945.
56. PRONI, COM7/45, 'Development of War Department sites 1944', report of Stormont ministers' meeting with the Distribution of Industry Committee, 29 March 1945.
57. PRONI, COM7/44, notes on a meeting in London between Brooke and Sir Andrew Rae Duncan and Oliver Lyttleton, the ministers of supply and production, February 1945.

58. PRONI, CAB9C/51/2 pt. 2, 'Postwar employment 1945–47', Gransden to Markbreiter, 2 March 1945.
59. Ibid., J.B. Howard, a principal secretary at the Home Office, to Gransden, 12 March 1945.
60. Ibid., Sinclair to Brooke, 16 March 1945.
61. NIHC Debates, vol. 28, col. 485, 20 March 1945.
62. PRONI, COM7/44, Gransden to Markbreiter, 27 March 1945.
63. Ibid., Sir G.H. Ince, permanent secretary to the Ministry of Labour and National Service, to Sir Frank Newsam, deputy under secretary at the Home Office, 16 April 1945.
64. PRONI, CAB9C/51/2 pt.2, Gransden to Brooke, 28 April 1945.
65. See file PROL, T 233/172/13/9/01, 'Papers leading up to Industries Development Bill 1945'.
66. P. Buckland, *A History of Northern Ireland* (Dublin, 1981), p.93.
67. PRONI, CAB 4/621/6, Cab. Conclus., 12 April 1945.
68. B. Probert, *Beyond Orange and Green* (London, 1978), p.69.
69. PROL, T 233/173/13/9/02, 'Northern Ireland: Treatment as a Development Area': see references in a letter from Compton to B.F.St J. Trend, a principal secretary at the Treasury, 6 June 1947.
70. Ibid., Hugh Dalton to Cripps, 19 June 1947.
71. PRONI, CAB4/635/14, Cab. Conclus., 27 September 1945. See also Bew et al., *Northern Ireland 1921–1966*, p.98.
72. PRONI, CAB4/636/5, memo by Grant, 2 October 1945.
73. PRONI, CAB4/635/14, Cab. Conclus., 27 September 1945, and CAB4/636/8, memo prepared by Freer and presented by Sinclair, 1 October 1945.
74. PRONI, CAB4/642/2, memo by Sinclair, 14 November 1945.
75. PRONI, CAB4/642/9, Cab. Conclus., 15 November 1945: cited in Bew et al., *Northern Ireland 1921–1996*, pp.98–9.
76. PRONI, CAB9F/165/4, 'Correspondence about the broadcast "The Week in Stormont" 1945–46', G.L. Marshall, Northern Ireland director-general of the BBC, to Gransden, 27 September 1945.
77. Ibid., Marshall to Brooke, 31 January1946. The BBC revived its plans for the series in August 1948, but Brooke maintained his opposition.
78. PRONI, CAB4/648/14, Cab. Conclus., 13 December 1945.
79. PRONI, CAB4/649/9, Cab. Conclus., 19 December 1945, and CAB4/652/9, Cab. Conclus., 17 January 1946.
80. For references to this cabinet debate, see D.W. Harkness, 'Back to Westminster or forward to greater authority', *Irish Times*, 16 November 1977.
81. Bew et al., *Northern Ireland 1921–1996*, p.99.
82. The first was 'The Cost of maintaining existing farm prices on our own', and the second was 'The Constitutional Position of Northern Ireland'. See also the Harkness article, 'Back to Westminster or forward to greater authority'.
83. PRONI, CAB4/676/7, Cab. Conclus., 25 June 1946.
84. PRONI, CAB4/690/21, Cab. Conclus., 14 November 1946, and CAB4/695/3, memo by Nugent, 11 December 1946. See also PROL, HO 45/23239/917747/1, 'Statistics of Trade (Northern Ireland) Act 1949', Gransden to Sir E. Holderness, an assistant secretary at the Home Office, 15 November 1946.
85. *Belfast Newsletter*, 16 November 1946.
86. NIHC Debates, vol. 31,col. 1603, 7 October 1947, and *Belfast Newsletter*, 5 November 1947.
87. *Belfast Newsletter*, 1 September 1947.
88. These speeches by Brooke and Warnock appeared in the *Northern Whig*, 21 October 1947 and 11 November 1947.
89. PRONI, CAB4/735/4, memo by Nugent, 10 November 1947.
90. PRONI, CAB4/735/5, memo by Brooke, 7 November 1947. See also an essay by D. Norman, 'No Tories Here', *Moirae*, vol. 4 (1979), pp.74–85.
91. PRONI, CAB9A/7/58, 'Visit of Right Hon. and Mrs. Herbert Morrison 1946', notes made by Brooke following an informal meeting, 15 September 1946.
92. B. Donoughue and G.W. Jones, *Herbert Morrison: Portrait of a Politician* (London, 2001), p.308 and p.386.
93. PRONI, CAB4/735/5, memo by Brooke, 7 November 1947.
94. PRONI, CAB4/735/27, Cab. Conclus., 13 November 1947.
95. *Belfast Newsletter*, 14 November 1947. See also Bew et al., *Northern Ireland 1921–1996*, p.103.
96. *Belfast Newsletter*, 22 November 1947.
97. Ibid., 27 November 1947. See also Bew et al., *Northern Ireland 1921–1996*, pp.103–4.
98. *Belfast Newsletter*, 4 February 1948.
99. Ibid., 21 February 1948.

100. PRONI, CAB4/746/9, memo by Brooke, 3 March 1948.
101. PRONI, CAB4/748/12, Cab. Conclus., 8 April 1948, and CAB4/749/8, Cab. Conclus., 14 April 1948.
102. For a fuller discussion, see K.O. Morgan, *Labour in Power 1945–51* (Oxford, 1984), p.5. The author has noted that 'consolidation' was urged by Morrison from 1948 onwards. See also D.N. Pritt, *The Labour Government 1945–51* (London, 1963), p.238, and R. Miliband, *Parliamentary Socialism* (London, 1973), p.298.
103. PRONI, CAB4/772/5, memo by Nugent, December 1948. For the full text of Nugent's memorandum, see A.C. Hepburn (ed.), *The Conflict of Nationality in Modern Ireland* (London, 1980), pp.174–6.
104. PRONI, CAB4/781/4, memo by Brooke, 16 March 1949.
105. *The Round Table*, vol. 38 (1948), pp.585–7. See also Bew et al., *Northern Ireland 1921–1996*, p.104.
106. PRONI, CAB9F/188/1, 'Correspondence relating to industrial development in Northern Ireland and measures taken by the British Government in relation to same 1949–50', Kelly to Gransden, 2 January 1950.
107. PROL, LAB43/28, 'C.R. Attlee CH, MP: personal minute about unemployment in Northern Ireland, 1950', copy of a note sent by Attlee to the Board of Trade, the Ministry of Labour and the Ministry of Supply, 9 January 1950.
108. Ibid., Wilson to Attlee, 23 January 1950.
109. PRONI, CAB4/831/11, Cab. Conclus., 28 November 1950.
110. PRONI, CAB4/847/4, Cab. Conclus., 15 May 1951, and CAB4/853/6, Cab. Conclus., 7 September 1951.
111. For a full discussion of the 1947 financial crisis and the rationing measures, see Morgan, *Labour in Power*, pp.330–58 and pp.369–70.
112. PRONI, CAB4/655/3, memo by Maginess, 29 January 1946.
113. PROL, HO 45/21265/916605, 'Trade Disputes and Trade Union Act (Northern Ireland), 1927: repeal rejected by Northern Ireland House of Commons. Imperial Parliament not empowered to intervene, 1946–1947', Edwards to G.H. Oliver, parliamentary under-secretary of state at the Home Office, 20 February 1947.
114. Ibid., this was the reply sent to a Post Office Engineering Union deputation, 13 March 1947.
115. PRONI, CAB9C/22/2, 'Arbitration in Strikes and Industrial Disputes 1943–47': see Kelly to Robinson, 17 April 1946, T. Hutson, a principal assistant secretary at the Home Office, to Gransden, 26 April 1946, and Kelly to Gransden, 11 May 1946.
116. NIHC Debates, vol. 30, col. 572, 14 May 1946.
117. PRONI, CAB9E/150/1, 'Correspondence and memoranda in connection with the Agriculture Bill 1946–47': see memo by Moore, 5 June 1946, and Gransden to Scott, 3 January 1947.
118. Ibid., memo by Nugent, 'Agricultural Policy', 13 January 1947.
119. PRONI, CAB4/697/5, Cab. Conclus., 16 January 1947.
120. PRONI, CAB9E/150/1, Brooke to Moore, 8 October 1947.
121. Ibid., Moore to Brooke, 8 October 1947, and CAB4/739/9, Cab. Conclus., 11 December 1947.

3

Stormont and the Minority

Since partition, the Unionist government's treatment of the minority had exacerbated the Northern Ireland problem and widened the divisions between the two communities. Successive Westminster governments had allowed this situation to develop, because they were unwilling to intervene in Northern Ireland to ensure equality of treatment for the province's nationalist community. Neglect by Westminster had given the Unionist administration a free rein in sensitive areas, and this contributed to the growth of institutionalized sectarianism. In the immediate post-war period the Unionist government had to deal with four key issues, which highlighted the problems in its relations with the minority. Stormont faced constant criticism of its security policy, as opponents focused on the notorious Special Powers Act. Frequently, this was linked to allegations of gerrymandering, particularly at local government level, and the Belfast government was repeatedly forced to defend its retention of the limited local government franchise, which Labour had abolished on the mainland. Both the restricted franchise and the redrawn electoral areas worked to the disadvantage of the minority. The nationalist community also believed that it suffered discrimination in education. In its attempts to reform the province's education system following Westminster's comprehensive Education Act, the Unionist government came under strong pressure from Nationalist MPs and the Catholic hierarchy to make concessions to Catholic education. At the same time, the Brooke administration was being pressed by the Protestant churches and many Unionist backbenchers to protect the privileges acquired by Protestant education in the inter-war period. Each of these issues had surfaced on many occasions since the establishment of the state, but the authorities at Stormont had to face a new problem, when decisions were required on the future of the large number of Éire workers who had secured employment in Northern Ireland during the war.

The formation of a Labour government in 1945 added a new dimension to Stormont's handling of such problems, because Unionist leaders were unsure of the new administration's attitude to these areas of controversy. Indeed, for a brief period following Labour's election success, there was speculation that the Attlee government intended to supervise Northern Ireland affairs more closely, paying particular attention to Stormont's handling of these issues. The presence of the thirty-strong Friends of Ireland group within the parliamentary Labour party ensured that the province's affairs were kept before the House of Commons.[1] These MPs frequently embarrassed the Brooke government, and the authorities in Belfast were forced, for the first time since the early 1920s, to consider potential Westminster opposition in the formulation of its policy towards the minority. Although Labour's return to power had initially unsettled the Unionists and prompted moderation in some of their policies, Brooke and his colleagues reverted to their more uncompromising style once they were convinced that the new administration in London would not be a threat.

ÉIRE WORKERS IN THE NORTH

The influx of labour from Éire during the war presented the Stormont administration with a delicate political problem. By October 1941 more than 1,000 Éire workers were obtaining employment in the province each month, exposing the Unionist government to stinging criticism, particularly from Midgley and the two Independent Unionists, Nixon and Henderson, who wanted restrictions placed on the immigration of labour from the South. When the minister of labour, J.F. Gordon, considered the issue, he warned his cabinet colleagues that any attempt to restrict the flow of labour northwards could provoke 'undesirable repercussions at Westminster'.[2] Indeed, even Bates, the leading right winger in the cabinet, acknowledged that Éire workers were essential for the war effort, though he also predicted that serious problems would arise if steps were not taken to control the movement of labour across the border.[3] When the cabinet discussed the problem, Andrews, the prime minister, was adamant that Éire workers should not obtain employment while suitable unemployed Northern Ireland workers were available on the register. Consequently, it was agreed that the Ministry of Home Affairs should approach the Home Office in March 1942 with a view to obtaining the necessary powers to permit only essential workers to enter the province.[4] Technically, the Stormont government had the powers to restrict the entry of Éire labour under the Defence Regulations, but Unionist ministers were afraid that such a controversial use of these provisions was likely to raise objections from the Westminster authorities, which would have opposed the 'wholesale restrictions' of Éire workers.[5] Although Stormont had been careful to follow strict protocol in attempting to restrict the flow of Éire labour into Northern Ireland, Westminster initially refused to introduce such a measure, leaving a frustrated Unionist administration open to further criticism for its inability to deal with the situation. The Andrews government responded by having Bates make a direct personal approach to Morrison, the home secretary, for assistance on the issue, emphasizing the danger of sensitive security information falling into the hands of 'ill-disposed persons' from the South.[6] There was a considerable delay, however, before Morrison was persuaded by the argument for restrictions, and the measure was announced simultaneously in both the Stormont and Westminster parliaments on 8 October. Under the new scheme any Éire worker seeking employment in the province had to apply for a residence permit. This enabled the authorities in Belfast to refuse permits to any worker who was not considered essential for the war effort. Significantly, Morrison's announcement also stated that the scheme would operate for a 'short period' after the war in order to give preference in the labour market to demobilized soldiers, and this became a major point of contention in 1945.[7] Not surprisingly, the Éire government registered a protest at the resident permit scheme. The high commissioner in

London, John Dulanty, warned the Dominions Office that the administration at Westminster had presented the Unionist government with a 'purely party political weapon', which it would use indiscriminately.[8] Attlee, the dominions secretary, sought to reassure the Dublin government by stressing that the Restriction Order would not result in the 'mass expulsion' of Éire workers from the province. Indeed, his reply to Dulanty even suggested that the Westminster government was optimistic about improved relations between the North and South in the post-war period, as Attlee thought 'matters of mutual interest' would provide a basis for some degree of reconciliation.[9]

Although, by March 1943, only 4,875 residence permits from a total of 15,071 applications had been granted under the 1942 order, Unionist backbenchers remained anxious about the influx of workers. The failure of the Stormont administration to satisfy supporters on the Éire workers issue was symptomatic of the wider problems undermining Andrews' beleaguered administration. Warnock, who had become a persistent critic of the government following his resignation as a minister in June 1940, told MPs that, while 38,000 Ulster workers had crossed to the mainland, the government continued to accept Éire immigrants, many of whom had 'brought their politics with them'.[10] Earlier, a nervous Gordon had questioned the wisdom of continuing to send Northern Ireland workers to the mainland, even though they had been urgently requested by the Ministry of Labour in London.[11] Concern about the number of Éire workers receiving residence permits continued to trouble the Brooke administration, and the need to strengthen the scheme became an important objective of the new government. Accordingly, in March 1944, Lowry, the minister of home affairs, highlighted an opportunity to impose new restrictions on Éire workers. The Americans were keen to control travel in the North prior to the Normandy invasion, and Lowry informed Brooke that Stormont should seek a tightening of the residence qualification at this juncture, as such a request might now escape 'close scrutiny in Whitehall'.[12]

The option of using its own powers to restrict the entry of Éire labour remained a possibility, but the Brooke government, like the previous administration, believed that such a move was likely to bring a swift reprimand from Westminster. The tactic was, therefore, to press the authorities in London to strengthen the residence permit scheme, though many Unionists could not understand Stormont's reluctance to assume direct responsibility for the matter. Nothing came from the Lowry initiative, and the issue became a constant source of anxiety for the Belfast administration. On 3 July 1944 the Unionist MP for the Westminster constituency of Down, the Rev. Dr James Little, claimed that the Unionist government had complete discretion in issuing residence permits. Both Brooke and Lowry expressed concern over Little's speech, because he was obviously implying that the order could be used to exclude southern Catholics. Anxious to clear up the confusion over the issue, the two leaders decided that a public statement should be issued, explaining that the Ministry of Home Affairs was responsible to the Home Office in London for the manner in which the order was administered and ruling out the possibility of any process of selection on a sectarian basis. Significantly, other members of the cabinet reacted strongly to this emphasis on the fact that permits could not be issued on a confessional basis, because they felt 'the repetition of this principle ... was like trailing one's coat and seemed to be unnecessary and particularly undesirable at the period of the 12th celebrations'. While Lowry acknowledged their concern, he was insistent that the Unionist authorities had to remind their followers of the realities of devolution. It was 'essential as a matter of policy to indicate quite clearly that discrimination according to religion was beyond the powers of the Government, although he was fully in sympathy with the view that unless some steps were taken to ensure the Protestant Ascendancy, the future of Northern Ireland was in jeopardy'.[13] As it happened, the opposition to the terms of the statement expressed by the majority of the cabinet had no effect, because Lowry had already issued his statement to the press, and it only remained for Grant to register his disapproval that the cabinet had not been consulted before such an important statement was made on behalf of the government.[14]

When Harry Midgley became minister of labour in June 1944, he alerted his colleagues to potentially more serious problems relating to Éire workers in the North. Midgley, who had been a persistent critic of the Andrews government for its failure to stem the flow of immigrant labour to the North, now urged the cabinet to focus its attention on the problems that large numbers of Éire ex-servicemen would create for the government in the post-war period. As the end of the war seemed in sight, the minister of labour anticipated that 'some modified form of demobilisation will take place at a comparatively early date, releasing more of these men to settle here and compete with our own ex-Servicemen and civilians in a falling labour market. Many of them will gravitate to the disloyal element in our population and increase our political difficulties.'

Midgley also stressed that Éire ex-servicemen would be encouraged to settle in the North if Beveridge's welfare proposals were implemented. Three different categories of Éire ex-servicemen were identified. The first two, those with rights under the Reinstatement in Employment Act and those with rights under the Disabled Persons Act, did not involve large numbers. However, the third group, comprising a large number of non-disabled Éire ex-servicemen with no rights of reinstatement, were granted residence permits in Northern Ireland under a 'gentleman's agreement with the Home Office'. Midgley recommended that a vigorous effort be made to have this agreement amended so that residence permits would only be granted to this third group, when it was justified by the labour situation. He was confident that his suggestion would be favourably received in London, because 'Mr. Morrison ... appreciates our difficulties arising out of the disloyal element on both sides of the Border ... he would not, if approached, oppose very strongly the suggested modification in our practice about the issue of permits.'[15] Midgley's proposal was enthusiastically supported by his colleagues, who decided to inform the Home Office before altering the existing procedure of granting residence permits to all ex-servicemen from Éire.[16] At the same time, the Unionist administration sought to reassure its supporters that it was dealing with the threat posed by the ex-servicemen from the South. It determined that Éire ex-servicemen would be excluded from the Northern Ireland version of the Disabled Persons (Employment) Bill.[17] After considerable hesitancy, Bevin, the minister of labour and national service, reluctantly agreed to Stormont's proposals:

> We should ... be sorry to see disabled ex-Servicemen from Éire excluded from the benefits of the Northern Ireland legislation. Nevertheless we recognise that the United Kingdom Parliament has given the Northern Ireland Parliament power to deal with this matter and if the Northern Ireland Government came to the conclusion that it must be dealt with as you propose we do not wish to press the other point of view.[18]

Still, the Brooke government was not immune to criticism from supporters who associated unemployment with the large number of Éire workers present in the North. Warnock, another critic of previous government weakness on the issue, had succeeded Lowry as minister of home affairs, and he warned his colleagues that a Unionist government 'could not survive if it had considerable numbers of our people out of work, and a considerable number of Éire workers in Ulster'.[19] The astute Brooke needed little reminding of wider dissatisfaction in the party. He described the control of Éire immigrants as a 'burning question' and assured his cabinet colleagues that the future allocation of residence permits would be kept to an absolute minimum.[20] Yet the reality was that the 1942 Residence in Northern Ireland (Restriction) Order was a temporary Westminster measure, and the Belfast government had no statutory power to extend the residence permit scheme. The Unionist government required Westminster backing for permanent legislation to ensure that the residence permit scheme would remain in operation after the war. When Brooke met Churchill and Morrison at the end of February 1945 to discuss this proposal, he found both men 'entirely sympathetic to our aims', though they pointed out that there were serious problems involved, because the Northern Ireland parliament was not a sovereign body.[21] The Unionist premier had based his argument for new legislation on the need to combat unemployment which was expected to rise sharply during the transitional period at the end of hostilities. Consequently, Stormont suggested that Westminster should give it the power to prohibit the entry of Éire labour, when the province's unemployment total exceeded 20,000.[22] Meanwhile, a 'critical situation' was developing in Belfast, where some trade unions were demanding that in the event of redundancies unskilled Northern Ireland workers should be laid off before skilled men from the South. The cabinet responded by agreeing that in such cases residence permits should be withdrawn even if a strike was threatened.[23]

A close examination of Stormont's operation of the 1942 order followed Brooke's move to raise the residence permit scheme with the authorities in London. Home Office officials were already aware of the tension caused by the administration of the scheme in the province, because Jack Beattie had written to the home secretary, complaining that the Unionist government was using the allocation of residence permits for 'political persecution'.[24] Indeed, C.G. Markbreiter, an assistant secretary at the Home Office, expressed his disapproval after considering the Northern Ireland government's proposals to extend the scheme: 'In refusing residence permits to volunteers from Éire Northern

Ireland are [sic] already going further than what was contemplated. A general and permanent power of exclusion for the purposes of maintaining unemployment within certain limits seems to be going too far.'[25]

Yet the Unionist government remained under pressure from supporters to defend the jobs of Northern Ireland workers. With unemployment rising above 23,000 by May 1945, Warnock told MPs: 'What happened after the last war shall not happen again … our returning soldiers shall not find in their jobs in Northern Ireland people who came up from Éire when they were fighting.'[26] The authorities at Stormont wanted to introduce their own permanent legislation, but Maxwell, the permanent under-secretary at the Home Office, reminded them that the residence permit scheme was only intended to operate during the war and 'for a reasonable time after'. While he understood Stormont's concern about the impact of attractive social services in Northern Ireland, Maxwell warned that any new measure for the extension of the scheme should be temporary. He was anxious, moreover, that such a bill should be introduced at Westminster, because Stormont legislation would raise the partition issue in a 'peculiarly acute form'. During this period the Home Office was receiving a string of complaints from Éire workers who had failed to have their residence permits renewed. Only prompt intervention by Kelly, the liaison officer at the Home Office, averted embarrassment for the government in Belfast, because he was able to deal with particular cases on the spot.[27] Kelly went on to play a vital role in the post-war period, helping to overcome problems that threatened to disrupt Stormont–Westminster relations. The experiment of attaching a Northern Ireland civil servant to the Home Office began in June 1940, and its success led the Stormont administration to retain a liaison officer after the war.

In spite of Warnock's earlier assurances, he was forced to tell Northern Ireland MPs that in the twelve months to July 1945 only 2,174 residence permits had been refused from a total of 12,935 applications.[28] As the province's unemployment total continued to rise, the minister of home affairs was under pressure to take action. Aware that Chuter Ede, the new Labour home secretary, was preparing to extend the residence permit scheme for a further two years, Warnock issued a warning to all Éire workers hoping to remain in the province.[29] In a speech delivered to a local Unionist association, he told the 20,000 Éire workers in the province to assume that their permits would not be renewed. He also infuriated Nationalist MPs by attacking the motives of Éire workers in coming to Northern Ireland to take up employment: 'The magnet which drew them here was not in a great many cases the war effort of the United Kingdom, but high wage rates and certainty of employment.'[30] Warnock's efforts to appease Unionist supporters provoked an outcry in Dublin. A furious de Valera protested to Maffey who contacted the Dominions Office, suggesting that the government should 'avoid precipitate action in implementing a policy pending a review of the consequences in the political field and some hearing of the Dublin point of view'.[31] Moreover, his follow-up correspondence revealed his frustration with the Unionist government: 'It is certainly unfortunate that the first discard of Irish labour should occur in Northern Ireland.'[32] Maffey was keen to warn the new Labour administration that its intention to extend the 1942 order would have serious political consequences in Ireland. In fact, Warnock's speech had caused disquiet among Home Office officials who found themselves having to defend the residence permit scheme following representations from the Fianna Fáil government. Fearing the mass expulsion of Éire workers from the North, the authorities in Dublin demanded participation in official discussions to settle the issue. Indeed, de Valera even threatened to postpone an important civil aviation agreement with Britain until the Éire workers issue had been resolved to his satisfaction.[33] While the Dominions Office was willing to accept the Éire government's presence at discussions, the Home Office flatly rejected such a move, because it knew that Stormont representatives would not attend and it did not want to defend the Unionist position in their absence.[34]

The Belfast government was also made aware of the impact of de Valera's protests, and Brooke had to warn his minister of home affairs not to raise the issue again: 'I am anxious that we should not make the position more difficult for our friends in the Home Office who are keeping our end up in a way that has been beyond praise.'[35] Undoubtedly, the close ties between Home Office officials and the Northern Ireland government eased many of the difficulties facing the Unionist administration during the initial phase of Labour rule at Westminster. Maxwell represented the Stormont case simply: 'So long as the social services in Northern Ireland and wage rates are above the level in Éire, there must be some protection against the flooding of the Northern Ireland labour market by Éire immigrants.' Yet Home Office officials had their own difficulties to consider, and Maxwell argued strongly that the Dominions Office should refrain from providing the Éire government with information on the residence permit scheme. He warned that any inkling of Westminster's decision to extend the scheme in Northern Ireland would result in the de Valera government raising the issue of the large number of Éire workers who had obtained employment in Great Britain during the war. Maxwell told Ede that, while Irish workers were still required, they might have to be sent home in changing employment circumstances. The permanent under-secretary also used the Westminster government's recent experiences of the benefits of partition to strengthen the Northern Ireland case:

> ... there is looming in the background the question whether any support will be given by the United Kingdom to the desire of the Unionists of Northern Ireland to prevent the Catholic minority becoming a majority. There is of course a danger that if Éire workers continue to flood North there will in some future election be a Nationalist majority and a Government that wants to break with the United Kingdom and join Éire. Having regard to our experiences in the recent war when it was of vital importance for the success of the Battle of the Atlantic that we should control the coast and ports of Northern Ireland, any such prospect may raise grave strategical problems.[36]

Therefore, although the Home Office was under considerable pressure to force the Stormont government to moderate its views, Maxwell responded by defending the Unionist position. This was in spite of the difficulties which Warnock's occasional outbursts created for Whitehall officials. His threat to expel 20,000 Éire workers was backed up by a claim that his department could administer the 1942 Residence in Northern Ireland (Restriction) Order without reference to London. Not only was this inaccurate, but it also gave de Valera the opportunity to accuse Westminster of ignoring maladministration in Northern Ireland.[37] Indeed, considering the problems that the Unionist government created for its 'friends' at the Home Office, it is remarkable to note the spirit with which Maxwell defended the Stormont cabinet's point of view during this critical period, when there was a possibility that the new Labour government would act against Stormont. At the time Kelly, who closely monitored these developments, reassured Stormont that the Labour leaders would be friendly, but he warned that this would only continue 'so long as Northern Ireland gives them no trouble'.[38] Of course, de Valera continued to highlight the threats posed by Warnock's injudicious public statements, and this caused alarm among British diplomatic representatives in Dublin. Maffey feared that any expulsion of Éire labour would be compared to evictions during the agrarian crises of the nineteenth century, and this could have a serious impact in the United States. In correspondence with Ede, Viscount Addison, the dominions secretary, reiterated the difficulties confronting his department, though he conceded: 'So long as we remain firmly on the footing that nothing is being done except to fulfil the undertaking to find employment for returning service personnel and that every case is considered individually on its merits, we are on strong ground.'

Addison was, however, very critical of the way in which the Northern Ireland government made the position even more difficult for the authorities at Westminster, when he added: 'Unfortunately the language used in certain quarters is apt to give colour to the suggestion that other motives beside this practical one lie behind the decision to terminate residence permits.'[39] This was a view widely held at the Dominions Office, because Stephenson had already stated that the real basis for de Valera's 'violent' complaints

> ... was not so much what was being done or the fact that people might be removed from employment in order to make room for returning Service personnel but the violent language used in certain quarters in Northern Ireland gave colour to the suggestion that there was a political rather than a practical economic motive behind the decision to terminate residence permits.[40]

In his reply to Addison, Ede assured anxious Dominions Office officials that he had successfully altered Stormont's policy, when he said that the Northern Ireland authorities now agreed 'there is no question of any wholesale termination of permits. Each case will be considered on its merits having regard in particular to the nature of the employment and the needs of the returning ex-servicemen.' The home secretary also agreed to the suggestion made by the Dominions Office that representatives of both departments should take the opportunity of having an 'informal talk' with Brooke on his next visit to London.[41] The Dominions Office was anxious to tone down statements by Northern Ireland ministers and prevent suggestions of mass expulsions. In using an informal briefing to encourage greater discretion on Stormont's part, the Labour government was following the strategy of previous Westminster governments by avoiding the risk of open confrontation with the Unionist authorities. Although there is no doubt that Stormont–Westminster relations were often strained during the early stages of Labour rule, the Attlee administration was just as keen as any previous government to ensure that Westminster kept its distance from the province's affairs. Nevertheless, the Labour government had demonstrated that where measures proposed by Stormont threatened to damage its relations with Dublin, resulting in the delay of a vital civil aviation agreement, swift and decisive action would be taken in order to force the Unionist government to toe the line. In this instance, however, the gentle pressure applied by Westminster succeeded, and controversial speeches by Stormont ministers on the residence permit issue ceased.

When Brooke travelled to London in March 1946, he sensed a feeling of antipathy among Labour leaders towards the Unionist government, but Kelly assured him that this was not the case. Yet shortly after this visit Kelly wrote to the cabinet in Belfast to amend his earlier judgement. The episode that altered his previous analysis was a meeting, at which he was present, between Ede and a deputation from the Friends of Ireland group of Labour MPs, who were demanding the revocation of the 1942 order on the grounds of maladministration.[42] It turned out that Mulvey had been working with the Friends of Ireland MPs on this issue, and he had supplied them with information on individual cases which they brought to the home secretary's attention.[43] Following the meeting, a dispirited Kelly reported Ede's comments on the Northern Ireland government: 'They were the remnants of the old ascendancy class and were very frightened both of Catholics and the general world trend to the Left.' Obviously alarmed, the Stormont liaison officer then expressed his opinion of Ede:

> I knew that the S/S [secretary of state] was a real socialist and that any other political creed was anathema to him … the S/S can be put in the same category as those others of the Labour Party who can find no good in political opponents and are prepared to use their power – now and while they have it – against them.

Kelly emphasized that the home secretary's agreement with the Friends of Ireland MPs was not just confined to general matters, because 'he permitted them to depart with so much comfort and a clear indication that on the political plane he was at one with them in their distaste for the present Northern Ireland Administration'. He also anticipated much closer supervision by Ede of Stormont's treatment of the minority, particularly in relation to the Éire labour issue. Indeed, the Home Office had requested reports on a number of individual cases, and Kelly expressed the hope that these had been handled fairly in order that 'the fullest possible details can be given'. He also advised the Northern Ireland government to treat each individual case with the utmost care, and to ensure that 'whatever is sent here in reply will be above reproach'. The Northern Ireland liaison officer then sounded a warning to his government:

I am quite satisfied that from Éire to the Dominions Office and through the Friends of Ireland and other ways there will be a steady and increasing pressure to do away with the Residence Permit Order at the earliest opportunity. For this reason we should ensure that the giving of benefits to Éire soldiers and workers is not so operated as to make another basis of objection to it. At the same time Home Affairs will need to continue to be very careful about their decisions as there are so many simply waiting to pounce on any mis-steps they may make.

Clearly, Stormont faced serious difficulties in its dealings with Westminster during the first two months of 1946. By following Kelly's advice, however, the Unionist government averted the possibility of any serious clash with London. This was a clear example of how discreet pressure from the Labour government had forced Stormont to re-examine its policy on such a critical issue for the Unionist party. On this occasion Brooke and his colleagues were anxious to avoid conflict with what appeared to be an unfriendly and unpredictable Labour administration. Although Kelly had indicated that Westminster had the management of the residence permit scheme 'under a magnifying glass', the close supervision ceased when it was clear that the Unionist administration was operating the scheme fairly.[44] Satisfied by the response he received from Stormont, Ede informed the House of Commons that he had no intention of terminating the Residence in Northern Ireland (Restriction) Order, because it had also been designed to give preference to Northern Ireland ex-servicemen in the post-war labour market.[45] More significantly from the Unionist government's viewpoint, the home secretary told Dr H.B. Morgan, the secretary of the Friends of Ireland group, that he was convinced that the 1942 order had been applied legitimately.[46] This reply was given after only one month's close investigation of Stormont's administration of the order.

Although the Labour government had forced Stormont to shelve its plans, the Unionist cabinet remained committed to a general policy of expelling Éire labour whenever possible. Consequently, a fresh attempt to remove Éire workers was likely once Westminster dropped its vigilance. However, the Dominions Office retained a watching brief on Stormont's handling of the issue, and Addison urged Brooke to proceed cautiously. While he acknowledged that Northern Ireland should have some protection, the dominions secretary wanted to know if it was 'absolutely essential to compel an Éire citizen to leave Northern Ireland if there was no work available for him'.[47] Nevertheless, mindful of their supporters' expectations, Brooke and his colleagues refused to alter their unequivocal stance on the Éire workers issue, arguing that they required additional safeguards as unemployment was higher in Northern Ireland than in Britain. Not for the first time, the Dominions Office came to realize that it should not expect any assistance from the Unionist government in its attempts to improve relations with the administration in Dublin.

By the beginning of 1947 the Northern Ireland government was again pressing the Home Office on the resident permit question. Two factors influenced the timing of the request. Firstly, there had been a marked improvement in

Stormont–Westminster relations, and, more significantly, the residence permit scheme, which had been extended after the war, was due to expire towards the end of 1947. Although Stormont recognized that Labour was opposed to any prolongation of the order, it continued to argue that restrictions were essential. Warnock, therefore, approached Ede with a suggestion that the question of residence in Northern Ireland should be decided by the Stormont government.[48] The Home Office, however, remained nervous about such a development. J.B. Howard, a principal secretary, informed the home secretary that, should it be necessary to pass new residence legislation, it would be 'less embarrassing' if this was done at Westminster. He emphasized that Stormont legislation would only arouse interest in the border question, whereas Labour's policy 'was to damp down controversy on this issue'. Any new bill dealing with residence permits would prove controversial, and Howard's only solution, which he thought might be acceptable to the administration in Belfast, would be for Stormont to legislate on a measure aimed at safeguarding employment.[49] The more senior Maxwell, however, told Warnock and Maginess that he was against any Stormont legislation, adding that there was free movement of citizens in every other part of the Commonwealth.[50] Of course, Unionist ministers never considered the issue of Éire labour in these wider terms, and they continued to demand their own legislation. Within a few weeks Maxwell relented and offered his support for Stormont legislation to control employment. Clearly, the Home Office had been edging towards such an outcome, but Maxwell's agreement that the new measure should be introduced at Stormont was surprising. He had changed his mind following a meeting with Maffey and Sir Eric Machtig, the permanent under-secretary at the Dominions Office. The Dominions Office officials had convinced Maxwell that new legislation should be left to the Belfast government. This would mean that anti-partition propaganda, which was steadily gaining momentum, could not accuse Westminster of 'using her power to keep the ascendancy class in Northern Ireland'.[51]

This change of heart at Westminster resulted in the introduction of the Safeguarding of Employment Bill. It received its second reading at Stormont in October 1947 and was scheduled to come into operation as soon as the residence permit scheme expired. During the drafting of the bill Warnock informed his colleagues that, as the emphasis would now be on employment rather than residence, it would be more appropriate for the new measure to be administered by the minister of labour. Maginess, too, was in favour of the change, as it 'would tend to discount any suggestion that the control would have a political as distinct from an employment background'.[52] When the bill was debated at Stormont, however, it aroused bitter controversy and was opposed by all sections of the opposition. Beattie claimed that there was no real difference between the new bill and the residence permit scheme that Westminster had dropped, because it was still aimed at Éire labour in the North.[53] Harry Diamond, the Socialist Republican MP for Falls, insisted that the sole purpose of the new bill was to keep the Unionist regime perpetually in power by ensuring that the numbers who were likely to support anti-partition candidates in future elections were kept to an absolute minimum.[54] The debate revealed the Nationalist party's growing disillusionment with the Labour government. In his criticism of the previous scheme Edward McAteer, the MP for Mid-Londonderry, complained that there had been frequent examples of abuse and discrimination 'practised under the somnolent eye of Mr. Chuter Ede'.[55] Nationalists were disappointed, because the Labour government's intention had been to control Stormont's administration of the residence permit scheme. In fact, Ede had earlier informed a Friends of Ireland deputation that the Stormont cabinet had been made aware in no uncertain terms that 'whether it was a slap in the face or not, matters reserved to London would be decided there'.[56]

Firm action by Westminster had prevented the Unionist government from implementing Warnock's plan, outlined in his October 1945 speech, of expelling large numbers of Éire workers who had obtained employment in the province during the war. Furthermore, the knowledge that the Home Office was closely supervising the administration of the 1942 order during the summer of 1946 undoubtedly influenced the Ministry of Home Affairs in its execution of the scheme. The influence of the Dominions Office and the pressure exerted by the Friends of Ireland group seemed likely to ensure that the scheme would not be continued in any form beyond 1947. However, the Brooke government never wavered in its demand for some form of protection, and the authorities at Westminster eventually gave way. The presence of A.J. Kelly in London ensured that the Brooke government was always kept well informed of the Labour government's intentions and was, therefore, always in a position to respond quickly and effectively as individual cases were considered. In this way the risk of open confrontation with Westminster was minimized, despite Warnock's clumsy attempts to appease Unionist supporters. The Northern Ireland government was also indebted to its 'friends' at the Home Office, particularly Sir Alexander Maxwell, and there were frequent examples of Home Office officials defending the Stormont position during 1946, when Ede had the matter under close investigation.

EDUCATION

Ever since the formation of the Northern Ireland state, education had been a particularly emotive issue for both sections of the community. The first minister of education, Lord Londonderry, had sought to lay the foundations for integrated schooling in the province with his 1923 Education Act. The fact that these schools were intended to operate under secular control antagonized the Catholic Church which refused to transfer control of their schools to the state. Their leaders reaffirmed their desire for 'Catholic children to be taught in Catholic schools by Catholic teachers under Catholic auspices'.[57] Even more formidable opposition to Londonderry's plans for education came from the Protestant churches. Although they disliked both the absence of religious instruction in the curriculum and the loss of control over teaching appointments, most Protestant churches agreed to place their schools under state control. Their mood changed, however, when they realized that Catholic schools would retain their independence. Soon leading Protestant churchmen were organizing a campaign against the Unionist government in an attempt to overturn certain provisions in the Londonderry act. To co-ordinate their opposition they formed the United Education Committee of the Protestant Churches in December 1924, and it quickly secured the support of the Orange Order and a number of Unionist backbenchers. Within three months of its formation, the committee enjoyed its first success, as the government revoked earlier undertakings by giving school management committees, on which Protestant clerics were usually represented, the powers to advise regional education bodies on teaching appointments. The United Education Committee then turned its attention to pressing for the inclusion of simple Bible instruction in the curriculum, and this was conceded by the government in new legislation in 1930.[58]

Naturally, the Catholic Church was furious at government concessions that effectively turned state schools into Protestant schools. By 1929 the Catholic hierarchy, working in tandem with Nationalist MPs who were now arguing the case in the Belfast parliament, was vociferously demanding some form of parallel concessions. In response to this agitation the government made a gesture to Catholic education by offering voluntary schools 50 per cent grants for building expenses, and this was also incorporated in the 1930 Education Act. Not surprisingly, both the 1925 and 1930 Education Acts aroused the attention of the authorities at Westminster, as there was some concern that the legislation contravened the powers given to the Northern Ireland government under the 1920 Government of Ireland Act. The government in London had the option of taking the legal route by referring any bill to the Judicial Committee of the Privy Council if it was thought to contravene the 1920 act. In political terms, of course, Westminster had the capacity to persuade, threaten or bribe the Northern Ireland government into altering its education policy, but neither legal nor political action was taken.[59] This reluctance by the authorities at Westminster to intervene during the inter-war period gave the Belfast government a free hand in many sensitive policy areas. In education the Unionist administration was able to allay the discontent of its traditional Protestant supporters by radically reshaping Londonderry's 1923 act.

Thus, when the Brooke government came to consider post-war educational reconstruction, it did so against a background of previous government capitulation to pressure from an alliance of the Protestant clergy and the Orange Order. The major reform of education expected in the wake of Westminster's 1944 Education Act was bound to reopen the debate about clerical influence, both Protestant and Catholic, in the province's schools. Tension was already beginning to mount, when in February 1944, Professor Robert Corkey, who had been minister of education for only ten months, was dismissed for alleged inattention to duties. Corkey defended himself by claiming that his dismissal had been the result of a clash with high-ranking civil servants in his department on questions of religious policy.[60] Controversy centred on those aspects of the 1930 act that required teachers in local authority schools to give simple Bible instruction. Acutely aware of the difficulties associated with this issue, the Brooke government refused to be drawn on its future plans for religious instruction. Secretly, however, Unionist ministers had already decided that compulsion on teachers to give religious instruction would be excluded from the new bill.[61] Indeed, the first indication of the government's thinking was only revealed in January 1945, when the White Paper was debated at Stormont. The new minister of education, Lieutenant Colonel Samuel H. Hall-Thompson, told MPs that compulsion on teachers to give Bible instruction would not be continued. In the same debate Lowry, who was now attorney general, announced 'that the religious provisions of the 1930 act were *ultra vires* under the Government of Ireland Act'.[62] The government's earlier silence gave Brooke the opportunity to gauge the level of Protestant opposition to such a change in direction, but the Unionist premier was also concerned about possible Westminster reaction to the new education proposals. Lowry had raised speculation on this matter. On becoming attorney general, he had informed his cabinet colleagues that the compulsion clause in the 1930 legislation clearly contravened section 5 of the 1920 act, adding that it was 'difficult to account for this not having been challenged long ere this'.[63] When the issue was explored with the Home Office in January 1945, Maxwell warned that any new legislation would have to meet the requirements of section 5 of the 1920 act, which dealt with the protection of minorities.[64] A further indication that Westminster was monitoring developments in the province came when the attorney general in London, Sir Donald Somervell, who, though questioning Lowry's assertion that the new proposals could be legally challenged under the 1920 act, informed the authorities in Belfast that Westminster 'on grounds of policy, viewed compulsion on teachers with great disfavour'.[65]

Hall-Thompson had already considered this matter and was adamant that the new bill should include a conscience clause to safeguard any teacher who did not wish to give religious instruction. To support his stance he argued that Westminster was opposed to compulsion, but he faced dissenting voices in the cabinet, opposing any tampering with the 1930 legislation. Although a majority of the cabinet favoured some form of conscience clause, there had been no agreement on the exact wording of a clause that would allow a teacher to opt out of religious instruction. The Unionist government was facing a dilemma. The Protestant churches were openly campaigning for the retention of Bible instruction, and Brooke was unsure about the level of support for their position both inside and outside parliament. The easy option would have been to give the Protestant clerics the guarantees they sought, but Brooke knew that he must not be bound by undertakings which would arouse opposition at Westminster. Hall-Thompson wanted to end the uncertainty by making an unequivocal statement on the future of religious instruction during the debate on the White Paper. Accordingly, he sought the cabinet's approval to state definitely: 'We are not continuing "compulsion" for two reasons: (a) we are not satisfied that it is in strict accordance with the Government of Ireland Act, and (b) equally important, we think it should not be continued whether legal or not.'[66] The minister was firmly opposed to clerical involvement in the province's schools on philosophical grounds, but his colleagues were unwilling to endorse his views and enter into conflict with the formidable alliance of the Protestant churches and the Orange Order. It was also true that a number of ministers viewed Hall-Thompson as a weak figure, too easily influenced by officials in the department who favoured the secularization of Northern Ireland education.[67]

Although the cabinet finally agreed to end compulsion, the precise terms of a new conscience clause to protect teachers who felt unable to give religious instruction had still to be settled. With the Protestant churches maintaining their opposition to major changes in education, Brooke and Hall-Thompson met a group of Unionist backbenchers on 23 May 1945 who were angry at the government's unwillingness to give the churches specific guarantees in relation to religious instruction.[68] Two days later Hall-Thompson, Brooke and Lowry met a deputation from the Protestant churches and the Orange Order. The deputation submitted a draft conscience clause, but it was rejected by Lowry who judged that it did not provide an effective safeguard for any teacher wishing to opt out of giving religious instruction.[69] With the Northern Ireland general election looming, Brooke found himself in a difficult position. Both Lowry and Hall-Thompson regarded the churches' demands as being *ultra vires* in regard to section 5 of the 1920 act, and Brooke believed that any agreement reached on such terms could be legally challenged at Westminster. Yet pressure from the Protestant clerics was mounting. Before polling day on 14 June, all Unionist candidates were sent circulars, asking them to vote against the repeal of the religious provisions in the 1930 act.[70] Brooke sought to regain control of the situation by staging a meeting with representatives of the churches and the Orange Order. On this occasion Hall-Thompson and Warnock, the minister of home affairs, accompanied Brooke. Lowry's absence was significant, because the clerics knew that he would never agree to their ideas on the conscience clause. Warnock did not share Lowry's liberal concerns, but the fact that he was a barrister may have persuaded the clerics that he was acting on the attorney general's behalf. Both sides presented new drafts, and an agreed conscience clause, which later became the subject of considerable confusion, was finalized. This stated:

> Where a teacher in a county school (whether appointed before or after the passing of this Act) finds himself unable, on grounds of religious belief, to conduct or attend collective worship in the school, or to give, or continue to give, religious instruction in the school, he may make application in writing to the local education authority to be excused from conducting or attending such worship and from giving such instruction; and if the authority after consultation with the school management committee are satisfied that the application is bona fide, they shall grant the application and the teacher shall be excused accordingly.[71]

Hall-Thompson's insistence that it would have to satisfy section 5 of the 1920 act was ignored by the Protestant clerics who, content with the new clause, agreed to withdraw their election circulars.[72]

The ambiguous nature of the conscience clause worked in Brooke's favour. He successfully smothered the clergy's attempt to disrupt party unity just before the Stormont elections, and then six months later his cabinet rejected the clause which was agreed at the June meeting, because it was considered to infringe section 5 of the Government of Ireland Act. Yet a minority within the cabinet continued to object to a more liberal conscience clause endorsed by Hall-Thompson, which offered greater protection to the individual teacher. By this stage, the minister of education was concerned that, in addition to probable legal complications, Westminster could raise political objections to the June clause. This implied that Stormont might come under some form of pressure to produce a clause more acceptable to the authorities in London. Lowry restated his opinion that Westminster could reject the June clause, because he was adamant that it infringed section 5 of the 1920 act. While Warnock, Moore and Grant favoured the retention of the June clause, a majority of the cabinet supported the adoption of the Hall-Thompson alternative. Significantly, Brooke 'felt there was no alternative' but to include the more liberal clause in the new bill, even though he believed that the provision acceptable to the churches and the Orange Order did not put the teacher 'in any disadvantage'.[73] The decisive factor in the Unionist cabinet's rejection of the clergy's demands was its desire to prevent possible intervention by Westminster. The permanent secretary to the Stormont Ministry of Education, R.S. Bromwell, warned of this, when he pointed out that Ede, a nonconformist who had worked closely with Rab Butler in the preparation of the 1944 Education Act and who was bitterly opposed to clerical control in education, would be 'hostile and suspicious' if teachers remained under compulsion to give Bible instruction.[74] Bromwell again emphasized the possibility of Westminster opposition, when he stressed that even if the Northern Ireland attorney general certified the June clause, the authorities in London would oppose it, and there were 'plenty of people waiting to make sure that it will not be passed'.[75] Hall-Thompson was equally convinced that if the June clause had been accepted, 'it would have been challenged in London and we should have got into trouble over it'.[76] Brooke, of course, had other concerns, as the Unionist government sought to create a favourable impression with the new government in London. Any controversy over the provisions included in the Education Bill could, therefore, have drawn the new Labour administration's attention to a number of other areas where the minority had a special interest.

With Westminster's position more clearly defined, the onus was definitely on the Northern Ireland government to satisfy the authorities in London that the forthcoming bill would not contravene any of the provisions laid down by the 1920 act. To consolidate his department's position, Hall-Thompson gained Home Office approval for his clause in the early part of 1946, though he warned his colleagues that the procedure involving the investigation by a committee of a teacher's conscience was unlikely to be acceptable. Again, on Home Office prompting, the new clause left the decision to opt out of giving religious instruction in the hands of the individual teacher, and such a decision could not be queried by the local school management committee on which Protestant ministers were frequently represented.[77] Although the Protestant agitators continued to demand a more favourable conscience clause, the Unionist government realized that, with the Home Office looking on, it had to reject the demands of its more extreme supporters. Following a further meeting between Hall-Thompson and representatives of the churches and the Orange Order, at which the government was urged to alter the terms of the conscience clause, Brooke informed the cabinet that 'the Government should now intimate the fact that they were not prepared to agree to any whittling down of the protection which they felt must be given to teachers'.[78] Earlier, Bromwell had urged the government to stand firm, as he warned that, apart from the legal considerations, any conscience clause acceptable to the Protestant churches would not 'pass the scrutiny of Mr. Ede'.[79] The crucial influence on the cabinet's decision to introduce a more liberal conscience clause was its desire to avoid confrontation with Westminster. In drafting the controversial aspects of its Education Bill, which was finally published on 28 September 1946, the Unionist authorities were convinced that the new Labour government would raise political, and not just legal, objections to any proposals that safeguarded Protestant privilege. Kelly had recognized this, and he warned the Unionist government that 'account must be taken of the political as well as the purely legal considerations'.[80] Not surprisingly, Hall-Thompson bore the brunt of backbench criticism when the Education Bill received its second reading in October 1946. Although the government had a comfortable majority, several MPs focused on the conscience clause, declaring it unnecessary, but the minister stuck doggedly to the principle that the teaching profession had to be given adequate safeguards on this key issue of conscience.[81]

The second major problem to confront the Unionist government in educational reconstruction was the question of representation on school management committees. At a cabinet meeting in June 1945 it was agreed that the rights enjoyed by the existing school management committees under the 1925 and 1930 acts would remain unaltered, subject, of course, to the conscience clause.[82] This legislation gave the transferrers of former public elementary schools, principally Protestant clergymen, 50 per cent representation on the new management committees, when the schools came under the control of the education authority. Nevertheless, Hall-Thompson informed his cabinet colleagues that the clerics would not have any claim to sit on the management committees of the new junior secondary schools (usually referred to as intermediate schools) which were to be established by fresh legislation. For the 'sake of peace', however, the minister of education accepted that the new committees could be comprised of the following representatives: one-third appointed by the education authority, one-third nominated by the parents and one-third appointed by the management committees of the local authority primary schools which would act as feeder schools to the new intermediate schools.[83] Nevertheless, the cabinet was aware that the Protestant clergy desired 50 per cent representation on the new committees, and this clearly frustrated leading Unionists. As the churches were not surrendering any property in the case of these new schools, Brooke claimed that their argument was without foundation. Moreover, he did not 'consider the representatives of the churches to be ideal for effective management'.[84] Nugent was equally critical of the churches. He argued that the composition of these new committees should reflect the financing of the new schools: 35 per cent to the local authority and 65 per cent to the Department of Education. He also drew the cabinet's attention to possible Westminster opposition, when he claimed: 'If the Roman Catholics make difficulties at Westminster it might be hard to defend giving one-third of the representation to the churches.'[85] Hall-Thompson, who never concealed his dislike of clerical interference in the province's education system, expressed the opinion that Ede, 'a Nonconformist and an ex-elementary teacher', would definitely oppose any proposal to give the churches 50 per cent representation on the management committees of the new junior secondary schools. The minister of education added that if concessions were made to the Protestant clerics on this issue, the Catholic hierarchy would raise an 'outcry' at Westminster. He stressed that the Unionist authorities could not risk the accusation of endowing Protestantism, because they would not 'fare well at the hands of the Home Secretary with his long history of opposition to clerical control in education'.[86] Only Warnock maintained that the composition of the new committees was outside Westminster's control, but this view was disputed by the attorney general, who was convinced that the proposal could be rejected on the grounds that it was an endowment of Protestantism.[87]

In March 1946 Northern Ireland officials met Maxwell in London to ascertain the Home Office's views on the Unionist government's proposal to allocate one-third representation on the new management committees to the Protestant churches. To their surprise they learned that Maxwell had no objection to even the 50 per cent representation on the management committees of the new schools demanded by the churches. Crucially, however, he added a proviso, stating that consent would only be given if the Home Office did not receive any complaints. Realizing that Catholic opposition to any such proposal was inevitable, the Stormont officials had no alternative but to follow Maxwell's advice of securing agreement in the province with all the parties concerned, including the Catholic representatives, to ensure that the legal validity of the proposal was not challenged.[88] Hall-Thompson quickly realized that the only way to prevent Catholic opposition was to make concessions to the province's voluntary schools.[89] It was apparent that the motivation for such a compromise came from the Home Office, which was able to influence the Northern Ireland Education Bill without resorting to direct intervention. This arrangement closely resembled the deal struck in 1930, when voluntary managers received 50 per cent construction grants in return for their acquiescence in the concessions on Bible instruction made to the churches.

Nearly all Catholic children were taught in voluntary schools. Previously, Lord Londonderry had attempted to extend some form of state control over the voluntary sector by providing grants towards the running of the schools if they would accept 'four and two' committees. The four and two system gave the representatives appointed by the voluntary manager, usually a local parish priest, double the representation of the education authority, but the Catholic Church repeatedly rejected the scheme. When the Brooke cabinet reviewed the voluntary system in late 1944, the schools were receiving 50 per cent grants for construction and for heating, cleaning and lighting, but nothing for internal repairs unless they had a four and two committee.[90] After some debate the cabinet decided to pay the full cost of heating, cleaning, lighting and internal maintenance, and to increase the capital construction grants to 65 per cent if the schools agreed to accept four and two committees. Yet again, Hall-Thompson had to overcome internal cabinet opposition to the raising of the building grant from 50 to 65 per cent. In the agreement that was finally reached it was stressed that the higher grant could only be given on the condition that a four and two committee was established. This went further than the Westminster act, but Brooke explained that conditions in Northern Ireland varied considerably from those in England, because 40 per cent of the total school population was being taught in Catholic voluntary schools.[91] Undoubtedly, the Home Office warning that the proposals in the new bill would be studied in Whitehall to ensure that adequate protection was given to the Catholic minority influenced the government's decision to defy many of its supporters and grant additional funding to the voluntary sector.[92]

Although the increased building grants represented a breakthrough for voluntary schools, Nationalist representatives and the Catholic hierarchy attacked the imposition of the four and two proviso in return for the 65 per cent grant.[93] Their most articulate lay spokesman, T.J. Campbell, the MP for Central, demanded a 100 per cent grant for new buildings and extensions, and he argued that as Catholics paid equal rates, it appeared as though 'Protestantism was being put on the rates.'[94] This was just the type of criticism that caused the Unionist government considerable embarrassment at Westminster. Privately, however, the leading Catholic cleric, Cardinal Joseph MacRory, the ageing archbishop of Armagh, was taking a more pragmatic approach, and this was recognized by Bromwell: 'There is a movement among Roman Catholics – of which my Minister and myself are aware – to stop "nagging" at the Government's policy towards R.C. schools and to concentrate instead on an amicable settlement the result of which would be more financial assistance from public funds for the R.C. voluntary schools.'[95]

Hall-Thompson expressed sympathy with Catholic grievances, and he told the cabinet 'that unless schools under Roman Catholic management were assisted to a greater extent the authorities in Great Britain might consider that the provisions of the Government of Ireland Act as to discrimination were infringed'. Nevertheless, in spite of the minister's concern, the cabinet remained opposed to giving extra assistance to Catholic education. Grant pointed out that if Catholic schools received more generous terms, complaints would follow from the Protestant churches which had already transferred their schools, while Brooke added that he disliked the idea of increasing grants to schools over which there was no public control.[96] Yet within six months the Stormont administration had performed a U-turn, as a Hall-Thompson proposal to increase building grants to 65 per cent without the obligation of a four and two committee was endorsed by the cabinet. Brooke, who had been a strong critic of any building grant increase without the four and two proviso, now argued that the government's main purpose was to secure the best possible education system in the interests of all children. Moreover, he was convinced that the whole scheme of educational reconstruction would be prejudiced if Catholic grievances were not addressed.[97]

While Brooke's statement made sound common sense, educational interests in themselves would not have been sufficient to bring about a reversal of the cabinet's earlier decision. The key motivation behind the government's decision to provide extra funding for the voluntary sector was its desire to escape possible legal and political opposition from the authorities in London. By allocating increased building grants to voluntary schools while permitting them to retain their independence, the Unionist government ensured that Catholic objections to the Protestant clergy's representation on the committees of the new junior secondary schools would be muted. Careful use of discreet pressure by Westminster had forced the Stormont government to adopt a more moderate approach to its plans for educational reconstruction. Usually, the authorities in London relied on informal personal contact to restrain the Belfast government, but the Home Office could, on occasion, issue a formal warning as it did in January 1945.[98] Certainly, Westminster's approach had been more effective than in 1925 or 1930, when the reservations of Home Office officials, which were expressed in private to individual Unionist ministers, were ignored by the Northern Ireland government. In the post-war period the authorities in London did not have to give Stormont positive directives on education policy. Instead, the prospect of legal, or even political, constraints was sufficient to persuade the Unionist cabinet to moderate its approach and defy its more extreme supporters as it restructured the province's education system. The Brooke cabinet's desire to avoid confrontation with Westminster, particularly when Labour came to power, ensured that a moderate line was taken in the two most controversial areas of the new bill: the conscience clause and the voluntary school building grants. The Home Office's task was considerably eased by the presence and actions of Bromwell and Hall-Thompson, both of whom were genuine moderates on educational matters. Furthermore, Ede's presence at the Home Office restrained the Unionist government. The Labour home secretary was a recognized expert in education and had taken a particular interest in the Northern Ireland reforms.

A significant number of Unionist backbenchers were incensed by the increased grants for voluntary schools, and the Education Bill, which received the royal assent on 27 March 1947, had a stormy passage through Stormont. Its fiercest critic was Harry Midgley, still leader of the Commonwealth Labour Party, who castigated the government for abandoning its earlier undertaking to maintain building grants at 50 per cent unless four and two committees were established.[99] While some Unionist ministers sympathized with this view, the cabinet was not prepared to follow a course that would risk confrontation with Westminster, especially when Labour came to power. Although Warnock, Grant and Moore expressed reservations on different occasions, a majority of the cabinet preferred to proceed cautiously on what they regarded as one of the most contentious issues facing post-war Northern Ireland. Consequently, the Home Office was able to persuade the Brooke government to reach an accommodation with representatives of the Catholic Church in order to prevent the legality of the Education Bill being challenged at Westminster. Discreet pressure from the Home Office, therefore, was the key factor in stiffening the government's resolve to overcome the united opposition of the Protestant churches, the Orange Order and a number of Unionist backbenchers. Angered by defeat, this powerful Protestant alliance was determined to prevent further concessions to Catholic education following the 1947 Education Act. Evidence of this opposition surfaced in May 1949, when Hall-Thompson attempted to pilot the Education

(Miscellaneous Provisions) Bill through Stormont. This was a short bill dealing with minor financial matters, one of which was a proposal that the Department of Education should meet the full cost of national insurance contributions for teachers in voluntary schools. Such was the scale of opposition, however, that the money resolution for the new bill was postponed indefinitely.[100]

Not surprisingly, Hall-Thompson became a target for militant Protestants who never missed an opportunity to attack the Department of Education. His difficulties were highlighted by the controversy surrounding the department's refusal to grant a boarding scholarship to a Catholic boy who lived close to both a Protestant voluntary grammar school and a local authority grammar school. With legal action pending, Hall-Thompson emphasized his dilemma in cabinet:

> If I hold to my decision it may be upset in court; it is possible, also, that I may be judged to have contravened the Government of Ireland Act. If I reverse my decision I shall be attacked by the 'strong Protestants' who are so anxious at present to find fault with my administration of the Education Act, and who seem to think that the development of education in this area should ensue to the benefit of Protestants alone.[101]

His anxiety, however, was short-lived. On 14 December 1949, at a meeting in Belfast to discuss the new Education Bill, Brooke informed the Grand Lodge of the Orange Order that Hall-Thompson had tendered his resignation.[102] On the previous day the minister of education had met a deputation of Unionist back-benchers in a failed attempt to negotiate an agreement on the Education (Miscellaneous Provisions) Bill. In the circumstances, it seems likely that Hall-Thompson resigned, probably under pressure from Brooke, to avoid a major split in the party. Ill feeling had persisted since his concession to voluntary schools in 1947, and it was clear that 'a section of the Party' resented the minister of education's defence of higher building grants.[103] An additional complication in the affair was the role played by Andrews, the former premier, in his capacity as imperial grand master of the Orange Order. Since his overthrow, he had consistently sought to embarrass the Brooke administration, and this undoubtedly played some part in the education crisis. For his part, Brooke was prepared to sacrifice Hall-Thompson in order to appease the hardliners and pre-serve party unity. By the end of 1949, moreover, the increase in sectarian ten-sion associated with Éire's secession from the Commonwealth made it more dif-ficult for the Unionist administration to defend politically the extra financial assistance for Catholic voluntary schools. Brooke himself accepted this and dropped his plans to have clerical influence removed from the province's edu-cation system.[104] The improvement in Stormont–Westminster relations during 1949 made Home Office opposition to any changes in education less likely. Without the threat of intervention by the authorities in London, Brooke was in a position to respond to the demands of his more extreme supporters, which had been spurned in 1947.

Once again, circumstances worked in Brooke's favour. Hall-Thompson's resignation gave the government breathing space, and the appointment of Harry Midgley, now a Unionist, as minister of education appeared to signal a major overhaul of the 1947 Education Act, which would satisfy the extremists. Midgley, who had impeccable anti-Catholic credentials, had been the sternest parliamentary critic of Hall-Thompson's treatment of voluntary schools. The new minister of education quickly settled the outstanding issues relating to the Education (Miscellaneous Provisions) Bill before taking up Brooke's suggestion to re-examine the whole education system. After a series of discussions with the interested parties Midgley formulated two proposals: firstly, the abolition of non-denominational religious instruction in the county schools and the placing of religious instruction under the control of the school's management committee, and, secondly, the continuation of the existing 65 per cent building grants, preferably for a five-year period, after which the grant would be reduced to 50 per cent if a four and two committee had not been established. These were similar to the demands which the government had refused to concede to the Protestant churches and the Orange Order between 1945 and 1947. Midgley said he would discuss his proposals with Major L.E. Curran, the attorney general, and if no 'insuperable objection' were raised, he would then initiate confidential discussions in London. However, when the attorney general asserted that the abolition of non-denominational religious instruction could be construed as an endowment of Protestantism, the cabinet decided to drop this proposal. In relation to voluntary school grants Curran agreed that the proposal to reduce the grants was within Northern Ireland's powers, though he found it 'distasteful and a breach of faith'. When the cabinet became aware of the attorney general's views, it deferred any decision to cut building grants in the voluntary sector.[105] In the end, Protestant agitation on the issue declined, and the government retained the 65 per cent building grants.[106]

REPRESENTATION

The allegation of discrimination against the minority on the issue of representation proved a constant source of concern for successive Unionist governments. Initially, the PR system operated for both Northern Ireland parliamentary elections and local government elections. Nationalists regarded the electoral system as crucially important, because PR was commonly associated with safeguarding the representation of minorities. Yet only one set of local elections in 1920 and two Northern Ireland general elections in 1921 and 1925 were held under the system, as PR was abolished in local elections by the 1922 Local Government Act and in parliamentary elections by the 1929 House of Commons (Method of Voting and Redistribution of Seats) Act. These two acts resulted in a reversion to the first-past-the-post system and the establishment of new local government boundaries. While the consequences of this switch had little impact on parliamentary elections, the effect on local government elections was considerable, as the Unionist party enjoyed significant gains, particularly in the west of the province.[107] Even though the Unionist government advanced the usual arguments against electoral reform, the real reason for the shift was political. While PR offered an opportunity to move away from single-issue politics, Unionists wanted every election to focus on the province's constitutional position. More particularly, the consolidation of a Unionist/Nationalist two-party system would facilitate the Unionist party's task of retaining Protestant working-class support and, thereby, deny the NILP a real foothold on the electoral map. Following the 1922 Local Government Act the Leech Commission was given the task of redrawing local government electoral areas. As Judge Leech's inquiries were largely boycotted by Nationalists, however, areas of doubt were always resolved in the Unionist party's favour, leaving the Belfast government open to the charge of gerrymandering. During the period between the wars the Unionist government's main defence against such an accusation was the failure of minority representatives to attend the inquiries, but this was widely interpreted as an admission of gerrymandering. Indeed, this was also the line taken by Maxwell at the Home Office, when he reviewed allegations made against the Northern Ireland government. Although he was in no doubt that gerrymandering of local government areas had taken place, he claimed that Nationalists had little room for complaint since they had boycotted the Leech Commission.[108]

Of course, the main challenge to the Local Government Bill had been mounted by the Westminster government which initially withheld the royal assent following the bill's passage in the Northern Ireland parliament. The authorities in Dublin had made strong representations to the government in London, claiming that changes in local government would inevitably prejudice the work of the proposed Boundary Commission, but Westminster hesitated in using its powers to force a U-turn by the Craig administration. Ultimately, the Unionist government's threat of resignation gave Westminster, which was keen to disentangle itself from Ulster politics, little alternative but to authorize the royal assent. Not surprisingly, this left the Westminster government open to the charge that it had failed to prevent the Unionist party from gerrymandering local government areas. While the case for malpractice in Northern Ireland parliamentary elections was inconclusive, Nationalists had little trouble in highlighting examples of gerrymandering in some of the redrawn local government electoral areas. Although both Tyrone and Fermanagh had narrow Catholic majorities, the effect of the 1922 legislation was to oust Nationalists from control of all public bodies in Fermanagh and leave only Omagh and Strabane urban district councils under Nationalist control in Tyrone. By 1936, moreover, Unionists had taken control of Omagh, following a further reorganization of local electoral areas.[109] In its efforts to weaken the arguments in favour of both counties being transferred to the Irish Free State and in order to overcome the problem of Nationalist-controlled councils, which had defied the government prior to 1922, the Unionist party attached great importance to securing control of as many local bodies in the west as possible. The restricted local government franchise, which favoured property owners, and the use of rateable value as well as population to determine electoral boundaries made it easier for the Unionist party to secure the necessary advantages.

The most spectacular instance of gerrymandering, however, occurred in Derry, where the Nationalists had won control of the corporation in 1920 under the PR system. Unionists regained control following the 1922 act, and a further rearrangement of local government boundaries in 1936 tightened their grip on the city, even though Catholics comprised roughly 65 per cent of local government electors. The 1936 changes created a position whereby 9,961 Nationalist supporters returned six councillors, while 7,444 Unionist voters returned twelve councillors in the smaller Waterside and North wards.[110] When pressed for an explanation of this anomaly, the Unionist government reiterated its claim that the higher population in the Nationalist-controlled South ward was balanced by the higher proportion of the rates paid in the other two wards.[111] Naturally, this did not satisfy the province's Nationalist MPs, who saw an ulterior motive in the Unionist party's gerrymandering schemes, because the control of local government enabled Unionist councils to exclude Catholics from public employment. The Home Office had repeatedly ignored such charges, though officials in London did acknowledge that Catholics were frequently overlooked in appointments where Unionists enjoyed a majority on the local council.[112] Subsequently, the growing tendency of Stormont's Nationalist representatives to abandon abstention brought further publicity to the link between gerrymandering and discrimination in employment. Michael McGurk, the MP for Mid-Tyrone, highlighted this injustice, when he told MPs that Catholics only filled 11 per cent of the public jobs in County Tyrone even though they comprised 55 per cent of the population.[113] Clearly, this shattered the minority's confidence in the impartiality of the Northern Ireland state, and the authorities in London had to bear some of the responsibility for their failure to curb Unionist excesses.

A possible threat to the Unionist party's hegemony in local government emerged in 1944, when the coalition government in London announced its intention to assimilate local government franchise with parliamentary franchise on the mainland. This put the spotlight on the different systems operating in Northern Ireland. In cabinet Lowry emphasized the advantages of following Westminster's lead. While there were obvious financial savings to be made by assimilating the franchises, Lowry also warned that it was becoming increasingly difficult to justify the province's restricted local government franchise. Although he favoured the extension of the franchise for local government elections, Lowry knew that such a change would have undesirable 'political' effects, as there would be an increase on the electoral register from 560,000 to 830,000.[114] However, Brooke had already been in contact with party representatives, and he firmly rejected Lowry's recommendation.[115] Yet Lowry's prediction that any discussion of the local government franchise would rekindle controversy proved to be accurate. Various opposition speakers commented on the uneasiness displayed by the usually brash Warnock, the new minister of home affairs, when he opened the debate on the second reading of the Elections and Franchise Bill.[116] In defending Stormont's decision not to follow Westminster's example, Warnock forecast that the experiment with a universal franchise in local elections would prove unsuccessful.[117] Although the new Labour government was unlikely to oppose the Brooke administration on the issue, Beattie attempted to exert pressure on the Unionist government by claiming that its handling of the local government issue was being closely monitored by the authorities in London.[118] Yet in his criticism of the new bill Cahir Healy offered evidence of the frustration that the Nationalist party was already feeling with the Attlee government: 'I would say that the British Government's acting hypocritically if they go wandering over the world to see that democracy is kept at its true value and close their eyes to what is happening at home.'[119] During the debate an outburst by the Unionist chief whip, Major Curran, laid bare the reasons for the retention of the restricted local government franchise. He wanted to prevent Nationalists, whom he believed had no stake in the country, from obtaining control of the three border counties and the Londonderry Corporation, and he thought that the best way to achieve this was to disenfranchise their supporters.[120]

Curran's admission merely confirmed the views of all Unionist opponents who saw the limited franchise as means of maximizing Unionist control of local bodies. Much to the displeasure of the opposition parties, the new Labour government, which had just introduced universal franchise for local elections in Britain, made no effort to pressurize the Belfast administration into following Westminster's example. Just after the Elections and Franchise Bill had received its second reading at Stormont, a deputation comprising J.H. McKie, the Independent Conservative MP for Galloway, Jack Magougan, the NILP chairman, and Frank Hanna, a Belfast councillor who subsequently won a Stormont seat, met Ede in an attempt to persuade the home secretary to intervene on the issue of local government franchise in the province. Although Ede sympathized with their arguments, he emphasized that local government franchise was 'completely' within the jurisdiction of the Northern Ireland parliament.[121] However, while the home secretary was content to leave the matter to the authorities in Belfast, officials at the Dominions Office were demanding an explanation for Stormont's refusal to follow Westminster's lead in extending universal franchise for local elections. Their interest in this issue stemmed from Maffey's demands in February 1946 for information on Northern Ireland's local government representation. The interference from the Dominions Office was not welcomed by Kelly, who attempted to play down the situation by informing Home Office officials that 'Maffey was far too inclined to scent intrigue and sinister motives where none existed.'[122] In spite of Kelly's reassurance, the Home Office felt obliged to ask the authorities at Stormont to repeat the arguments in favour of the limited local government franchise. The reply given by Gransden was firm and effectively ended any further investigation by the Home Office: 'I am not quite clear how "controversial" issues arise in relation to Éire in respect of a domestic Measure, which has passed both Houses of Parliament in Northern Ireland.'[123] Further evidence of the Home Office's lack of enthusiasm for intervention emerged in June 1946, when Ede received a request from the Birmingham Borough Labour party, urging him to use his powers to revoke the recent Northern Ireland franchise legislation. The home secretary replied that such a course of action would be irreconcilable with the constitutional function created by the Government of Ireland Act, and he emphasized that under its constitutional powers the control of local government franchise was entirely within the jurisdiction of the Stormont parliament.[124] Kelly immediately sent a copy of the correspondence to the Northern Ireland cabinet, suggesting that this statement of Northern Ireland's constitutional position was one worth preserving.[125]

With Westminster unwilling to intervene, Nationalists introduced a motion at

Stormont in December 1946 demanding a public inquiry into the gerrymandering of local government areas, but it had little impact on the Unionist government or its supporters.[126] The issue received further attention, however, when the Northern Ireland Bill was introduced at Westminster in the following year. This was an innocuous, technical measure enabling the Stormont government to conclude minor agreements such as the Lough Erne drainage scheme with the Éire government, but it gave the Friends of Ireland group, and Geoffrey Bing in particular, an excellent opportunity to highlight the anomalies of local government representation in the province. Bing asserted that the limited franchise was blatant discrimination and, more significantly, contended that the issue of local government franchise and elections should not be left to the Stormont parliament: 'This is the supreme Parliament. It is our duty to see that the Government of Ireland Act, 1920, is carried out, not only in the letter but in the spirit in which it was intended.'[127] In defending Stormont's actions, Sir Hugh O'Neill, the Unionist leader at Westminster, rehearsed the party line that the charge of gerrymandering was without foundation, because the province's local government electoral areas were based on rateable value in addition to population.[128] On this occasion criticism of Northern Ireland's local government arrangements came not only from Labour MPs in the Friends of Ireland group. A Liberal backbencher, Wilfrid Roberts, concluded: 'I think the case of local elections ... is really discreditable to a parliament of a British Government.'[129] In addition, Mulvey, the Nationalist MP for Fermanagh and Tyrone, highlighted the consequences of gerrymandering for the Catholic community, as Unionists frequently used their control of local government to allocate houses and public jobs to their supporters. In his conclusion he reiterated the standard criticism that section 5 of the 1920 act, which was intended to protect the minority, was frequently ignored by the Northern Ireland government: 'Everything possible has been done ... to strike at the Catholics of Northern Ireland, and to deprive them of the right of control in counties where they form a majority of the population.'[130] Considering the publicity given to these attacks on the treatment of the minority, Ede's response to the criticism must have come as a relief to the Unionist government. The home secretary was unequivocal on the Labour government's general policy towards Northern Ireland's internal affairs:

> Rightly or wrongly, this House has specifically delegated to the Northern Ireland Parliament the oversight of certain matters. I have no more right to inquire into how they discharge their functions in that matter than I have to inquire into the way in which the Dominions of South Africa, Canada, Australia, or New Zealand discharge the self-government which this Parliament has, in time passed, bestowed upon them. I have no such powers.[131]

Quite apart from confirming the view that the issue of local representation was entirely a matter for the Stormont parliament, Ede's statement greatly reassured Brooke and his colleagues about the general attitude of the Labour administration towards Northern Ireland. Although the home secretary was mistaken in attributing virtual sovereignty to the devolved legislature, his action clearly demonstrated the reluctance of the new Labour administration to become involved in the province's internal political disagreements. While Ede had some sympathy with the arguments expressed by the Unionist government's opponents, and had privately expressed his preference for the application of universal suffrage in local government elections, he rejected several pleas for intervention, rigidly adhering to a policy of non-intervention in the province's affairs. Significantly, a lack of unity among the opposition parties eased the pressure on the Unionist government. While Nationalists sought to force a revision of gerrymandered local electoral areas, the more left-wing parties concentrated on the demand for an extension of the franchise in local government elections. Indeed, this divergence of interest reflected the geographical footprint of support for the opposition parties in the province. The Nationalist party, which was much stronger in the west of the province, recognized that it would derive major benefits from the redrawing of local government areas, whereas a wider franchise would bring advantages to the NILP and the Socialist Republican party in Belfast. Although the Brooke administration steadfastly refused to consider any measure of local government reform, a stance facilitated by Ede's reluctance to intervene on the issue, allegations of gerrymandering and the restricted franchise remained contentious issues in Northern Ireland, and they were to surface dramatically during the 1960s when Labour returned to power.

SECURITY

In denouncing the Unionist government, Friends of Ireland MPs frequently linked local government representation with the use of the Special Powers Act. The Civil Authorities (Special Powers) Act had been rushed through the Northern Ireland parliament in the spring of 1922 during a period of violent sectarian conflict. In the period 6 December 1921 to 31 May 1922, a total of 236 people were killed: 16 were members of the Crown forces, 73 were Protestants and 147 were Catholics.[132] Originally intended to operate for a year, the Special Powers Act conferred power on the civil authority, defined as the minister of home affairs, 'to take all such steps and issue all such orders as may be necessary for maintaining order', and the minister could delegate this authority to his junior minister or to any police officer.[133] More specifically, the legislation gave sweeping security powers to the Belfast government. These included flogging and the death penalty for arms and explosive offences, the detention of suspects without trial and the imposition of curfews on the recommendation of the police. Craig believed that the use of such draconian measures would enable his government to bring the violence under control. Not surprisingly, the Special Powers Act was fiercely criticized by Unionist opponents at Westminster, but a combination of Craig's influence and the fact that the legislation closely resembled the 1920 Restoration of Order in Ireland Act, used by the Lloyd George government during the War of Independence, gave the authorities in Belfast a relatively free hand on the security front. More serious criticism, however, was reserved for the Ulster Special Constabulary (USC), an exclusively Protestant force, comprising full-time and part-time elements, which began recruiting in

November 1920 and quickly acquired a brutal reputation. The activities of the USC, particularly the part-time 'B' Specials, confirmed nationalist fears and attracted powerful condemnation from the British press.[134] For its part, the new Unionist government regarded the use of both the 'B' Specials and the Special Powers Act as necessary to reassure anxious Protestant supporters who were convinced that the Specials provided the only effective restraint on the IRA. Nevertheless, the behaviour of the USC alienated the nationalist community and destroyed what little prospect there was of Catholics becoming reconciled to the new state. While Craig did attempt to restrain his followers and impose discipline on the Specials, this was partly intended to make his government's security policy more acceptable at Westminster, because the Unionist administration relied on Westminster to pay for the USC.[135]

Although the Westminster government had responsibility for financing the Special Constabulary, it made no significant attempt to influence the Unionist administration's security arrangements during this critical formative period. This was in spite of its reservations about the consequences of using such a partisan group as an auxiliary police force and the obvious lack of impartiality associated with the operation of the Special Powers Act. While no effort was made to modify the Belfast administration's approach to civil unrest, there was a specific case in 1924, involving the release from internment of Cahir Healy, which demonstrated that a Westminster government could influence security decisions made by the Unionist government.[136] Healy, a Sinn Féin MP for the two-member constituency of Fermanagh and Tyrone, had been one of the first to be detained under the Special Powers Act. When he was re-elected in December 1923, however, Labour backbenchers demanded his release, and this pressure intensified in the following month when the Labour government took office. Direct ministerial pressure was now applied, and by threatening to withhold payments to the Northern Ireland exchequer Westminster secured Healy's release in February 1924 in spite of protests from the Ministry of Home Affairs in Belfast.[137] On the only other occasion when finance and security measures were directly linked, Craig, acting without cabinet approval, agreed to the release of all nationalist political prisoners in January 1926, when Baldwin threatened not to meet additional expenditure incurred by the Northern Ireland government in its use of the Special Constabulary.[138] Still, the Unionist government retained both the Special Powers Act and the 'B' Specials, even though relative peace had been restored by the summer of 1922. When they abandoned abstention in 1925, Nationalist MPs used the annual renewal of the legislation to argue that the reduced security threat undermined the case for the retention of both the 'B' Specials and the Special Powers Act. Unionists countered with the claim that it was the presence of the Specials, supported by such tough security powers, which effectively discouraged further IRA activity in the North. Though inactive for long periods, Unionists were convinced that the IRA remained a constant threat, and it was the government's duty to respond quickly to any sign of renewed activity. This, of course, required a high state of alert on the security front. Yet despite their intransigence, Craig and his colleagues were disturbed by Nationalist criticism of their security policy, because it attracted

Westminster's attention and highlighted the repressive measures used by the government in its efforts to maintain peace and order. Consequently, in 1928 the cabinet decided to renew the Special Powers Act for five years until 1933, when, in view of the mounting tension caused by de Valera's recent election victory, it was made permanent.[139]

Nationalists also had little difficulty in producing examples of double standards in the operation of the Special Powers Act, which was practically never used against the Protestant community. Certainly, this was the case in 1935, when serious sectarian rioting erupted in Belfast during July. While Nationalist demands for an official British inquiry into the 1935 riots had the support of a number of British MPs, the prime minister, Stanley Baldwin, refused an inquiry, emphasizing that responsibility for law and order rested with the Northern Ireland government. Such was the publicity surrounding these events, however, that the London-based National Council for Civil Liberties undertook an inquiry in 1936 investigating Stormont's handling of law and order issues. Its report constituted a scathing indictment of the Unionist government, and particular criticism was reserved for its use of the Special Powers Act.[140] Yet the Westminster government ignored this independent body's findings. Indeed, when the Home Office subsequently examined the application of the Special Powers Act, it concluded that the regulations made under the act had been sparingly used, and, furthermore, these regulations had tended to discourage terrorism. Although the Home Office acknowledged that the powers held by the Unionist government were objectionable, it stressed that the act itself was not directed against Catholics, but against the IRA.[141] When pressed by the Dominions Office for further analysis of the Belfast administration's treatment of the minority, the Home Office continued to defend the Unionist government's record on law and order. It emphasized that the Éire government had also found it necessary to rely on similar legislation to combat the threat posed by the IRA in the South. Moreover, while the Home Office recognized that the powers at the disposal of the Northern Ireland Ministry of Home Affairs were draconian, they were in practice 'administered with great moderation'.[142] Still, officials at the Dominions Office remained unconvinced, arguing that, while there were only a few specific complaints against the Unionist government's administration of the act, 'the whole system wants overhauling'.[143] In spite of the concerns expressed by the Dominions Office, the Westminster government continued to follow the principle that issues relating to the province's minority, including law and order, remained the responsibility of the government in Belfast. Subsequently, the argument that vigilance had to be maintained to combat the IRA was underlined by the bombing campaign in England during 1939. Clearly, this strengthened the Unionist government's contention that the IRA remained a significant threat, and that special measures were required to meet this threat. Any lingering doubt about the need for such repressive law and order measures was dispelled by the events of the war, as the Stormont government realized that its tough security policy was no longer in question. Indeed, during the war the government found it necessary to mobilize a small number of 'B' Specials for full-time duty to assist the regular police in carrying out their normal duties.[144]

Inevitably, the issue of security was raised at the end of the war, when the Unionist government considered the question of IRA suspects who had been interned during hostilities. Together, Brooke and Warnock decided to release all of these prisoners, even though it was noted that de Valera had been forced to re-intern some of those released in Éire. There was no dissenting voice in the cabinet, but Grant urged an early announcement of the decision in order to avoid the appearance of yielding to Nationalist pressure that would undoubtedly be exerted in the new parliament.[145] The release of the internees, however, was not followed by a general relaxation of Stormont's security policy. In December 1945 Warnock reported to his colleagues that at a recent nationalist meeting, at which a number of MPs were present, 'very extreme views' had been expressed, thus confirming the case for maintaining an efficient Special Constabulary.[146] Yet this would present problems. The minister of home affairs recognized that extra expenditure would be required to revitalize the force, because towards the end of the war 'the enthusiasm and interest of the personnel and the general efficiency of the Force waned to an alarming extent'.[147] Clearly, Warnock believed that the £50,000 per annum which Stormont had received to run the Specials over the ten years before the war was now inadequate. Responding to Warnock, Sinclair warned that a major increase in expenditure on security after the war would spark confrontation with the Treasury, which wanted any increased costs to be met by local revenue. More significantly, the minister of finance offered the opinion that increased spending on security could have 'serious political repercussions at Westminster'.[148] Sinclair's argument in favour of caution was based on his fear of the new Labour government and his desire to deflect attention from Stormont's handling of security. Nevertheless, these fears were unfounded. Shortly after opening negotiations for additional finance, the minister was able to inform the cabinet that the Treasury had agreed in principle to increase the annual expenditure for the Special Constabulary to approximately £137,500 per year.[149] Obviously, the new Labour government was content to leave responsibility for law and order in the hands of the Northern Ireland administration, even though individual Labour MPs were highly critical of the repressive measures employed by the Unionist government.

Bing used the debate on the 1947 Northern Ireland Bill to launch a vehement attack on the Special Powers Act, claiming that its real purpose was to give the Unionist party a political advantage.[150] The Ulster Unionist leader at Westminster, Sir Hugh O'Neill, responded by stressing that both the London and Dublin governments relied on similar draconian measures when threatened by an upsurge in IRA violence. He did, however, appear to make one concession in his suggestion that the act should be reviewed annually in the Northern Ireland parliament.[151] Before the debate the Unionist government had produced a pamphlet, warning that the IRA menace was still present, but Mulvey dismissed this as Unionist propaganda, timed to provide some defence for the operation of the Special Powers Act during the Westminster debate.[152] In his speech winding up the debate Ede struck a familiar note and reassured the authorities in Belfast by insisting that the Northern Ireland government had the authority to administer its own internal affairs as it saw fit. He also took this opportunity to reject calls for an inquiry into various matters, including the Special Powers Act, which concerned the Catholic minority.[153]

While the Labour government provided little incentive for opposition parties in the province, they were, nevertheless, encouraged by the activities of outspoken Friends of Ireland MPs who constantly criticized the Unionist administration. Harry Diamond, the MP for Falls, called on the government to take up Sir Hugh O'Neill's suggestion that the Special Powers Act should be reviewed annually, and when the Offences against the State Act was suspended by the Éire government, he asked Warnock to consider the repeal of the entire act.[154] Earlier, Diamond had introduced a motion at Stormont demanding repeal. In his speech he claimed that there was no justification for the retention of such legislation in the peaceful climate of 1947, but the attorney general dismissed the idea, arguing that, while the IRA was attempting to reorganize, 'not one jot or tittle would be taken from the Act'.[155] Yet in spite of this uncompromising approach, Warnock informed his cabinet colleagues only one year later that he intended to suspend certain provisions in the act which infringed the liberty of the subject, though it would be possible to revive these powers at very short notice should the need arise.[156] A further sign of the government's change of heart emerged with Warnock's suggestion that the time was approaching when the RUC could be disarmed for normal duties, but before reaching a definite decision he wanted to confer with the force's inspector-general.[157] In the end, opposition from within the force ensured that the RUC was not disarmed. Moreover, the reluctance on the part of the police to countenance any diminution of its powers made it even more difficult for the government to alter its security strategy.[158] Of course, the other great obstacle to any easing of the Special Powers Act was the attitude of Unionist supporters, who required constant reassurance of Stormont's ability to respond immediately to renewed activity by the IRA.

In reaching its decision to modify the Special Powers Act, the Unionist cabinet carefully considered the benefits which such a move would have at Westminster. While the authorities in London did not intervene directly, it appears as though the Labour government was applying some degree of gentle pressure in an effort to persuade the Northern Ireland government to adopt a more conciliatory approach to the question of law and order. During a cabinet discussion on the amendment of the Special Powers Act, Sinclair expressed the hope that the proposed changes would be made before the measure dealing with reinsurance came up for discussion at Westminster. Warnock was in full agreement, and he assured the cabinet that everything possible would be done to have the changes expedited.[159] This was yet another example of the Stormont cabinet's thinking being influenced by its desire to present a better image to the authorities in London, because the Stormont ministers appreciated that this made it easier for their government to secure financial assistance from Westminster in other areas. The cabinet's decision to reconsider some aspects of the Special Powers Act eventually led to the revocation in 1949 of forty-one of the regulations made under the act.[160] At Stormont Harry Diamond was in no doubt that the Unionist government had been influenced by the authorities in London. He claimed that the main reason for the suspension of certain sections of the act was 'the whispering of Chuter Ede to the then minister of home affairs to indulge in some face-saving and to indicate to the world that Northern Ireland is not actually what it is, a police State'.[161] Not surprisingly, Diamond's argument was rejected by Brian Maginess, who had succeeded Warnock as minister of home affairs in November 1949. Maginess dismissed any idea that pressure had been applied by Westminster, instead claiming that the 'peaceable state' of the country had enabled Stormont to tone down the legislation.[162]

The decision to remove some of its more repressive powers was due to a combination of the desire to promote better relations with Westminster and the more peaceful state of the province in the immediate post-war period. Indeed, with the encouragement of the liberal Maginess, the cabinet even considered repealing the Special Powers Act. Only weeks after his appointment, Maginess presented a memorandum, arguing the case for an early repeal of the entire act. He explained that the Council of Europe was in the process of considering a draft convention on human rights, which was basically opposed to arrest without trial, and argued that if this was ratified by the Council of Europe, as it almost certainly would be, the Special Powers Act should be revoked immediately. The minister of home affairs indicated, however, that the inspector-general and his Crime Special Staff were not in favour of repeal. They were concerned about any delay, which might have serious consequences, in rushing appropriate legislation through the Stormont parliament in the event of an emergency.[163] During the ensuing cabinet discussion, Nugent, now minister in the Senate, re-echoed the concern expressed by the police in relation to the effect of any delay in an emergency situation. However, Maginess rejected the idea of contingency legislation which would take effect immediately, arguing that the government would still be open to the same criticism as long as there was any law on the statute book giving the authorities the power to make regulations for arrest and detention without trial. The new minister of education, Harry Midgley, supported Maginess's argument, emphasizing that 'the existence of the Acts was a continual source of embarrassment when the matter was raised in Great Britain and elsewhere, especially as the facts were usually distorted and exaggerated'. Finally, a compromise was reached. In the event of the repeal of the Special Powers Act it was agreed that provisions should be included in the Public Order Bill which would allow the necessary powers for dealing with an emergency to be revived at very short notice.[164]

Yet the Special Powers Act was not repealed, and the Public Order Act, which became law in 1951, gave the government even more specific powers to impose control on disorderly meetings and processions. Furthermore, the 1954 Flags and Emblems Act gave the police new powers to seize provocative emblems.[165] This represented a dramatic reversal of the Unionist government's earlier intentions, as the authorities in Belfast responded to the escalation of street politics associated with Anti-Partition League (APL) demonstrations in the 1949–51 period. Moreover, nervousness among rank-and-file Unionists had increased following Éire's withdrawal from the Commonwealth, and there was mounting pressure on the Stormont authorities to take some action to alleviate these concerns. In acceding to its supporters' demands for firm action, the

Brooke government abandoned its previous strategy which had offered evidence of a more enlightened approach to the crucial question of law and order. For example, an earlier request from the Ulster Unionist Council for the playing of the national anthem at the close of every entertainment in the province had brought an unequivocal response from Lowry, who dismissed 'this most foolish desire', explaining that the government was responsible for promoting peace, order and good government, whereas such a measure would have the opposite effect.[166] The Unionist government had also appreciated that the more peaceful state of the province had created the conditions in which the government could consider moderating its security policy. In addition, gentle prompting from Westminster, coupled with the Stormont government's desire to promote a better image in London in order to stifle criticism of the Unionist administration, had encouraged the cabinet to formulate definite proposals for modifying the Special Powers Act. The revocation of forty-one of the regulations made under the act indicated that the government was prepared to compromise, but the fact that nothing further was achieved in this direction demonstrated the Stormont cabinet's unwillingness to upset its supporters by appearing soft on the vital issue of law and order. Of course, a greater degree of pressure from Westminster could have forced the Belfast administration to make many more concessions on security, but as this did not materialize, Unionist ministers realized that they did not have to risk losing Protestant support by appearing to drop their guard against the IRA. Of course, the RUC remained opposed to any tampering with the Special Powers Act, and any major overhaul of the province's security provisions would, therefore, have required a bold move on the part of the Unionist government.

Unlike the other issues concerning the minority, the Stormont authorities found it much easier to defend their use of the Special Powers Act if challenged by Westminster. The existence of similar legislation in both Éire and Britain, aimed at combating the threat posed by the IRA, helped the Unionist government to present a robust case for the retention of such draconian powers. Although it was clear that the Special Powers Act operated to the detriment of the Catholic community, the Labour government made little attempt to secure the changes necessary for a more impartial system of law and order. In the postwar period, however, Unionist ministers, and Maginess in particular, had demonstrated that there was more awareness of its general responsibilities on the part of the Unionist government. There was also much greater sensitivity about the projection of the province's image at Westminster, and this clearly encouraged the Brooke administration to give some consideration to fairer treatment for the province's Catholic minority.

NOTES

1. Correspondence with James Callaghan.
2. PRONI, CAB4/496/5, memo by Gordon, 15 January 1942.
3. PRONI, CAB4/503/2, memo by Bates, 16 March 1942.
4. PRONI, CAB4/503/6, Cab. Conclus., 18 March 1942.

5. PRONI, CAB4/504/4, Cab. Conclus., 31 March 1942. The Defence Regulations had been designed 'to promote the prosecution of the war'.

6. PRONI, CAB4/507/6, memo by Gordon, 24 April 1942, and CAB4/507/7, Cab. Conclus., 28 April 1942.

7. PRONI, CAB4/525/8, Cab. Conclus., 30 September 1942.

8. PROL, DO 35/1229/WX123/2, 'Labour – Conditions of residence in the six Irish Counties', memo by Dulanty, 21 January 1943.

9. Ibid., Attlee to Dulanty, 6 February 1943.

10. NIHC Debates, vol. 26, col. 364 and cols 396–7, 25 March 1943.

11. PRONI, CAB4/533/7, memo by Gordon, 26 February 1943.

12. PRONI, CAB9C/47/2, 'Infiltration of Éire workers into N.I. March 1944–December 1945', Lowry to Brooke, 14 March 1944. In fact, the United States government had made representations to the Éire government on this matter.

13. See Bew et al., *Northern Ireland 1921–1996*, p.92. The authors record the cabinet discussions and cite Lowry's speech.

14. PRONI, CAB4/592/2, Cab. Conclus., 10 July 1944.

15. PRONI, CAB4/597/7, memo by Midgley, 9 September 1944. See also Bew et al., *Northern Ireland 1921–1996*, p.92.

16. PRONI, CAB4/597/17, Cab. Conclus., 15 September 1944.

17. PRONI, CAB4/597/8, memo by Midgley, 9 September 1944.

18. PRONI, CAB9C/47/2, Bevin to Midgley, 1 November 1944.

19. PRONI, CAB9C/47/2, memo by Warnock, 'Control of entry of Labour from Éire into Northern Ireland', 21 February 1945.

20. PRONI, CAB4/615/5, Cab. Conclus., 15 February 1945.

21. PRONI, CAB4/618/5, note on Brooke's visit to London, 27 February to 1 March 1945.

22. PROL, HO 45/21985/900542, 'Infiltration and Immigration into Northern Ireland: control, 1942–1948', Markbreiter to Maxwell, 22 March 1945. The correspondence included a note by Gransden.

23. Bew et al., *Northern Ireland 1921–1996*, p.93.

24. PROL, HO 45/21985/900542, Beattie to Morrison, 7 February 1945.

25. Ibid., Markbreiter to Maxwell, 22 March 1945.

26. NIHC Debates, vol. 28, col. 884, 22 May 1945.

27. PROL, HO 45/21985/900542, Maxwell to Gransden, 21 June 1945.

28. NIHC Debates, vol. 29, col. 235, 31 July 1945.

29. PROL, HO 45/21985/900542, note by Markbreiter, 17 October 1945. Ede had indicated to Brooke at a meeting between the two on 10 October 1945 that the scheme would be extended for two years.

30. *Belfast Telegraph*, 20 October 1945. There were actually 24,000 Éire residents in the province, but 4,000 (retired doctors, clergymen, teachers, bank officials, etc.) would be certain to have their permits renewed.

31. PROL, HO 45/21985/900542, Maffey telegram to Dominions Office, 16 October 1945. A copy was sent to Markbreiter.

32. PROL, DO 35/1229/WX123/5, 'Discarding of Éire Labour in N. Ireland', Maffey to Dominions Office, 17 October 1945.

33. PROL, HO 45/21985/90052, Maffey telegram to Dominions Office, 16 October 1945.

34. Ibid., Maxwell to Stephenson, 2 November 1945.

35. PRONI, CAB9C/47/2, Brooke to Warnock, 25 October 1945.

36. Ibid., Maxwell to Ede, 30 October 1945. Kelly sent a copy of this correspondence to the cabinet secretariat at Stormont.

37. PROL, HO 45/21985/900542, Home Office minute, 24 October 1945. Warnock's statement was described as 'unfortunate and inaccurate'.

38. PRONI, CAB9C/47/2, Kelly to Gransden, 31 October 1945.

39. PRONI, CAB9C/47/3, 'Infiltration of Éire workers into N.I. 1946–47', Addison to Ede, 7 December 1945. A copy, which also contained Maffey's comments, was sent to the Stormont cabinet secretariat by Kelly.

40. PROL, DO 35/1229/WX123/5, note by Stephenson, 20 November 1945.

41. PRONI, CAB9C/47/3, Ede to Addison, 19 December 1945. A copy was sent to the Stormont cabinet secretariat by Kelly.

42. Ibid., Kelly to Gransden, 2 April 1946.

43. PROL, HO 45/21985/900542, see Hutson to H.C. Montgomery, an assistant secretary at the Ministry of Home Affairs, 11 April 1946, and Mulvey to Ede, 11 March 1946.

44. PRONI, CAB9/47/3, Kelly to Gransden, 2 April 1946.

45. HC Debates, 5th series, vol. 421, col. 229, 4 April 1946. He was replying to a question by Beattie.

46. PRONI, CAB9C/47/3, Ede to Morgan, 13 May 1946. A copy was sent to the Stormont cabinet secretariat by Kelly.
47. Ibid., note on Brooke's meeting with Addison, 29 May 1946.
48. PROL, HO 45/21985/900542, Warnock to Ede, 23 January 1947.
49. Ibid., memo by Howard, 10 February 1947. The idea was first suggested by Sir E. Holderness, an assistant secretary at the Home Office.
50. PRONI, CAB9C/47/3, note on Maxwell's meeting with Warnock and Maginess, 15 March 1947.
51. Ibid., note on Maxwell's meeting with Maffey and Machtig, 16 April 1947, and Maxwell's meeting with Gransden, 24 April 1947.
52. PRONI, CAB4/724/7, Cab. Conclus., 17 July 1947.
53. NIHC Debates, vol. 31, col. 1825, 21 October 1947.
54. Ibid., col. 1912, 22 October 1947.
55. Ibid., col. 2068, 30 October 1947.
56. PRONI, CAB9C/47/3, Kelly to Gransden, 2 April 1946.
57. D.H. Akenson, *Education and Enmity: The Control of Schooling in Northern Ireland 1920–1950* (Newton Abbot, 1973), p.52. The Catholic school managers met in Dublin in October 1921 and issued this declaration.
58. Farren, *The Politics of Irish Education*, pp.66–85.
59. Buckland, *The Factory of Grievances*, pp.266–7.
60. Akenson, *Education and Enmity*, pp.159–63.
61. PRONI, CAB4/595/6, Cab. Conclus., 20 July 1944. At this meeting the cabinet reaffirmed an earlier decision: see CAB4/590/18, Cab. Conclus., 22 June 1944.
62. NIHC Debates, vol. 27, cols 2747–9, 23 January 1945, and cols 2844–55, 24 January 1945.
63. PRONI, CAB9D/1/12, 'Educational Reconstruction 1944–45', memo by Lowry, 15 November 1944. Lowry had been appointed attorney general on 3 November 1944.
64. PRONI, CAB4/611/5, Maxwell to Gransden, 16 January 1945.
65. PRONI, CAB4/611/7, note on London meeting between Stormont and Westminster officials, 11 January 1945.
66. PRONI, CAB4/611/4, memo by Hall-Thompson, 15 January 1945, and CAB4/611/10, Cab. Conclus., 18 January 1945. For the Protestant churches' reaction to the conscience clause, see Farren, *The Politics of Irish Education*, pp.168–9 and pp.173–4.
67. Information from Unionist source.
68. PRONI, CAB4/626/5, Cab. Conclus., 25 May 1945. See also Farren, *The Politics of Irish Education*, pp.176–8.
69. PRONI, CAB4/627/5, memo by Brooke, 9 June 1945.
70. W. Corkey, *Episode in the History of Protestant Ulster 1923–47* (published privately, Belfast, not dated), p.119.
71. PRONI, CAB4/647/5, memo by Brooke, 9 June 1945, and CAB4/647/4, copy of the draft clause.
72. Corkey, *Episode in the History of Protestant Ulster*, p.119 and pp.125–6.
73. PRONI, CAB4/647/8, Cab. Conclus., 10 December 1945.
74. PRONI, CAB9D/1/12, memo by Bromwell, 'The Educational System of Northern Ireland as it might be seen by Mr. Chuter Ede, the Home Secretary', 1 October 1945.
75. PRONI, CAB9D/1/16, 'Religious Education in Schools 1946'. Bromwell said that if the June clause 'is certified in Belfast and publicly repudiated in London, it will not be to the credit of Northern Ireland': note by Bromwell on a letter from the bishop of Down and Dromore to Brooke, 1 January 1946.
76. Ibid., Hall-Thompson to the primate of the Church of Ireland, 21 January 1946.
77. PRONI, CAB4/662/5, Cab. Conclus., 28 March 1946.
78. PRONI, CAB4/679/8, Cab. Conclus., 1 August 1946.
79. PRONI, CAB9D/1/16, memo by Bromwell, 'The Education Bill: Reconstruction and the attitude of the Protestant Churches and the Roman Catholics to the proposals of the Government for management and finance', 4 March 1946.
80. PRONI, CAB9D/1/17, 'Education Act 1946–51', correspondence from Kelly, 29 August 1946. Kelly also added that even if a bill's legal validity was in doubt, it could still receive the royal assent if it was 'non-controversial'. Of course, all the parties concerned knew that this would not apply to the Education Bill.
81. NIHC Debates, vol. 30, cols 2002–3, 15 October 1946. For backbench criticism of Hall-Thompson, see col. 2136, 17 October 1946, and col. 2263, 23 October 1946.
82. PRONI, CAB4/627/20, Cab. Conclus., 1 June 1945. See also Farren, *The Politics of Irish Education*, p.177.
83. PRONI, CAB4/637/4, memo by Hall-Thompson, 5 October 1945.
84. PRONI, CAB4/637/9, Cab. Conclus., 15 October 1945.

85. PRONI, CAB4/647/8, Cab. Conclus., 10 December 1945.
86. PRONI, CAB9D/1/16, Hall-Thompson to the primate of the Church of Ireland, 21 January 1946.
87. PRONI, CAB4/647/8, Cab. Conclus., 10 December 1945.
88. PRONI, CAB9D/1/16, note on Maxwell's meeting at the Home Office with Gransden, Kelly and Bromwell, 16 March 1946.
89. PRONI, CAB4/662/5, Cab. Conclus., 28 March 1946.
90. PRONI, CAB4/601/7, memo by Hall-Thompson, 9 October 1944. See also Farren, *The Politics of Irish Education*, pp.170–1.
91. PRONI, CAB4/606/16, Cab. Conclus., 16 November 1944. Voluntary grammar schools could receive the 65 per cent building grant without having a four and two committee.
92. PRONI, CAB4/611/5, Maxwell to Gransden, 16 January 1945.
93. Farren, *The Politics of Irish Education*, pp.172–3.
94. PRONI, CAB4/637/4, memo by Hall-Thompson, 5 October 1945. Campbell's comments were quoted by the minister of education.
95. PRONI, CAB9D/1/11, 'Religious Education in schools 1922–44', Bromwell to Gransden, 29 March 1945. Bromwell favoured offering 75 per cent building grants in return for the establishment of four and two committees, because it would have been more difficult for the Catholic hierarchy to refuse.
96. PRONI, CAB4/637/9, Cab. Conclus., 15 October 1945.
97. PRONI, CAB4/662/5, Cab. Conclus., 28 March 1946. The cabinet also decided that grants for maintenance, heating, cleaning and lighting of voluntary primary schools and non-academic secondary schools would also be set at 65 per cent, thus altering a previous decision to bear the full costs of these. If a voluntary manager would accept a four and two committee, however, his school would receive 100 per cent grants for heating, cleaning, lighting and internal maintenance.
98. PRONI, CAB4/611/5, Maxwell to Gransden, 16 January 1945.
99. NIHC Debates, vol. 30, cols 2110–11, 16 October 1946.
100. Akenson, *Education and Enmity*, p.186. The author noted, 'Hall-Thompson suffered a humiliation rare for a Unionist minister.'
101. PRONI, CAB4/797/5, memo by Hall-Thompson, 24 October 1949. There were about sixty-eight similar cases of Catholic children seeking boarding scholarships to attend Catholic voluntary grammar schools. The total cost per annum to grant these scholarships would have been approximately £1,400. See also Farren, *The Politics of Irish Education*, p.214.
102. PRONI, CAB4/803/10, Cab. Conclus., 15 December 1949. Brooke had met Hall-Thompson on the morning of the Orange Order meeting. For the Order's criticism, see CAB9D/1/17, Harry Burdge, general secretary to the Grand Lodge of Ireland, to Brooke, 8 December 1949.
103. PRONI, CAB4/803/10, Cab. Conclus., 15 December 1949. This was cited in Brooke's review of the education system. See also CAB9D/1/17, memo by Hall-Thompson on grants to voluntary schools, which was written on 14 December and sent to Brooke.
104. PRONI, CAB9D/1/17, Brooke to Lord Glentoran, 15 December 1949.
105. PRONI, CAB4/813/9, memo by Midgley. Indeed, Midgley had suggested changes along these lines only four days after his appointment. This memorandum on an investigation into the educational system has subsequently been removed from the file, though references to it appear in the agenda and in the cabinet conclusions: see CAB4/813/14, Cab. Conclus., 27 March 1950.
106. PRONI, CAB4/825/11, memo by Midgley, 11 September 1950. For Midgley's solution, see Farren, *The Politics of Irish Education*, pp.211–13.
107. Buckland, *The Factory of Grievances*, p.226. Following the 1920 local elections under PR, Sinn Féin, Nationalists and Labour controlled 32 per cent of the province's local public bodies, but by 1927 Nationalists and Labour controlled only 16 per cent of these.
108. PROL, DO 35/893/X11/123, memo by Maxwell, 22 April 1924.
109. Buckland, *The Factory of Grievances*, p.226 and p.244. See also D. Fitzpatrick, *The Two Irelands 1912–39* (Oxford, 1998) pp.155–6.
110. Buckland, *The Factory of Grievances*, p.245. The Waterside ward included 2,339 unionists and 1,443 nationalists, and returned four councillors, while the other unionist ward, the North ward, contained 3,515 unionist electors and 2,021 nationalist electors, and returned eight councillors. The South ward contained 6,227 nationalist and 1,590 unionist electors, and returned eight councillors.
111. PROL, DO 35/893/X11/251, correspondence from the Ministry of Home Affairs to Londonderry Corporation, 11 December 1936. Robinson, an assistant secretary at the Ministry of Home Affairs, sent a copy to the Home Office to defend the Belfast government against charges of gerrymandering made by de Valera. It showed that the North ward with 5,469 electors paid £105,824 in rates, while the South ward with 7,844 electors paid £63,065 in rates.
112. Ibid., memo by Home Office on allegations made in connection with partition, November 1938.

113. NIHC Debates, vol. 28, cols 80–1, 21 February 1945.
114. PRONI, CAB4/597/6, memo by Lowry, 8 September 1944.
115. PRONI, CAB4/597/17, Cab. Conclus., 15 September 1944.
116. NIHC Debates, vol. 29, col. 1721, 9 January 1946. Beattie was just one who drew attention to Warnock's unusual lack of confidence.
117. Ibid., cols 1715–21, 9 January 1946.
118. Ibid., col. 1728, 9 January 1946. The bill proposed the retention of the seven-year residence qualification for any voter not born in Northern Ireland and the maintenance of the £5 dwelling house valuation, in addition to raising the valuation of qualifying premises other than dwelling houses from £5 to £10. The bill also proposed the retention of the company vote, which gave limited companies an extra vote for every £10 of valuation up to a maximum of six extra votes.
119. Ibid., col. 1741, 9 January 1946.
120. Curran's outburst was made in reply to an interjection. Although it was edited out by Stormont Hansard, the offending remarks were reported in the press: see Northern Whig, 11 January 1946, and an editorial in the Irish News, 11 January 1946. In fact, the offending sentence was later quoted by a Liberal MP in the House of Commons during the Westminster debate on the Northern Ireland Bill, HC Debates, 5th series, vol. 438, col. 1503, 13 June 1947.
121. PRONI, CAB9B/125/1, 'Equal franchise: Representation of the People Bill. Correspondence and memoranda concerning the laws governing elections in N. Ireland 1928–37', Kelly to Gransden, 29 January 1946.
122. PROL, HO 45/21996/915158, 'Elections and Franchise Bill (Northern Ireland) 1946; Elections and Franchise (Amendment) Act (Northern Ireland) 1948, 1945–1948', C.T.H. Morris, a senior administrative assistant at the Home Office, to Hutson, 26 February 1946. Morris repeated Kelly's views.
123. Ibid., Gransden to Morris, 29 April 1946.
124. PRONI, CAB9B/125/3, 'Correspondence and memoranda regarding the franchise in N. Ireland 1942–49', Ede to secretary of Birmingham Borough Labour party, 27 June 1946.
125. Ibid., Kelly to Gransden, 5 July 1946.
126. NIHC Debates, vol. 30, cols 3050–85, 3 December 1946, and cols 3248–384, 10 December 1946. Fourteen MPs voted for the motion. The ten Nationalists were supported by Beattie and by the NILP's Hugh Downey (Dock), Robert Getgood (Oldpark) and Frank Hanna (Central).
127. HC Debates, 5th series, vol. 438, cols 1491–2, 13 June 1947.
128. Ibid., cols 1503–4, 13 June 1947.
129. Ibid., col. 1509, 13 June 1947.
130. Ibid., col. 1522, 13 June 1947.
131. Ibid., col. 1556, 13 June 1947: cited in Hepburn (ed.), The Conflict of Nationality in Modern Ireland, p.170.
132. Buckland, A History of Northern Ireland, p.46.
133. Ibid., p.40.
134. Phoenix, Northern Nationalism, p.93. For the formation and structure of the USC, see A. Hezlet, The 'B' Specials (London, 1973), pp.22–3 and p.28. For criticism of the Special Constabulary, see M. Farrell, Arming the Protestants: The Formation of the Ulster Special Constabulary and the Royal Ulster Constabulary 1920–27 (London, 1983), pp.104–231 passim.
135. Buckland, A History of Northern Ireland, p.41. For Westminster opposition to the USC, see Canning, British Policy towards Ireland, pp.57–61.
136. Earlier attempts to secure the release of IRA prisoners and to obtain clemency for convicted IRA volunteers usually resulted in failure, though the lord lieutenant successfully intervened in a small number of serious cases in 1922: see Buckland, The Factory of Grievances, pp.207–10. The Dublin government had less success when it attempted to secure the release of six internees in 1923. Five of these men were normally resident in the Free State, and the authorities in Dublin were prepared to ensure that the men would not return north if released, but their request was rejected by the Craig government. See SPOI, S5750/5, Cosgrave to Craig, 21 July 1923, and Craig to Cosgrave, 30 July 1923.
137. Phoenix, Northern Nationalism, pp.300–2.
138. Buckland, The Factory of Grievances, pp.216–18 (notes). See also PRONI, CAB4/155/4, Cab. Conclus., 7 December 1925.
139. Buckland, The Factory of Grievances, p.219.
140. Buckland, A History of Northern Ireland, p.71.
141. PROL, DO 35/893/X11/123, note by Markbreiter, March 1938.
142. PROL, DO 35/893/X11/251, Home Office memo on allegations in connection with partition, not dated.
143. Ibid., memo by Batterbee, 18 November 1938. See also Canning, British Policy towards Ireland, pp.234–7.

144. Hezlet, *The B Specials*, p.139.
145. PRONI, CAB4/629/12, Cab. Conclus., 5 July 1945.
146. PRONI, CAB4/646/7, Cab. Conclus., 4 December 1945.
147. PRONI, CAB4/646/4, memo by Warnock, 27 November 1945.
148. PRONI, CAB4/646/7, Cab. Conclus., 4 December 1945.
149. PRONI, CAB4/649/9, Cab. Conclus., 19 December 1945.
150. HC Debates, 5th series, vol. 438, cols 1485–8, 13 June 1947.
151. Ibid., col. 1502, 13 June 1947.
152. Ibid., cols 1514–15, 13 June 1947.
153. Ibid., cols 1554–8, 13 June 1947.
154. NIHC Debates, vol. 31, col. 874, 5 June 1947, and cols 1360–1, 26 June 1947.
155. Ibid., vol. 30, cols 4124–5, and col. 4252, 11 February 1947.
156. PRONI, CAB4/745/13, Cab. Conclus., 26 February 1948.
157. PRONI, CAB4/746/11, Cab. Conclus., 11 March 1948.
158. Several officers who served in the immediate post-war period have recalled that there was a move towards a 'pulling-in' of arms around that time, but the idea appears to have been mysteriously dropped. There is some evidence that the inspector-general, Sir Richard Pim, a former high-ranking Whitehall civil servant who took up his duties in 1945, favoured the withdrawal of arms in certain instances.
159. PRONI, CAB4/766/8, Cab. Conclus., 28 October 1948.
160. F.H. Newark, 'The Law and the Constitution', in T. Wilson (ed.), *Ulster Under Home Rule: A Study of the Political and Economic Problems of Northern Ireland* (Oxford, 1955), p.48.
161. NIHC Debates, vol. 33, col. 2187, 13 December 1949.
162. Ibid., col. 2191, 13 December 1949.
163. PRONI, CAB4/810/5, memo by Maginess, 20 February 1950.
164. PRONI, CAB4/810/13, Cab. Conclus., 22 February 1950.
165. Newark, 'The Law and the Constitution', p.51.
166. PRONI, CAB9B/264, 'Correspondence with Attorney General concerning the playing of the National Anthem 1946–7', Lowry to Brooke, 15 January 1947.

4

Stormont and the Border

In the 1945–51 period there was renewed interest on Northern Ireland's constitutional position, as each of the three governments in London, Dublin and Belfast became embroiled in the issue. While the war had strengthened the Stormont government's position, Labour's surprise election victory created some concern among the Unionist community, because it was unsure of the precise line that the Attlee government would take on the crucial question of the border. At the same time, the end of the war presented an opportunity for nationalists to reopen their campaign for the removal of the border, and Labour's election success gave them added encouragement. This led to the establishment of the APL which sought to highlight the injustice of partition and influence the new Labour administration. Further encouragement for nationalists was provided by the formation of the Friends of Ireland group, comprising Labour backbenchers, many of them newly elected, who sympathized with the goal of Irish unity and expressed concern about the treatment of the province's minority. Naturally, these developments added to the apprehension felt by the Brooke administration, and in the 1945–48 period it adopted a more circumspect approach to the constitutional question. Events in the South also contributed to the Unionist government's initial sense of unease. The emergence of a new republican party, Clann na Poblachta, and its impact in the 1948 general election rekindled interest in the partition issue in Éire. Soon, the new Inter-Party government, which included the Clann na Poblachta leader and former IRA chief of staff, Seán MacBride, in the crucial post of minister for external affairs, threw triangular relations into turmoil with its decision to pull out of the Commonwealth and establish a republic. De Valera, freed from the constraints of office, responded with a new militancy on the border question in an attempt to cover Fianna Fáil's republican flank and re-establish his pre-eminent position in Irish politics. These changes undoubtedly damaged Dublin's relations with the administration in London. Meanwhile, the change of direction in southern politics further alienated Unionist opinion, but Brooke managed to exploit the change in Éire's status by negotiating a formal guarantee of Northern Ireland's constitutional position with the Labour government at Westminster. The 1949 Ireland Act demonstrated Labour's goodwill towards the province and effectively dispelled any lingering apprehension among Unionists on the fundamental issue of partition.

Two distinct phases can be identified in the 1945–51 period. The first three years witnessed the reorganization of anti-partition forces in the North, initially encouraged by the formation of a Labour government and then by the activities of the Friends of Ireland group. During the same period southern interest on the border question was revived, as Clann na Poblachta achieved greater prominence. By 1948, however, Nationalist leaders in the North had begun to express their frustration at the Labour government's lack of interest in the partition issue. They were also dismayed by the failure of the parties in the South to raise the issue above the level of party politics. Moreover, the Inter-Party government's decision to leave the Commonwealth had unexpected repercussions for northern nationalists, as the balance of relations in the London–Dublin–Belfast triangle was altered. Between 1948 and 1951 pressure for the removal of the border was dramatically intensified, but this only reinforced partition. The Unionist government, which had adopted a cautious approach on the border question since the end of the war, now went on the offensive, seizing the opportunity to cement the province's constitutional position and, in the process, strengthening its position in Northern Ireland politics at the expense of the NILP.

1945–1948

Northern Ireland's participation in the Second World War and the Éire government's policy of neutrality had combined to consolidate partition and strengthen the bond between London and Belfast. Moreover, the war had been responsible for boosting the Unionist leadership's confidence in the future security of the province's constitutional position following the low point of the 1938 Anglo-Irish Agreement, when Chamberlain had privately expressed sympathy with de Valera's unity aspirations. The events of 1938 had left the Unionists in their weakest position since partition, and the authorities at Stormont naturally welcomed the transformation in triangular relations brought about by the war. Éire's neutrality had given the Unionists a powerful argument for the retention of the border, and it was obvious that any post-war Westminster government would recognize the province's strategic importance in the formulation of its defence policy. Of course, while the war had effectively entrenched partition, de Valera had used the border's existence to justify neutrality, particularly when British and American pressure to abandon that policy intensified. Nevertheless, having conclusively demonstrated Éire's sovereignty by maintaining neutrality, it appeared as though he would be free to focus on his one remaining political goal, the ending of partition.

Earlier, de Valera's stance on partition changed once Fianna Fáil took office in 1932, as rhetoric gave way to pragmatism. While he continued to believe that Irish unity was inevitable, it was felt that only a long-term approach to the problem would yield success. Indeed, earlier doubts about the seriousness of Fianna Fáil's commitment to ending partition had emerged in 1926, when the new party chose not to organize in the North.[1] In power, de Valera also rejected a proposal from Éamon Donnelly, the self-appointed intermediary between Fianna Fáil and the northern Nationalists, to develop a united anti-partition strategy by extending Fianna Fáil's organization to the North and admitting Nationalist MPs to the Dáil.[2] Throughout his long political career de Valera enjoyed an awkward relationship with northern Nationalist representatives, and he did his utmost to ensure that he set the agenda on the border question for party political purposes in the South. Although Irish unity had been one of Fianna Fáil's founding principles, de Valera pursued a course in government that actually rendered partition more intractable. While his desire to marginalize republican extremism during the 1930s was central to his strategy,[3] his efforts to protect Fianna Fáil's strong republican flank limited his ability to make any constructive moves on partition. For Unionists, the Fianna Fáil leader had long been a dangerous opponent, and Unionist opinion was further alienated by the 1936 External Relations Act and the 1937 Constitution, both of which de Valera had hoped would restrain Fianna Fáil's more militant wing. On the other hand, the Unionist leadership had been equally unenthusiastic about Irish unity during Cosgrave's period in power, but de Valera's actions enabled the Unionist administration to present itself as the victim of a militant aggressor and reap the reward in all Northern Ireland elections. Yet such a negative reaction did not appear to cause de Valera any concern. He had recognized, from the outset, that progress on partition, which effectively meant wooing the Unionists, was incompatible with his more immediate objectives of retaining power and establishing stable government in the South.

Still, de Valera's manipulation of the border issue raised expectations among the nationalist community in the North. Frustration with the Unionist government, coupled with de Valera's 1932 victory, had encouraged the Nationalist MPs to adopt a more militant stance on partition, as they hoped that the impact made by the Fianna Fáil government would expedite the removal of the border. Nationalists faced a dilemma, because they had to decide whether to concentrate their energies on seeking an end to partition or on defending the rights of the North's Catholic minority. Indeed, their inability to resolve this dilemma contributed not only to their political ineffectiveness during the inter-war period but also to their action in periodically abstaining from the Northern Ireland parliament.[4] The Nationalist party also suffered from structural difficulties, and this often led to a lack of cohesion among its representatives. Devlin's death in January 1934 was another major blow for the Nationalist party. Without his influence the party was devoid of political direction, and it made little impression in the period up to the end of the war. It was apparent, moreover, that Nationalist MPs felt increasingly isolated, as they had received little practical help or encouragement from the South. Indeed, just before the war they expressed their deep concern at 'the apathy and indifference existing in the Twenty Six Counties on the vital matter of partition'.[5] These problems undoubtedly contributed to a decline in the party's electoral fortunes. In November 1942, in the Falls by-election, the Nationalist candidate, who had pledged to attend Stormont, was soundly beaten by Donnelly, standing as an abstentionist.[6] Further evidence of the Nationalist party's weakness in Belfast emerged in the 1945 Northern Ireland general election, when it could win only one seat in Belfast. In Falls the party was humiliated when the Nationalist candidate trailed in third behind Harry Diamond.[7] Although support was significant in selected rural areas and in Derry, it was clear that working-class Catholics in Belfast had little affinity with the Nationalists. Their votes went to Socialist Republicans and various brands of Labour including the Communist party. Only outside Belfast, therefore, where these more radical parties had little presence, could the Nationalist party still rely on a solid anti-Unionist vote from the Catholic minority.

During the war the minority community, influenced by Éire's neutrality, expressed indifference to the outcome of the war.[8] Nevertheless, as the struggle drew to a close, nationalists realized that the ending of hostilities would present a suitable opportunity to reopen the partition debate. By this stage, however, Unionist confidence had been restored, and the Stormont government felt more secure on the border question. Still, optimism among the nationalist community increased considerably, when the results of the British general election were announced in July 1945. The Labour party had supported Irish self-determination in the 1920s, and many of the party's MPs were thought to be sympathetic to Irish unity. Indeed, Labour's victory in 1945 proved to be the deciding factor in persuading all Nationalist MPs at Stormont to take their seats. Although it was difficult to estimate the new Labour government's attitude to Northern Ireland, an *Irish Times* editorial on the British general election results warned that Labour would not sweep away the border, because Stormont had its defenders, notably Herbert Morrison, in the Labour cabinet, and Northern Ireland's strategic value was very much in Labour's mind.[9] Certainly, there appeared no immediate threat to the province's constitutional position. This was confirmed by Maffey, the United Kingdom representative to Éire, when he completed a comprehensive survey for the Dominions Office, entitled 'The Irish Question in 1945'. His analysis was not clouded by the usual diplomatic language, and it included the remarkably bold statement: 'If I were a Protestant or Presbyterian resident in Northern Ireland, nothing would induce me to accept citizenship under a Dublin government.'[10] Of course, Maffey's thinking on Ireland was dominated by Britain's defence requirements. While he sympathized with the long-term goal of unification, it was also clear that support from the British representative for such a move would be conditional on the state becoming a member of the Commonwealth.

The new dominions secretary, Viscount Addison, one of Attlee's closest political allies, drew upon some of Maffey's observations, when he presented a cabinet memorandum on the general lines of policy which the new government should follow in its relations with Éire in the immediate post-war period. In his assessment Addison remarked: 'Never in our history have we been in such a strong position in relation to world opinion so far as Ireland is concerned, and Éire's position has never been weaker.'[11] Addison's judgement was based on his assessment of Éire's alienation of American opinion, which developed with the South's refusal to abandon neutrality and then intensified following de Valera's condolence visit on the occasion of Hitler's death. The dominions secretary also noted the 'strong if latent feeling of resentment' against Éire in Great Britain, which he feared could easily be provoked into active hostility if the Labour government radically revised its existing policy of 'distant relations with Éire'.[12] There was little prospect, therefore, of the Attlee administration even contemplating a pro-Irish policy, even if it had wanted, as this would be exploited by the Conservatives, who would seize the opportunity to play the Orange card. Consequently, the cabinet endorsed Addison's suggestion that Westminster should attempt to improve relations with Dublin, particularly in less controversial areas such as trade, by a gradual process 'without any ostentation'.[13] This reference to the need for caution had its origin in Maffey's earlier survey in which he warned that on no account should Irish statesmen be invited to London for general discussions, because: 'From Dublin they go forth as warriors to fight the battle of Ireland against England. They are aware that no British Government likes to admit a failure or breakdown in negotiations. The Irish bargaining position in London is strong.'[14]

THE ANTI-PARTITION LEAGUE AND THE FRIENDS OF IRELAND GROUP

With no knowledge of Labour's thinking on Ireland during its first few months in office, the Nationalist leadership was optimistic that some progress could be made on partition.[15] Accordingly, in November 1945, Eddie McAteer and Malachy Conlon, two of the new Nationalist MPs at Stormont, organized a convention in Dungannon of all 'nationally minded' groups at which the APL was launched. At this meeting James McSparran, a prominent barrister and the MP for Mourne, was elected chairman, with Conlon taking up the position of secretary, and an executive including all Nationalist MPs and senators was elected.[16] The APL was intended to act as an umbrella movement which would unite the various anti-partition groups, but it quickly ran into difficulties. At the outset, Harry Diamond denounced the convention as sectarian, because his own Socialist Republican party and the Ulster Union Club, both of which opposed partition but had substantial Protestant memberships, had not been invited.[17] Clearly, Catholic clerics were expected to play a prominent role in the development of the APL, and the *Irish News* report on the Dungannon convention highlighted the large number of clergy in attendance. From the beginning the APL made little headway in Belfast, instead drawing its strength from Derry city and those rural areas where the minority made up a substantial proportion of the population.[18] As a consequence, support largely mirrored support for the Nationalist party, and the APL's identification with the Catholic middle class obviously limited its influence. The League suffered a further early blow when Campbell accepted a county court judgeship, a position which many nationalists perceived as condoning the Belfast government, because he did not even consult the APL before accepting the post.[19]

In spite of these shortcomings, however, the leading figures in the APL were hopeful that Labour's victory in Great Britain would lead to a revision of Westminster's policy on Northern Ireland, which would at least take cognizance of the minority's grievances. They were further encouraged by the formation of the Friends of Ireland group of approximately thirty Labour MPs under the chairmanship of Dr Morgan, the MP for Rochdale, which was committed both to Irish unity and the redress of the minority's grievances in the North.[20] The other office bearers in the group were Hugh Delargy, the MP for Platting, Manchester, who worked as a journalist and occasionally wrote articles for the *Irish Press*, while R.R. Stokes, the MP for Ipswich, and Dublin-born Valentine McEntee, the MP for Walthamstow West, acted as joint treasurers. Another prominent member was Henry McGhee, the MP for Penistone, Yorkshire, whose father had been a Protestant member of the old Redmondite party from Tyrone. There is no evidence that the man who was to become the group's most effective spokesman, Geoffrey Bing, the MP for Hornchurch, took any interest in the formation of the group. The group itself was a combination of left wingers and MPs who were either of Irish extraction or had considerable numbers of exiled Irish in their constituencies, and they were supported by the two Communist MPs, Willie Gallacher and Phil Piratin.[21] Initially, the potential difficulties of these Labour left wingers working effectively with the traditionally conservative, middle-class leadership of the APL were ignored. Perhaps not surprisingly, the Friends of Ireland made an early impact, because they unsettled the Unionist administration, which was already anxious about the new Labour government's attitude to Northern Ireland.[22]

The first significant move by the Friends of Ireland was the organization of a visit to Dublin in January 1946 by two of its prominent members, McEntee and Fred Longden, the MP for Deritend, Birmingham. The visit was supposed to be a fact-finding exercise dealing with issues such as wages and social security benefits, but McEntee, probably encouraged by the considerable press interest in Dublin, gave the visit a political twist by announcing that the present Labour government was much more sympathetic to Ireland than its predecessor.[23] Westminster expressed concern at this development, and Addison, the dominions secretary, regarded the Dublin trip as an unwelcome interference, and he conferred with Ede in an attempt 'to limit the somewhat undesirable activities' of the Friends of Ireland group.[24] Contact was also made with Morgan, who sought to reassure the Dominions Office that the Friends' immediate policy was simply to cultivate friendly relations between North and South, while long-term policy was to assist in the reunification of Ireland under a Labour government in Dublin. Indeed, Morgan was highly critical of the public statements made by McEntee and Longden during their Dublin visit, because he thought that the premature focus on the border question would only prejudice the group's long-term strategy.[25] Maffey also expressed frustration at the Dublin visit, complaining that the MPs had been too easily impressed by de Valera's promise to review Dublin's relations with Westminster in the event of an agreement on the border. In addition, he was anxious that the Friends of Ireland should not force the partition issue onto the Labour government's long agenda, because it would only benefit those people 'who would welcome the opportunity to play the deadly Orange Card once more'. Instead, he favoured a policy of keeping the Belfast government 'strictly in order', and forcing it to comply with Westminster's policy of forbearance towards Éire, which effectively meant moderating the Unionist administration's attitude to the minority, particularly on the question of Éire labour in the North. Maffey's personal preference, which he had intimated to Longden and McEntee, was to submit the partition issue to international arbitration, because he argued that the United Kingdom could never hope to obtain more favourable results from arbitration 'than we could to-day, when the factor of Éire's neutrality stands out so starkly and when the North still has a strong individuality'. This argument for early action was based on Maffey's assumption that the long-term trend was moving inexorably towards Northern Ireland's instability and against London's strategic interests, because the higher Catholic birth rate would eventually produce a nationalist majority in the North.[26] However, officials at the Dominions Office took an even stronger line than Maffey on the activities of the Friends of Ireland group, and there are several references to the Westminster government's failure to prevent the Friends from carrying on their 'extremist campaign' in conjunction with Dulanty, the Éire high commissioner in London.[27] Earlier, both Attlee and William Whiteley, Labour's chief whip, had met the group in an effort to curb its activities, but their admonition had failed to achieve the results that the officials at the Dominions Office desired.[28] For the Dominions Office, the Friends of Ireland had become an obstacle to its policy of gradually improving Anglo-Irish relations, while seeking to play down the partition issue.

Brooke, meanwhile, having taken steps to moderate Stormont's stance on the Éire labour issue, felt entitled to demand that the authorities in London should respond effectively to the threat posed by the Friends. He received some reassurance from Addison at a meeting in May 1946, when he learned of the government's attempts to control the most active members of the group. For his part, Brooke informed the dominions secretary that the Friends' activities were creating political difficulties for him at home, but he 'was doing his best to keep the brake on his Orangemen'.[29] The Unionist premier understood the importance of creating the right impression at the Dominions Office, and Stephenson had advised Addison that he should use the meeting to assure Brooke that, in pursuing the policy of preserving good relations with Éire, Northern Ireland's interests would never he overlooked.[30] Such support was welcome, because at this time Brooke was concerned by the British Labour party's involvement in a by-election for the two-member Westminster constituency of Down which took place in June 1946. Labour had offered both moral and financial support to the NILP candidate, Flying Officer Desmond Donnelly, who had previously been active in the British Labour movement, and he enlisted the enthusiastic support of a number of Friends of Ireland MPs. Although Donnelly insisted that he was opposed to Irish unity without the North's consent, Delargy used the by-election campaign to emphasize the Friends' support for unification.[31] While references to the border worked to the Unionist party's advantage, enabling it to overcome the challenge of two independent Unionist candidates by calling for solidarity on the constitutional position, Donnelly still polled nearly 30,000 votes in a constituency that certainly did not suit the NILP.[32] Previously, individual Labour figures, such as Harold Laski, the party chairman, had been critical of the Belfast administration, but Donnelly's high poll and the impact made by his by-election campaign caused much more anxiety among Unionist leaders. They feared that further intervention by the Labour party in Northern Ireland elections would put a major strain on Stormont–Westminster relations. Yet, in spite of such concerns, Brooke refused to be flustered, and he retained his very friendly approach to relations with the Labour government in London.

Consequently, relations between London and Belfast had improved by

September 1946, when Morrison made a short visit to both Éire and Northern Ireland. At a meeting with Brooke on his return to London, Morrison asked the Stormont premier to use his influence to restrain the Ulster Unionist MPs at Westminster, whose conduct had been partly responsible for arousing criticism of the Belfast government on the Labour backbenches. At the same time, however, he expressed his admiration for Stormont's restraint in refraining from scoring cheap party points after the war by stirring up feeling in the province against Éire.[33] Interestingly, further evidence of such discretion surfaced at Stormont in the following month in the government's response to a Diamond motion on partition. Both government speakers, Brooke and Warnock, largely ignored the traditional arguments and concentrated on highlighting the economic differences between Northern Ireland and Éire.[34] During his meeting with de Valera in Dublin, Morrison had mentioned the strong feelings on the border, which he knew existed among Unionists from his wartime experience as home secretary, when he warned that it would be unwise for the Éire government to raise the partition issue in the immediate future. De Valera responded by suggesting a federal solution, adding that a new united Ireland could then become a member of the Commonwealth. On his return to London Morrison reported this discussion to Brooke, who, he noted, was 'always most reasonable and co-operative', and was told that any attempt by the Labour government to raise the partition issue would create 'a storm in Ulster'. Brooke knew that he could rely on Morrison to present the Unionist case in any cabinet discussion on the border question. Indeed, Morrison was keen to explain to his Labour colleagues that they should not think of the Unionist party as a Conservative party. He argued that it contained 'Conservatives, Liberals and Radicals' and noted that, if Grant, the minister of health and local government, were a politician on the mainland, he would almost certainly be in the Labour party.[35] Much of the credit for Morrison's consistent defence of Stormont's interests must be given to Brooke. His friendly personality and easy style of leadership enabled him to develop excellent relationships with key individuals at Westminster and convince them of his administration's more moderate approach on issues relating to the minority.[36]

Not surprisingly, Addison took a different view of the border question. He did agree, however, that as the Éire government appeared likely to intensify pressure for the ending of partition, Westminster would have to take account of two essential considerations: the attitude of the Unionist majority in the province and Great Britain's strategic interests. Nevertheless, the dominions secretary wanted Westminster to promote friendly relations with Éire: 'I have no desire that we on this side should discourage the North and South of Ireland in any move that they may make with the object of getting together. As a long-term policy it is no doubt right and indeed inevitable that Northern Ireland and Éire should enter into some kind of closer relation.' Yet, in the meantime, he insisted that the Dominions Office should concentrate on the steady improvement of relations with Éire, while steering clear of the border question, particularly in view of the attempt by the Friends of Ireland to have a cabinet mission sent to Ireland to investigate partition.[37] During these early years of Labour rule, when relations with Éire were conducted on a deliberately low-key basis, officials in London, particularly at the Foreign Office, were more concerned by the prospect of Irish–American groups raising the partition issue in the United States and of the implications that this might have for relations between London and Washington.[38] Although Éire had lost considerable sympathy in the United States during the war, the Foreign Office still felt it necessary to supply detailed arguments for its embassy staffs to counter Dublin's claims on partition.[39]

Of course, keeping the Northern Ireland problem out of American politics required the co-operation of the authorities at Stormont, but this could not always be guaranteed. To combat increasing anti-Ulster propaganda in the United States immediately after the war, Brooke suggested a personal visit to put Northern Ireland's case. The Home Office had approved the visit, but later the Foreign Office intervened and successfully pressurized the Stormont premier into abandoning his plans. British representatives in the United States informed the Dominions Office that such a move would be 'disastrous': 'Emphasis on Ulster particularism would … awaken sleeping dogs, which we had every reason to hope were not merely somnolent but lethargic.'[40] A similar situation arose later in the year, however, when the Stormont government proposed that Major-General Brooke-Purdon, the Ulster agent in London, should visit the United States to present Northern Ireland's case. Although Maxwell at the Home Office thought that it would be unreasonable to object to Brooke-Purdon's visit, the Foreign Office continued to disapprove, arguing that publicity in the United States to defend the province's constitutional position should be left to the British Information Services.[41] Subsequently, the Foreign Office withdrew its opposition to the visit, but only when it learned that Stormont had planned the Brooke-Purdon trip to prevent 'some non-official and more outspokenly loyalist body, such as the Orange Order' organizing its own mission across the Atlantic. With this information, which had reached the Foreign Office from an unnamed source, the Brooke-Purdon visit was considered as the 'lesser evil', if the Belfast authorities pursued their interest in sending a representative to the United States.[42]

SOUTHERN POLITICS AND THE BORDER

The concern expressed by the authorities at Westminster could not be dismissed as paranoia, because the Dublin government was under constant pressure to launch a worldwide campaign to end partition. In addition, anti-partition rhetoric was an integral part of southern politics, and de Valera frequently took a tough line on the border question. During a by-election campaign in November 1945, the taoiseach informed his Wexford audience that he had 'not the slightest doubt' that unity could be achieved, and that Fianna Fáil's policy continued to be the old Sinn Féin policy.[43] While such a hawkish stance may have brought political benefits to Fianna Fáil and encouraged the fledgling APL, it also enabled Brooke and his colleagues to assert the Unionist viewpoint in both London and Belfast. On other occasions, however, the taoiseach took a more moderate approach to the border issue. In the annual St Patrick's Day broadcast to the United States in 1946 the taoiseach's central theme was the condemnation of the 'wrong' of partition, and he claimed that while it persisted it would be a barrier to real reconciliation between Dublin and London. As a way forward, de Valera proposed a repartition scheme that would restore four counties, where he argued a combined majority would be in favour of unity with the South.[44] Nevertheless, he acknowledged that propaganda alone would be insufficient to solve the Northern Ireland problem, emphasizing instead that it would only be resolved by the 'persistent national endeavour of the Government'.[45] It was apparent that the border was again becoming a party issue in the South, following its deferment during the Emergency, and de Valera was keen to use his record on partition in order to retain electoral support for his party.

Of course, partition also provided a welcome diversion for a Fianna Fáil government that faced mounting criticism immediately after the war for its handling of the economy. Meanwhile, Fine Gael TDs were anxious to demonstrate that they 'differed fundamentally from Fianna Fáil in their approach to this great question', and they stressed that partition could not be rectified 'unless they were prepared to appreciate the viewpoints of those who preferred to deny allegiance to the Irish state'. They argued that in such circumstances 'the only hope of reunion lay in conciliation, tolerance and a closer approach to their divided countrymen'.[46] This divergence of opinion between the two main parties in the South disappointed Nationalist leaders in the North who had wanted a common approach to take the issue above party politics. The APL was particularly disappointed with Fianna Fáil's lack of urgency on the border, and it came as no surprise when delegates at the party's 1946 árd fheis criticized Fianna Fáil for its 'slow progress' on partition.[47] Indeed, there was some evidence to suggest that the Fianna Fáil leadership was divided on its anti-partition strategy. Seán McEntee, a native of Belfast and the minister for local government, consistently advanced more moderate proposals and stressed that there was no simple solution to partition. He argued that Dublin should attempt to cultivate a desire among Unionists to co-operate with the South, rather than emphasize the need to reclaim lost territory.[48] Mulvey also expressed his frustration with the Fianna Fáil government at an APL meeting in County Down. Although the League had made progress in Northern Ireland and Britain, he angrily insisted that the Dublin administration should now recognize its responsibility and begin to exert pressure on the Labour government at Westminster.[49]

Not surprisingly, the authorities at Westminster did not share the League's disappointment with the performance of the Fianna Fáil government. Significantly, Westminster had been impressed by de Valera'a firm action against republican extremists, which had resulted in the death of Seán McCaughey on hunger strike in Maryborough jail in May 1946.[50] When the Dáil debated a motion alleging ill-treatment during McCaughey's imprisonment, de Valera was unequivocal in outlining his government's attitude to the IRA:

> Is anybody in this House going to suggest that if a person commits murder and is found guilty of that act of murder that we should distinguish between those who commit murder because they have a political reason

and those who commit murder for some other motive? Is there any single Deputy in this House who can honestly say that such a distinction should be made? Such a distinction cannot be made.[51]

In the following month Fianna Fáil reiterated its tough stance on republican violence, when Gerald Boland told a Roscommon audience that the IRA remained a 'menace' and would not be allowed to reorganize following its setbacks during the war.[52] As the minister for justice, Boland was responsible for containing IRA activity, and he had been a consistent advocate of additional security measures. When the authorities in Dublin learned that the IRA intended to reorganize, following the release of its prisoners in May 1945, Boland was adamant that ordinary police powers would not be sufficient to deal with the threat. Consequently, the government backed his proposal to give his department powers to intern suspects under the 1940 Offences Against the State (Amendment) Act.[53]

Differences between the two main parties also emerged on the question of Éire's relationship with the Commonwealth, and de Valera hoped that such an arrangement would facilitate eventual reunification. Nevertheless, his claim that Éire was in effect a *de facto* republic angered Fine Gael, which favoured a much closer link with the Commonwealth. Its leaders were convinced that unity could only be accomplished within the Commonwealth, but de Valera rejected this view, arguing that a united Ireland would probably sever its links with the Commonwealth. There would be no olive branch offered to the Unionist 'minority' in the North, because it

> ... will have to agree that the form of Government we have here and the relationship we have with other States must be determined by the people of this island in the ordinary democratic way, that is by majority rule ... Why should a member of the majority think that he would have to give up his fundamental aspirations in order to satisfy the aspirations of the minority?[54]

Such an uncompromising attitude only served to entrench partition. Patrick McGilligan, a leading spokesman in Fine Gael and a frequent visitor to the North, warned the Fianna Fáil government that unless it adopted a much softer line on partition, 'we are going to be met with the completely cold and unresponsive attitude which the Northerners have so far given us'.[55]

In his dealings with Westminster, however, de Valera was much more restrained. This moderation was also reflected in Dulanty's approach, and the Éire high commissioner in London assured Addison that Éire would be glad 'to come back to the fold' if Westminster would remove partition.[56] The authorities in London were also aware that de Valera was anxious to attend certain Commonwealth meetings, though he never sought an invitation as this could have created political difficulties at home.[57] By July 1946 the dominions secretary was even considering a new departure in Anglo-Irish relations, as further evidence of de Valera's softer line on the border question emerged. Following a meeting with the taoiseach, Norman Archer, Maffey's principal secretary in Dublin, reported that de Valera was 'unusually moderate' on the partition issue, adding that his strategy had changed from 'obvious fanaticism' to a 'reasonably balanced approach'.[58] This prompted Addison to ask if there was 'any useful action' which Westminster could take with a view 'to furthering closer association between Éire and Northern Ireland'.[59] The civil servants at the Dominions Office were taken aback by this suggestion, however, and they responded by emphasizing two separate considerations which could not be ignored. Firstly, there would be bitter opposition from the Unionist community in the North, both on political and religious grounds, to any move designed to bring Éire and Northern Ireland closer together. Secondly, it was stressed that in view of Éire's recent neutrality it would be impossible for Westminster 'to take the initiative in throwing away the security provided by a base in Northern Ireland'.[60] While officials at the Dominions Office attached great significance to Britain's defence requirements, they were, nevertheless, successful in curbing Addison's enthusiasm for initiating a major review of Westminster's Irish policy. When the dominions secretary subsequently led a cabinet discussion on Anglo-Irish relations, he reminded his colleagues of the problems caused by Éire's neutrality. He suggested, moreover, that Labour's future policy should be one of silence on partition, refusing even to give the matter consideration as this in itself, in view of the strong feelings existing on both sides, would only lead to serious trouble.[61] By the summer of 1946, therefore, de Valera appeared as a moderate to the authorities in London and as an extremist to the electorate in Éire. In so doing he hoped to make progress in London on issues involving Anglo-Irish relations, while simultaneously curbing republican extremism and retaining nationalist support at home. The future course of Anglo-Irish relations and the prominence of the partition issue in southern politics would depend on how successfully de Valera could balance the two.

By far the most significant development in southern politics during the immediate post-war period was the appearance in July 1946 of Clann na Poblachta, a new political party that appeared to be a mirror image of Fianna Fáil in 1932. In its early stages the party was closely identified with Seán McCaughey, the IRA hunger striker. Seán MacBride, the Clann na Poblachta leader, had represented the family at the subsequent court hearing that alleged ill-treatment of the prisoner, and both Noel Hartnett, the junior counsel, and Con Lehane, the solicitor in the case, were members of the party's Provisional Executive. Other members of the executive included Mrs Austin Stack and Captain Peadar Cowan, both prominent republicans, and it was evident that the new party had secured the involvement of former IRA leaders who had decided to enter constitutional politics.[62] Initially, the most striking feature of the new party was its serious commitment to the removal of the border. Later, it emerged that Clann na Poblachta's electoral appeal would be twin-edged, because it hoped to attract voters with its radical approach to social and economic issues.[63] The leading exponent of this social radicalism was a young doctor, Noel Browne, who was later to achieve notoriety for his part in the 'mother and child' controversy. Not surprisingly, however, it was the party's militant nationalist image that first aroused public interest and represented the most serious challenge to the Fianna Fáil establishment. In a Sligo speech MacBride explained Clann na

Poblachta's nationalist policies in more specific detail. He highlighted three distinct areas: the admission of northern MPs to the Dáil, the detachment of Éire's currency from sterling and the prevention of emigration by using the national credit for undeveloped resources.[64] It was clear, therefore, that in addition to its strong line on the border the Clann intended to pursue a policy of economic nationalism which was likely to lead to conflict with Westminster if the party ever attained power.

The emergence of Clann na Poblachta provided some encouragement for the APL, which had become frustrated not only by the lack of interest shown by the main political parties in the South but also by the inflexibility of the Labour administration in London. Coincidentally, while the new republican party was being launched in the South, the League was opening its anti-partition campaign in Britain with a rally in Birmingham.[65] This marked the beginning of a period of great activity for the League, as its small band of MPs and senators attended numerous meetings in British cities where there was a large Irish immigrant population.[66] This upsurge in activity on the mainland caused the Unionist authorities some concern, as it contrasted sharply with the inactivity and demoralization of the anti-partition forces in the province before and during the war. Yet while the League was keen to exert pressure on the Labour government by influencing public opinion in Britain, little thought was given to how this could best be achieved. At a rally in London in December 1946 Diamond, who had been reconciled after the early disagreement, informed his audience that there were seventy-five Westminster seats in which the votes of exiled Irishmen could be decisive.[67] While this type of intervention had proved a partial success in the Parnell era, the League failed to develop an election strategy for the mainland, even though it recognized the significance of the Irish vote in Britain.

Earlier, Healy had sent a pamphlet to every Westminster MP which concentrated on the minority's grievances, but he was criticized by Delargy, who felt that too much emphasis had been placed on the Catholic persecution angle, something that was 'peculiar to handle in England', rather than on the persecution of minorities, such as Labour and progressive associations.[68] Nevertheless, Delargy's advice was ignored, and Nationalist MPs addressing British audiences soon began to attack the Labour government, claiming that it was ignoring their grievances. As a consequence, relations between the League and the Friends of Ireland became strained, because the Labour MPs found themselves defending their government's refusal to intervene in Northern Ireland. This frustration with the League was illustrated when Morgan, the chairman of the Friends, gave an interview to the *Irish News* in which he criticized the League's impatience with the Labour government.[69] Instead, the League had to rely on southern politicians to woo Labour support by participating in the campaign in Britain. At a Liverpool rally T.L. Mullins, the general secretary of Fianna Fáil, appealed directly to Labour supporters when he said: 'The Six County regime exists for the sole benefit of a small group of reactionary capitalists with a terrible record as employers, worse even than their political record.'[70] MacBride was equally aware of the potential value of exploiting Labour support for the League's campaign, and he appealed to the British Labour movement to relinquish its support for 'the most intolerant group of reactionary capitalists in Europe'.[71] Only a few days later the Clann na Poblachta leader gave this idea further publicity, when he urged the League to make partition a live issue in the British Labour movement by directing its anti-partition propaganda at Labour supporters, and not simply at Irish exiles in Britain.[72]

However, the Attlee government's continuing lack of interest in the province's internal troubles further alienated prominent Nationalist MPs, who now began making more frequent attacks on the Labour administration at APL meetings in Great Britain during the spring and summer of 1947.[73] At the League's annual convention in Dungannon, McSparran emphasized his frustration with the Labour government, adding that not one Labour minister had yet declared himself in favour of a united Ireland.[74] Later in the same year, Ede dispelled any hope of Labour intervention on behalf of the minority, which Nationalists at Stormont still retained, when he refused to meet a Nationalist deputation to discuss these issues during a visit to the province.[75] On this occasion, Ede had arranged to meet all Nationalist MPs and senators at the Law Courts in Belfast, but they were furious when the home secretary announced on his arrival that he could only spare the deputation six minutes of his time.[76] By the end of 1947, therefore, the Nationalists had become disenchanted with the Labour government, and McSparran made their feelings public when he addressed an anti-partition rally in Glasgow:

> ... no Tory Government ever treated the Irish people or the minority in the Six Counties with such contempt and injustice as the present Labour Government has done since they came into office, and no Tory home secretary has, in my opinion, in recent years been more indifferent, if not actively hostile, to the legitimate grievances of the Irish people and the oppressed minority in the Six Counties than Mr. Chuter Ede.[77]

Of course, part of the APL's frustration was due to its tactic of making a direct approach to the Labour administration for some form of dramatic intervention in Northern Ireland. More progress could have been made by developing grass-roots support among local Labour party branches, as this would have produced a stronger movement in Britain capable of influencing a future Labour government.

The impact made by the League on the mainland was further undermined by the failure of the Friends of Ireland group to make a more decisive contribution. Later, Eddie McAteer, who was recognized as one of the driving forces in the APL, recalled that the Friends of Ireland MPs contributed little to the anti-partition movement, because they tended to look at the Irish problem 'through socialist eyes'.[78] The League's hopes had been raised temporarily by Bing's performance in the House of Commons during the debate on the Northern Ireland Bill in June 1947, when he attacked the Stormont government for its hostile attitude to the minority. By this time it was evident that Bing was clearly the Friends' most able spokesman, but his approach to the Northern Ireland problem differed from some of his associates in the group. While Bing's focus was on the redress of the minority's grievances, Delargy, the APL chairman in Britain, was much more militant on the border question. He argued that partition was primarily a

British responsibility, and he wanted a motion to abolish the border introduced in the House of Commons.[79] McGhee, on the other hand, had declared on a visit to Belfast that the Labour party was 'completely hamstrung on Partition until Northern Ireland changed its representation from Tory to Labour'.[80] This view was shared by the more left wing MPs in the group, who argued that the only prerequisite for unification was the establishment of Labour governments in both Dublin and Belfast.[81] Naturally, such a range of views rendered the Friends of Ireland group less effective, and it underlined the dilemma for politicians interested in the Northern Ireland problem, who had to decide between concentrating on the removal of the border and alleviating the problems faced by the nationalist community. Bing had achieved prominence by highlighting issues such as the Special Powers Act and the limited local government franchise, both of which he maintained could be altered by Westminster if it chose to assume its powers as the supreme parliament. The MP for Hornchurch had also laid great emphasis on the need to raise economic standards in the South, and he frequently advanced the idea that partition was an Irish problem, an argument which led to bitter criticism from Fianna Fáil leaders, who regarded partition as exclusively a British responsibility.[82] Ultimately, this neglect of the border dismayed the APL. The League found it difficult to endorse such ideas as the need to raise economic standards in Éire and the wish to see Labour governments in Dublin and Belfast as a prelude to unification.

THE 1948 ÉIRE GENERAL ELECTION

Clann na Poblachta's success in two of the three by-elections held in late 1947 clearly rattled de Valera. He did not share the view of an *Irish Times* editorial, which attributed the new party's success to the existence of an element in the South that was always ready to identify with anti-British sentiment.[83] De Valera's intention was to call a snap general election designed to stifle the Clann before it made further inroads into Fianna Fáil's support. In the election Clann na Poblachta fielded ninety-three candidates, the largest number by any party except Fianna Fáil, and this created the impression that the contest was a two-horse race between the established Fianna Fáil and a youthful Clann na Poblachta.[84] The announcement of the election gave the APL the opportunity to make its most overt intervention in any southern election. Questionnaires were sent to the competing parties, and voters were asked to support only those parties which would give support as a government to the League.[85] Surprisingly, in spite of the Clann's militant stance on the border and its pledge to admit northern MPs to the Dáil, the League did not identify closely with MacBride's party. While this was partly due to de Valera's continuing reputation as the South's pre-eminent political leader, MacBride's uneasy relationship with Nationalist leaders in the North was also significant. None of them doubted his exceptional ability, but they did not consider closer ties, as they were of the opinion that he was much 'too detached and remote'.[86]

The by-election successes in late 1947 had led some Clann na Poblachta members to predict an overall majority for the new party, but MacBride himself was much more cautious. It was also noticeable that he took a softer line on the border issue during the election campaign. Indeed, he expressed the view that, unless the South could establish economic conditions and social services which at least approximated to those available in the six counties, 'it would be very difficult to arouse any enthusiasm among the people of the North for the ending of partition'.[87] In spite of the efforts made by the APL, the lack of attention paid to the border question during the campaign was an indication of its relative insignificance as an issue in the election, and this apparent lack of interest did not go unnoticed by Unionist leaders in Northern Ireland. Warnock even remarked that the reference to partition in the Clann na Poblachta manifesto could have been written by a member of the Ulster Unionist Council and observed that it was not even mentioned in the Fine Gael manifesto.[88] Interestingly, Fianna Fáil also chose to play down the partition issue, probably fearing that unnecessary emphasis on the continued existence of the border would only benefit MacBride. The party adopted a cautious approach, typified by a Lemass speech in Carlow in which he declared that Fianna Fáil did not have a 'cut and dried plan' to end partition, but it would strive to keep partition a live issue until an opportunity emerged to remove the border.[89] During the campaign the taoiseach himself admitted that his government had no policy for ending partition,[90] but he did promise that after the election he would bring Irish opinion throughout the world to bear on Great Britain.[91] Only a few months earlier, de Valera had made his most revealing statement on the border question in the post-war period during the annual Dáil debate on the estimates for the External Affairs department. The taoiseach stated that a 'concurrence of wills' between Stormont, Dublin and Westminster would be a necessary prerequisite for the removal of the border.[92] At the same time, he was adamant that his government should not make the running by opening negotiations with the North to end partition. While he acknowledged that Westminster would not stand in the way if Stormont and Dublin could reach agreement, the taoiseach believed that the onus should be on the London government to make the first move by declaring that it desired to see the removal of the border.

Fianna Fáil failed to retain its overall majority in the February general election, winning only 68 of the 147 seats. Still, de Valera and his colleagues looked on with astonishment as the opposition parties came together to form a coalition government. This Inter-Party government included Fine Gael, Clann na Poblachta, Clann na Talmhan and both Labour factions, and few observers expected the new administration to survive. Clearly, the only common objective of these diverse parties was a determination to keep de Valera out of office. As Fine Gael was the largest party in the coalition with thirty-one seats, it supplied the taoiseach and the greatest number of cabinet ministers. However, Clann na Poblachta refused to serve in a government led by Richard Mulcahy, the Fine Gael leader, because of his role in the Civil War, and John A. Costello, a distinguished barrister, was nominated as taoiseach with Mulcahy accepting the Education portfolio. The new taoiseach had no Civil War baggage, and he and MacBride shared a mutual respect that had developed from their contact on the legal circuit.[93] Costello's close colleague and political ally, Patrick McGilligan, became minister for finance, while William Norton, the leader of the official Labour party which had won fourteen seats, became minister for social welfare and acted as tánaiste. But the most interesting appointment to the new government was that of MacBride as minister for external affairs. Clann na Poblachta's electoral performance in winning only ten seats had disappointed many of its supporters, but the party had polled 13.2 per cent of the first preference vote, enough to establish itself as a major force in Irish politics.[94] These ten seats enabled MacBride and Noel Browne to take their places in the cabinet, and both took advantage of their new positions to exercise considerable influence in the Inter-Party government.

The formation of the Inter-Party government also raised eyebrows in the North, where MacBride's appointment was highlighted as a 'surprising choice'.[95] Yet the diversity of parties in the new government made it very difficult to predict Dublin's approach to Anglo-Irish relations. While MacBride's opinions were well known, the cabinet also included James Dillon, an independent TD and the new minister for agriculture, who was widely regarded as the most pro-British member of the Dáil. Although the Costello government inherited a situation in which political relations between London and Dublin had been cool, economic relations had improved considerably since the end of the war. In particular, the 1947 trade negotiations between the two countries had been of mutual benefit. Éire imported plant, coal and other raw materials, while agricultural produce was exported to Britain in much greater quantity. The Fianna Fáil administration also agreed to the formation of a Joint Standing Committee to consider ways to promote trade between the two countries.[96] Earlier, in April 1946, the Attlee government had signed a Civil Aviation agreement with the Éire government, creating a joint organization in which Éire was given a controlling interest.[97] This latter arrangement caused the Stormont authorities some concern, as they only learned of the full terms of the air transport agreement when it was reported in the press, even though the new company was given the right to pick up and set down passengers in Belfast.[98] The Unionist government subsequently protested both at this lack of consultation on such an important issue and at the use of the term 'Éire' in the agreement, but, despite enlisting Home Office support, the Dominions Office ignored Stormont's requests.[99] On other occasions, however, the Belfast and Dublin governments managed to work together on a small number of economic projects. The best example was the Lough Erne drainage scheme which planned to provide hydroelectric power and drain large areas of land in Fermanagh. Yet while the project offered obvious economic advantages for the province, it was evident that the Unionist government entered into the arrangement with some reluctance. Brooke himself expressed doubts about the political aspects of such co-operation, indicating that any contact with Éire carried the risk of alienating the party's less tolerant followers.[100] Clear evidence of the Unionist government's pandering to its more militant supporters emerged in February 1948, when Stormont banned a proposed St Patrick's Day anti-partition demonstration in Derry following representations from prominent local Unionists led by the city's mayor, the Rev. Godfrey MacManaway.[101] The decision provoked an outcry by

Nationalists at Stormont, but Warnock defended the ban in typically vigorous fashion. MacManaway, meanwhile, boasted that, had the government not intervened, he and his supporters would have suppressed the demonstration.[102]

Yet this incident had wider repercussions for the authorities in Belfast. Bing quickly seized the opportunity to bring the facts surrounding the ban before the House of Commons, where there was considerable interest, as two of the speakers at the proposed demonstration, Delargy and Mulvey, were Westminster MPs. The MP for Hornchurch informed the House that 100 MPs had signed a motion on the order paper in relation to the banning of a meeting to be addressed by MPs, which he regarded as a violation of MPs' rights. He also called on the government to amend the 1920 act, thus preventing Stormont from prohibiting such meetings.[103] The nationalist press eagerly reported Westminster's interest in the Derry march, and when Warnock flew to London a few days later, it appeared as though he had been summoned to the capital to account for the Unionist government's action.[104] Further controversy emerged following Bing's statement at Westminster, because in his response Morrison claimed that Stormont was not a subordinate parliament.[105] Bing immediately challenged this interpretation of the 1920 act: 'Unfortunately the Northern Ireland papers have taken up your statement as a correct interpretation of the constitutional position and I am certain that it would be most unfortunate if they were led into any further departures from democratic practice through thinking they were not subject to British Parliamentary control.'[106] When the Privy Council Office sought advice on the correct interpretation, however, the Home Office responded by fully endorsing the Morrison viewpoint, adding:

> The effect of the Government of Ireland Act is to place on the Northern Ireland people responsibility for the management of their own internal affairs, and this transfer of responsibility would be nullified if the Northern Ireland Parliament were required to exercise their powers in accordance with the views of United Kingdom Ministers or of the United Kingdom Parliament.[107]

In his reply to Bing, Morrison repeated this argument and stressed that Stormont was only subordinate in the sense that Westminster could legislate to amend the 1920 act.[108] Therefore, while it was apparent that Bing and his followers in the Friends of Ireland group could still embarrass, if not really threaten, the Unionist administration, Brooke and his colleagues were delighted with Morrison's exposition of Stormont's constitutional powers. Moreover, the debate on the 1947 Northern Ireland Bill marked the high point of the Friends/APL alliance, as difficulties soon emerged to undermine the relationship.[109]

Earlier in the 1945–8 period, it was evident that the Unionist government was occasionally uneasy about its relationship with the administration in London. Clearly, this contributed to the remarkably muted response that frequently greeted anti-partition propaganda. The establishment of the Anti-Partition League, the formation of the Friends of Ireland group and the appearance of Clann na Poblachta had all given cause for concern, but in the immediate post-war period the Unionist leadership usually followed a cautious approach to the partition question. Brooke was well aware that the events of the war had strengthened Northern Ireland's position within the United Kingdom. Yet he realized that there was little to be gained by placing unnecessary emphasis on partition, while a new and potentially unsympathetic government was in office at Westminster. Labour's intervention in the 1946 Down by-election had embarrassed the Unionist government, and it threw up the prospect of unwelcome difficulties in Stormont's relations with the Labour government. By 1948, however, as the Stormont government's confidence in the Attlee administration increased and anti-partition pressure intensified, there were growing signs that Unionist leaders were ready to take the offensive on the border issue. Morrison's influence at Westminster had done much to ensure that Northern Ireland's interests were not overlooked by the Labour government. He had been particularly effective in handling criticism of the Belfast administration by Labour backbenchers. Still, the Attlee government had never posed any threat whatsoever to Northern Ireland's constitutional position. British defence requirements dominated the post-war Labour administration's thinking on Ireland, and there are numerous references in the London archives to the lessons of the war and the need to retain control of the North. The Labour government was also keen to restore friendly relations with Éire, particularly in less controversial areas such as trade. At the same time, Labour ministers were anxious to avoid the partition question, and there is some evidence to suggest that they secured the Belfast government's co-operation in playing down the issue in the immediate post-war period.

The return of a Labour government and the impact made by Clann na Poblachta had encouraged the nationalist community in the North to believe that progress on partition was possible. By 1948, however, it was clear that their hopes of a sympathetic hearing from the new administration at Westminster had been without foundation. The Attlee government followed the line taken by its predecessors on partition and on other controversial areas affecting the minority, preferring to keep Northern Ireland affairs out of British politics. Indeed, the Labour administration was particularly keen to prevent discussion of the Northern Ireland problem at Westminster, because it realized that the emergence of such a potentially divisive issue would only benefit its Conservative opponents. In the circumstances the Attlee government's position was eased by the ineffectiveness of the Friends of Ireland and the APL. The Friends consisted of a small nucleus of activists, and though they managed to attract the interest of approximately thirty Labour backbenchers and cause concern at Stormont, there was little real support for the group within the parliamentary Labour party.[110] One reason for the group's ineffectiveness was the difference in emphasis between Bing and Delargy, the two most prominent Friends of Ireland MPs. Delargy, who had grown up on the Falls Road, was instinctively anti-partitionist. Bing, on the other hand, maintained that political and economic advances for the province ultimately depended on the British connection.[111] An equitable society could be created in Northern Ireland, he argued, but only if Westminster recognized its responsibilities under the 1920 legislation and took the appropriate action. Of course, the Friends also struggled to make an impact because of the wide range of domestic and foreign issues that preoccupied the Labour party in the immediate post-war period.

For its part, the APL reflected the organizational weaknesses of the Nationalist party. It also failed to devise a clear strategy for the promotion of the partition issue both in Great Britain and in Éire. This was partly attributable to the inability of the rural and socially conservative League to combine effectively with the Friends of Ireland MPs, most of whom were on the left of the Labour party. Naturally, this lack of cohesion weakened the anti-partition cause. By 1948, however, partition had emerged as a live issue in southern politics, and this rejuvenated the APL. The rise of MacBride's new party had forced the other main parties in the Dáil to turn their attention to the border question. Crucially, de Valera, still the dominant figure in Irish nationalism, raised the border question on the international stage, but a realistic assessment of these developments brought little comfort to Nationalist leaders in the North. The primary aim of Fianna Fáil's promotion of the anti-partition cause was to strengthen the party's republican credentials against attacks from Clann na Poblachta, while an obvious secondary objective was to divert the electorate's attention away from Éire's serious post-war economic difficulties. Yet de Valera's approach to the border question demonstrated a lack of imagination. He continued to hector the British, demanding that they undo partition, while underestimating the intensity of feeling among Ulster Unionists in their opposition to partition. Frequently, moreover, his actions only served to further entrench this opposition.

1948–51

The presence of a new coalition government in the South, which included two members of Clann na Poblachta, increased speculation on Dublin's future relationship with London. It was widely expected that the Inter-Party government, with MacBride exercising considerable influence from his key post at the Department of External Affairs, would attempt to raise the border question in the hope that it would receive a sympathetic hearing, while Labour remained in power at Westminster. Meanwhile, Fianna Fáil, freed from the constraints of office, adopted a less cautious approach to partition, and this added to interest in the South. Lord Rugby had earlier warned the authorities at Westminster to expect this, following a meeting that he had with de Valera in October 1947. Although he acknowledged that the taoiseach was anxious not to force the partition issue, Rugby was afraid that 'the extremists on his left may start a campaign which will have in it a reproach against him for doing nothing'.[112] Subsequently, de Valera became convinced that a more militant stance on the border was the most effective response to the challenge posed by the new coalition government which had threatened his leadership of the anti-partition cause. Following the election defeat, the Fianna Fáil leader decided to embark on a tour of the United States, Australia and New Zealand in an effort to secure international support for the ending of partition.[113] Though out of office, this world tour ensured that Fianna Fáil was not overshadowed on the partition issue by the Costello government, and it kept de Valera in a position of prominence. Little influence was exerted on international opinion, however, because de Valera's audiences invariably consisted of exiled Irish, and his anti-partition rhetoric was principally for home consumption.[114] Certainly, this was a view endorsed by Delargy, who chaired many of de Valera's meetings during his visit to Britain in 1949. Reflecting on the period, Delargy was very critical of de Valera's approach, claiming that he was either ignorant of, or indifferent to, English public opinion. He described these meetings as 'tribal rallies', from which Englishmen sympathetic to Irish unity went away bewildered.[115]

Despite raising expectations in the South for progress on partition, MacBride began cautiously. In listing ten tasks for the new government, no mention of partition was made, and he even speculated that certain elements of Clann na Poblachta's long-term policy, such as the repeal of the External Relations Act, would have to be shelved because of the diverse composition of the new administration.[116] Such a moderate line did not surprise the Foreign Office. In the month before the general election Rugby had expressed his admiration for MacBride and stressed that he was not an irresponsible extremist.[117] The United Kingdom representative confirmed this assessment following his first meeting with the new minister for external affairs, and he confidently informed the authorities in London that MacBride would adopt a restrained approach to relations with Westminster, even though this would anger factions within Clann na Poblachta.[118] In fact, MacBride's early remarks on the border were confined to the possible creation of an all-Ireland customs union through which economic unity could be achieved.[119] On the other hand, Costello's first radio broadcast as taoiseach claimed that Irish unity was his new government's main objective, but, even in the North, this was dismissed as empty rhetoric. Indeed, the Inter-Party government's early caution on the border question was noted by Brooke, who had detected a 'less aggressive and more ingratiating' tone from the new government. Of course, the Stormont premier quickly dismissed any notion that a more conciliatory and flexible approach by Dublin could lead to a closer relationship between North and South.[120] Nevertheless, there were signs that the authorities in London welcomed the change of government in the South.[121] When MacBride met Bevin in Paris during a conference of foreign ministers in April 1948, the Foreign Office observed that he was not aggressive on partition. Instead, he was content to develop his idea of economic unity, stressing that this would leave Stormont free to continue in its existing form. Although Bevin himself was sympathetic to Dublin's aspirations for political unity, he felt it necessary to emphasize the Westminster view that partition was an Irish problem.[122] Bevin's main interest was to ensure that Britain's defence requirements were met. When he subsequently discussed the Northern Ireland issue with Ede and Philip Noel-Baker, the secretary of state for Commonwealth relations, it was again stressed that London should be very careful not to intervene on partition, leaving the whole question to be resolved between North and South.[123] MacBride's conciliatory stance on the border question greatly impressed Rugby. Indeed, he offered the opinion that 'It would not be the first time that a reputed firebrand turned out to be a pillar of the State.' Rugby's correspondence during this period also conveys the impression that he was much happier in his role as

United Kingdom representative now that he no longer had to deal with de Valera: 'It is a change to be able to discuss the pros and cons of the Partition issue dispassionately and to state arguments which would make Dev go pale and shake with emotion.'[124]

Yet, in spite of Rugby's optimism, MacBride retained very strong views on both the border issue and relations with Westminster, and these were to be revealed in due course. Elsewhere, the authorities at Westminster were delighted by James Dillon's inclusion in the new government. His presence at the Department of Agriculture was one of the factors that persuaded Westminster to reopen economic negotiations with Éire. Faced with the prospect of serious food shortages, the authorities in London were anxious to increase substantially imports of agricultural produce from Éire. This would necessitate a reorganization of Irish agriculture to meet British demand, and, while Fianna Fáil had considered this during the trade negotiations in 1947, Rugby believed that Westminster could obtain a more favourable response from Dillon. In May 1948 he reported that 'Dillon is working for a reversion to the old order of things. He is very alive to the need of maintaining the English market and for not letting down the old customer.'[125]

Partition was mentioned informally during the negotiations with the British government, which preceded the 1948 Trade Agreement, but it was clear that the Irish delegation failed to link the partition issue with economic and commercial relations, as de Valera had done in 1938. Westminster's determination to avoid any discussion of partition was illustrated by the arrangement for Attlee's visit to Dublin in July 1948 for the formal signing of the agreement. The Labour premier only agreed to make the trip on the condition that he would not be expected to discuss partition in any form.[126] These economic discussions were also significant, because they revealed a divergence of opinion within the Inter-Party government. Treasury officials in London had sought a much closer economic relationship with Éire, and they assumed that the new Costello government would also favour such a course. Fianna Fáil had been moving in this direction, and it made particular appeal to the Ministry of Finance in Dublin. Obviously, such an arrangement would have boosted Irish agriculture, but it would also have been of considerable benefit to the British. In addition to much needed food imports, close co-operation would have helped Westminster to protect sterling and reduce the dollar expenditure of the sterling area pool.[127] Perhaps not surprisingly, any move towards closer economic ties with Britain was bitterly opposed by Clann na Poblachta, which had campaigned during the 1948 general election for the separation of Éire's economy from Great Britain's. On this occasion, however, MacBride, who had taken a keen interest in the Ministry of Finance's close relationship with the Treasury, was forced to accept a measure designed to establish increased interaction between the two economies. Later, MacBride was to allege the Ministry of Finance's 'complete subservience to the British Treasury'.[128] Costello subsequently recalled that it was his experience at the 1948 trade negotiations that had coloured his impression of Herbert Morrison, who could not conceal his dislike of Éire. At one stage during the negotiations, Morrison declared that even if the North agreed to co-operate in the formation of a united

Ireland, Westminster could not grant her approval, until the matter was considered from Britain's point of view. On another occasion, Costello recalled that Morrison had left an official function abruptly, remarking that he had 'to visit his friends in the North'.[129]

THE DECLARATION OF THE REPUBLIC AND THE IRELAND ACT

De Valera's international anti-partition tour put the Costello government under pressure during its early period in office. Designed primarily for home consumption, the Fianna Fáil leader's passionate appeals for the removal of the border threatened to undermine the new administration.[130] MacBride, in particular, thought it essential to respond to de Valera's initiative, as Fianna Fáil attempted to limit Clann na Poblachta's republican advantage. Accordingly, the Inter-Party government was obliged to give greater consideration to the border question and to Anglo-Irish relations in general, as de Valera set the agenda in southern politics. Attention became increasingly focused on the 1936 External Relations Act, the legislation that had made Éire an external associate of the Commonwealth. De Valera had hoped that this would facilitate reunification at some stage in the future. Since the end of the war, the Fianna Fáil government had been subjected to criticism for its retention of this tenuous link that had cast doubt over Éire's constitutional status. Norton, the Labour leader, had been a persistent critic of the act, and he had advocated the establishment of a republic in order to remove the continuing ambiguity.[131] When he again raised the issue in August 1948, describing the 1936 act as a 'fraud on the people', his comments carried much more weight, as he was now the tánaiste in the Inter-Party government. Rugby attached great significance to Norton's comments, though he noted that politicians of all shades in the Dáil were eager to make political capital out of the External Relations Act, just as they had done with partition. Although he had earlier been critical of 'this strange device', Rugby was now arguing that the act had served a useful purpose, but he feared, 'since extreme Nationalists can quote it as implying subservience to the Crown of England and to the Union Jack, no man in public life dare defend it. Moreover, no political party is willing to hand over to any other party, the "credit" for removing this so-called offence to Éire sentiment.'[132] Evidently, recent developments in Éire had caused concern at Westminster, and Noel-Baker, the secretary of state for Commonwealth relations, repeated Rugby's fears and warned his colleagues that the Éire government appeared to be contemplating the repeal of the External Relations Act.[133] Subsequently, MacBride indicated that the Inter-Party government gave several signals that the cabinet had already taken the decision to withdraw from the Commonwealth, but that these had been missed by Rugby.[134]

It was not, therefore, Costello's decision to withdraw from the Commonwealth that surprised the authorities at Westminster. Rather, it was the occasion on which he chose to make the announcement. The leader of the Inter-Party government made public his intention in somewhat controversial circumstances during a visit to Canada. Although the coalition had been steadily moving towards such a decision, Costello's announcement on 7 September 1948 that the External

Relations Act would be 'ditched' was a spontaneous event which took his cabinet colleagues by surprise.[135] The taoiseach had continually felt snubbed during his Canadian visit, and the announcement at his press conference in Ottawa was, at least in part, a reaction to the provocation that he had endured from his pro-British hosts during the previous few days. Of course, there were other significant political factors that had contributed to Costello's decision. Clearly, MacBride and Norton were advocates of such a course, and Costello was also extremely nervous that a private member's bill, proposing the repeal of the act, would be brought before the Dáil. Here, suspicion fell on Peadar Cowan, the militant anti-partitionist, who had been expelled from Clann na Poblachta on 3 July. Cowan repeatedly sought to embarrass the government by demanding clarification of Éire's constitutional status.[136] Surprisingly, both Costello and MacBride believed that the repeal of the 1936 act would not affect Éire's association with the Commonwealth, but Rugby saw the Inter-Party government's decision as 'slapdash and amateur'. Claiming that Fine Gael 'had a sudden brainwave that they would steal the "Long Man's" clothes', Rugby feared that the announcement would raise tension on the partition issue on both sides of the border. He also warned the government in London to expect trouble, as the various parties in Éire switched their attention to the border issue: 'No leading politician dare to appear reluctant to join the anti-Partition bandwagon or to seem doubtful about the wisdom of giving it a shove.' Yet, as Rugby added, the move to establish a republic, following Éire's wartime neutrality, would only further entrench partition.[137] For his part, de Valera, though his official biographers suggest otherwise, must have viewed the Inter-Party government's dramatic gesture as ill-judged, because it made the task of removing the border more complicated.[138] Clearly, the Fianna Fáil leader had the opportunity to repeal the External Relations Act during 1947 when it was a source of contention. Such a move, moreover, would have stolen Clann na Poblachta's thunder, but de Valera rejected this short-term political advantage in favour of retaining Éire's tenuous link with the Commonwealth.

The announcement of Éire's intention to repeal the 1936 act was discussed at a Commonwealth conference which, by coincidence, had already been planned for October 1948. Under the auspices of this conference an Irish delegation was invited to meet senior figures in the Commonwealth on 17 October. MacBride and McGilligan represented the Dublin government, and they were joined by Attlee, Noel-Baker and the lord chancellor, Lord Jowitt, and by Peter Fraser, the New Zealand prime minister, L.S. St Laurent, the Canadian prime minister designate, and Dr Herbert Evatt, the Australian deputy prime minister. Significantly, Costello, who apparently found it difficult to contain his emotion on the subject of Éire's relationship with the Commonwealth, did not attend. At these talks the Commonwealth leaders were generally sympathetic towards Éire, but the British ministers were keen to put pressure on the Dublin administration by threatening existing trade preferences and querying the nationality of Éire citizens in Britain.[139] In the following month, further talks in Paris failed to resolve these issues, as the Commonwealth leaders stressed that Éire should not be treated as a 'foreign country', while British ministers continued to stress the legal consequences of Éire's intention to pull out of the Commonwealth. In the end, Labour ministers recognized that if they continued to argue that the repeal of the External Relations Act categorized Éire as a foreign state, 'they would find themselves alone in maintaining that view'.[140] Over the course of these discussions, Attlee was mindful of events in India, where a new constitution establishing the state as an independent republic was being planned, and the prime minister hoped that some mechanism could be devised to keep India in the Commonwealth.[141]

Under pressure from Commonwealth governments, Westminster conceded special treatment for Éire in the areas of trade and commerce, though the cabinet minutes record that the decision was taken 'with reluctance, as they felt that Éire would thereby succeed in retaining many of the practical advantages of Commonwealth membership while renouncing its obligations'.[142] There was also the fear that a dangerous precedent had been created which might prove attractive to other Commonwealth countries. In Éire there was a widely held view that secession might be an obstacle to unification, but Costello was confident that progress on partition would not be impeded, when he introduced the Republic of Ireland Bill.[143] The Unionist government had responded to Éire's move by lobbying Westminster for reassurances on the constitutional position, but the Labour government reacted cautiously, judging that it would be 'embarrassing' for Westminster 'to be put in the position of having to support the continuance of partition'.[144] The Attlee cabinet was also concerned by the prospect of Éire joining the United Nations and availing of the opportunity to raise partition in an international forum.[145] Initially, the only crumb of comfort for the Stormont authorities was a statement by Attlee in the House of Commons on 28 October, when he declared: 'The view of His Majesty's Government in the United Kingdom has always been that no change should be made in the constitutional status of Northern Ireland without Northern Ireland's free agreement.'[146] Yet this was not sufficient to placate the Belfast administration. Indeed, Brooke even considered the possibility of military intervention by the South. He informed Westminster that a 'Sudeten' situation could arise in which republican elements would provoke disturbances in the North and then exert pressure on Dublin to send in troops to protect the nationalist minority.[147] What Brooke did not realize, however, was that the Labour cabinet had secretly decided to shift their position on partition. Previously, Westminster had always maintained that 'partition was an issue for the Irish themselves', but it now believed 'that for defence reasons it was not possible any longer to maintain that position'.[148] Brooke's strategy during this period was to take advantage of Westminster's attitude to uncompromising anti-partition propaganda which had escalated since Costello's government took office. His task was facilitated by militant declarations in the South, such as the statement made by Cowan during the debate on the Republic of Ireland Bill, when he claimed that the only way to solve partition would be 'by marching across the Border and ending it'.[149]

While the Labour government remained nervous of a public debate on partition, it felt obliged to furnish the authorities in Belfast with a report on recent discussions with the Éire representatives in Paris. Significantly, Labour ministers

were also aware that the favourable treatment given to Éire, following its decision to leave the Commonwealth, could 'prejudice the good relations' between
Belfast and London.[150] In a further attempt to reassure the Unionist government,
Brooke was invited to Chequers on 20 November for an important meeting with
Attlee. The prime minister informed Brooke that Northern Ireland's constitutional position would be fully safeguarded, and he was at liberty to make public this assurance. When the Unionist leader learned that Éire would not be treated as a foreign state, he empathized with Attlee, suggesting that Westminster
'could not have reasonably adopted any other policy'. Nevertheless, he took the
opportunity to remind Attlee that Stormont had to be aware of 'the ultimate
objectives of the Éire Government as regards partition'. A major concern for
Brooke was the fear that a 'large influx of Éire citizens' could threaten the
province's long-term constitutional position by obtaining the franchise and voting against the Unionist party. Although the existing residence requirement was
seven years, Brooke argued that Stormont might need 'to tighten up still further'
the franchise qualifications for Northern Ireland elections. Attlee regarded this
as a transferred matter, on which his government would raise no objections, but
he cautioned against the imposition of a residence qualification for voting in
Westminster elections. Brooke also mentioned a number of other points, including the future of southern peers in the House of Lords and the change of name
from 'Northern Ireland' to 'Ulster', which he thought his government might
raise formally.[151] On his return to Belfast, Brooke oversaw the establishment of
a working party under the chairmanship of W.D. Scott, the permanent secretary
to the Ministry of Finance, to consider all issues relating to the consequences for
Northern Ireland of Éire's withdrawal from the Commonwealth and present a
case for stronger constitutional powers.[152] Yet, while Attlee had been supportive,
he had also indicated in his Commons speech that any legislation which might
be necessary following Éire's secession would be confined to 'clearing up one
or two small points'.[153] Indeed, in his reply to the prime minister's statement,
Churchill expressed the view that the province had already benefited: 'It is obvious that the position of the people of Northern Ireland ... has been simplified
and consolidated by the decisions which the Dublin Government have taken.'[154]
However, Brooke was determined to seize this opportunity to press for a statutory guarantee on the province's constitutional position, because he feared that
some future Westminster government might be persuaded to support a Dublin
initiative to bring partition to an end.[155]

Accordingly, the Unionist cabinet drafted the following constitutional declaration which it hoped would appear in legislative form: 'Any alteration in the law
touching the status of Northern Ireland as a part of the United Kingdom or the relation of the Crown to the parliament of Northern Ireland shall require the assent of
that parliament as well as of the parliament of the United Kingdom.'[156] At
Westminster, meanwhile, a working party, consisting of senior Whitehall civil servants under the chairmanship of the cabinet secretary, Sir Norman Brook, had been
established to examine the Northern Ireland proposals. By this stage the Labour
government had accepted that some legislation would be required following Éire's
secession. At one of the working party's early meetings, however, it was

established that the Stormont proposal on legislation to safeguard the province's constitutional position 'went a great deal too far and was quite unacceptable'.[157] Furthermore, the working party quickly rejected Brooke's demand for the continued use of 'Éire', and it only agreed to give further consideration to the replacement of 'Northern Ireland' by 'Ulster'.[158] These early decisions convinced Scott that Whitehall wanted the 'minimum legislation necessary', as it tried 'to preserve the status quo as far as possible'.[159] Still, one member of the working party, Sir Frank Newsam, the permanent under-secretary at the Home Office, was sympathetic to the Unionist government's position. While he recognized that 'few if any' of the Northern Ireland proposals were really consequential on the repeal of the External Relations Act, he urged his colleagues to appreciate Stormont's motives in seeking new legislation:

> ... the Northern Ireland government contend that Éire's secession from the Commonwealth has killed any lingering hope of a united Ireland and ... there is therefore no ground for the continuance of arrangements which are based on the assumption that partition might some day be ended. At the same time the Northern Ireland government fear that Éire's latest move is a prelude to a violent campaign for the ending of partition and are naturally anxious to strengthen their hands against any such campaign. In my view we cannot brush aside these considerations and treat the Northern Ireland proposals as though all we were concerned to do was to recommend such changes as are consequential in the strictest sense of the word.[160]

Only two days later Newsam expressed agreement with the Unionist analysis of partition by stressing that Éire's intended withdrawal from the Commonwealth had created an 'entirely new situation'. Westminster would have to face the fact, moreover, that 'there was now no practical possibility of ending partition'. Significantly, he went further, arguing: 'Even if Ulster should want to join with the Republic of Ireland, we could not let her do so now that the Republic of Ireland no longer owed allegiance to the King. The North must, therefore, be defended, if necessary against itself.'[161] Newsam's analysis obviously influenced other members of the working party. When its report was submitted to the cabinet office, it emphasized the importance of holding the province, if necessary against its own wishes. In addition, it argued that the Unionists should be given 'a binding assurance that Northern Ireland shall never be excluded from the United Kingdom without her full and free consent'. Political factors were also assessed in the wake of Éire's secession from the Commonwealth. Recognizing the existence of strong support for Northern Ireland's position on the mainland, the Whitehall working party suggested that 'there is positive political advantage in doing everything possible at this stage to strengthen the position of the North'.[162] Following the submission of the working party report, Attlee organized a meeting in London between representatives of the Westminster and Stormont governments on 6 January 1949. The Labour leader was joined by Jowitt, Ede, Shawcross, Noel-Baker and Patrick Gordon Walker, a junior minister at the Commonwealth Relations Office, while Brooke was accompanied by Warnock, Sinclair and Curran, the attorney general.[163] At the meeting Attlee rejected the Stormont proposal for a constitutional guarantee, because it was considered to be 'too wide in scope'. Further discussion on this point, however, led to a provisional agreement that the new bill should include a guarantee that Northern Ireland would not cease to be part of the United Kingdom without the consent of the Northern Ireland parliament. Although it was recognized that a subsequent Westminster parliament could revoke such a declaration, Brooke welcomed the proposal and succeeded in securing Attlee's approval for the declaration to include specific references to the existing boundaries of Northern Ireland. When the proposed titles for the North and South were discussed, it was revealed that a majority of the working party had supported the Stormont proposal for the introduction of the title 'Ulster'. However, this was rejected by Attlee and his colleagues, who argued that such a change would be difficult to defend, as Cavan, Monaghan and Donegal were not part of Northern Ireland. While there was little support for the continued use of 'Éire', the British ministers did agree that while statutory provision would have to be made for the use of 'Republic of Ireland' in Westminster legislation, the phrase 'the Irish Republic' could be used in less formal contexts.

The most contentious subject to be discussed at the meeting was the franchise issue. When Brooke requested the imposition of a six-month residence qualification for the Westminster franchise in Northern Ireland, he was opposed by Ede, who warned that any attempt to secure even a three-month residence qualification would provoke strong criticism of the province's local government franchise in the House of Commons. The home secretary refused to consider the Stormont delegation's proposals, unless the Unionist government was prepared to reduce substantially the seven-year residence qualification for voting in Northern Ireland elections. Interestingly, Labour ministers had also formed the opinion that Stormont should not be allowed to legislate on all Supreme Court matters, because they 'felt themselves to be in some sense trustees for the minority in Northern Ireland'. The only surprise for the Westminster representatives at the meeting was Brooke's reference to 'the renewed activities of the IRA in the South and to the state of anxiety which existed in Northern Ireland'. The Stormont premier informed those present that such concern had led to speculation about the revival of the Ulster Volunteers. To prevent this occurrence Brooke wanted Attlee to provide an assurance that Northern Ireland 'would be defended from any possible attack, just as any other part of the United Kingdom'. The Unionist leader's concern about possible incursions across the border was not dismissed by the Westminster representatives. Indeed, in the following week, a Foreign Office official recalled Rugby's recent warning of the grave signs that a new terrorist campaign could erupt in Éire.[164]

The meeting between Westminster and Stormont ministers on 6 January 1949 was crucial in determining London's response to Éire's Republic of Ireland Bill, enacted on 21 December 1948. After the discussions, Attlee produced a constitutional guarantee for Northern Ireland, and this was to become the key clause in the 1949 Ireland Act: 'that Northern Ireland remains part of His Majesty's dominions and of the United Kingdom and ... that in no event will Northern Ireland or any other part thereof cease to be part of the United

Kingdom without the consent of the parliament of Northern Ireland'. The prime minister's memorandum on the subject demonstrated that the only major point of contention between Attlee and the Whitehall working party concerned nomenclature. A majority of the working party had favoured the use of the term 'Ulster' to replace Northern Ireland, but this was rejected by Attlee.[165] When the cabinet discussed Attlee's proposals on 12 January, only Frank Pakenham, later Lord Longford, the minister for civil aviation, appeared to raise any objection to the prime minister's recommendations:

> ... he thought it would be a mistake to give any guarantee of the territorial integrity of Northern Ireland. In two Northern Ireland counties there was a majority in favour of an ending of partition and, if the issue of partition ever came before an international court, the view might be expressed that these counties should be transferred to Éire. He believed that the right solution lay in the political unity of Ireland and the strategical unity of Ireland and the United Kingdom.

Pakenham carried little weight in the Labour administration, however, and the cabinet took the line that

> it was by no means certain that an international tribunal ... would consider that ... Tyrone and Fermanagh should be transferred to Éire: recent discussions on the partition of India and Palestine provided examples of the arguments which might be used in favour of treating these counties as essential to the viability of Northern Ireland. Unless the people of Northern Ireland felt reasonably assured of the support of the people of this country, there might be a revival of the Ulster Volunteers and of other bodies intending to meet any threat of force by force; and this would bring nearer the danger of an outbreak of violence in Ireland. From the point of view of Great Britain, experience in the last war had amply proved that Northern Ireland's continued adhesion to the United Kingdom was essential for her defence. There was nothing in past experience to give any reasonable assurance to Great Britain that Éire would not be neutral in a future war. In 1940 Éire had jeopardised her chances of ending partition by remaining neutral, and her recent legislation had shown that she laid more store on formal independence than on the union of Ireland.[166]

Attlee then raised a potential difficulty, when he anticipated that the Unionist leaders might seek an assurance from London that British troops would be available to defend the North against possible aggression. After consideration the cabinet decided that Westminster would avoid taking the initiative, though ministers acknowledged that a suitable assurance would have to be given if the question was raised by the authorities in Belfast. The Labour cabinet remained undecided on the franchise question, deferring any decision on the possible imposition of a three-month residence qualification for the Westminster franchise until Attlee ascertained whether the Unionist government was prepared to reduce the residence qualification for the franchise in Stormont elections. In fact, Westminster had already failed in one attempt to persuade Stormont to lower the residence qualification for the Northern Ireland parliamentary franchise from seven to five years.[167]

Brooke, accompanied by Gransden, the cabinet secretary, next met Attlee and Ede in London on 18 January, and much of the discussion centred on nomenclature. Recognizing that Labour was firmly against the use of 'Ulster', Brooke concentrated his efforts on persuading Attlee to withdraw the title 'Republic of Ireland' from the forthcoming Westminster bill.[168] The Unionist case emphasized the 'political and psychological effects' in Northern Ireland of giving statutory recognition to the title 'Republic of Ireland', considering the significance that political leaders in Éire were attaching to the title. Some indication of the concern which the Unionist leadership felt on this issue emerged, when Brooke informed those present at the meeting:

> If he was not satisfied on what he regarded as a question of principle, he could not conceal this from his political supporters. He might then be pressed to put forward the demand that Northern Ireland should be given Dominion status, so that the Northern Ireland parliament might have full power to do all that it thought necessary, for the protection of the North. This, he thought, would be an unsound solution of Ulster's difficulties and he did not wish to be put in a position in which he would have to advocate it.

On this occasion Brooke attempted to extract a concession by claiming that failure to appease his supporters on this issue might put him in a position where he had no alternative but to demand dominion status for the province, even though he regarded it as an 'unsound solution'. Yet this argument did not impress the Labour leadership, and Ede pointed out that dominion status would place the province in greater danger, because at present 'Northern Ireland was, for defence purposes, as much a part of the United Kingdom as Kent or Sussex.' Attlee then attempted to allay Unionist fears by assuring Brooke and Gransden that Westminster would use the title 'the Irish Republic' in all official documents. In addition, the Labour leader responded to Unionist concern on the franchise question. Although the Stormont authorities maintained their opposition to any lowering of residence qualification for Northern Ireland elections, Attlee agreed to recommend the imposition of a three-month residence qualification for the franchise in Westminster elections. While such a change would have had little effect on the actual results in future Westminster elections, it was, nevertheless, a significant concession, because the Labour government realized that any alteration of the province's franchise qualifications would raise general questions in the House of Commons about the conduct of all elections in Northern Ireland, which would have to be answered by the home secretary. However, a further Unionist proposal received a negative response from Attlee. Unionists wanted the Stormont parliament to be given powers to disqualify MPs in certain circumstances, an obvious attempt to prevent abstention by Nationalist MPs under threat of disqualification, but Attlee steered clear of such controversy. The meeting on 18 January marked the end of the serious negotiations on the new bill, as the authorities at Westminster learned of the Dublin government's plans to delay implementing the Republic of Ireland Act until Easter Monday. Westminster did not want to proceed with its Ireland Bill until the Republic of Ireland Act had come into operation, because it was anxious to avoid any suggestion that it had forced Éire out of the Commonwealth. Moreover, the switch of dates from 21 January to Easter Monday did not pass without comment by the authorities in London. Sir Norman Brook recorded that the Costello government's new choice of date, the anniversary of the 1916 rising, was 'hardly in accord with their professed desire for friendlier relations with the United Kingdom'.[169]

Indeed, the intense political activity in the South, following Costello's Canadian announcement, threatened to create further problems in Anglo-Irish relations. The influence of Clann na Poblachta in the Inter-Party government and de Valera's response had made partition a prominent issue, and there had been a significant increase in anti-partition propaganda emanating from Dublin. During a meeting with Brook, the cabinet secretary, and Sir Percivale Liesching, the permanent under-secretary at the Commonwealth Relations Office, F.H. Boland complained that all the political parties in the South were very anxious to prove that 'they were not backward about partition'. What angered Boland even more was that since the end of the war he believed that there had been a growing acceptance in Éire of the view that partition could not be terminated without Northern Ireland's agreement, but the present anti-partition campaign only made such agreement even more difficult to achieve.[170] When Rugby contacted London in February 1949, he was scathing in his assessment of recent anti-partition rhetoric: 'The Irish Nationalist view, justified by past experience, is that it is only necessary to worry and harry the British long enough for them to throw up the job and clear out. Irish Nationalists do not realise that this technique no longer applies.' Of greater interest to officials at Westminster was his warning that de Valera had recently expressed anxiety over the consequences of rising anti-partition feeling in the South. The United Kingdom representative was convinced that the Fianna Fáil leader was genuinely concerned about the increasing likelihood of an outbreak of violence on the border issue.[171] In earlier correspondence Rugby had expressed his concern that partition might become a subject for international debate, a development that could result in considerable embarrassment for the British government.[172] Yet such fears were exaggerated. Rugby consistently overlooked the extent of Éire's isolation from the rest of the world in the immediate post-war period.

Certainly, the Stormont authorities were indifferent to the possibility of an international debate on partition. Their main concern was to persuade the Westminster government to take firm action against the anti-partition campaign directed from Dublin. The delay in the implementation of the Republic of Ireland Act had, moreover, increased tension on all sides, and Brooke was quick to see the possibility for further Unionist gains. Consequently, he informed Attlee of 'the current uneasiness' in Northern Ireland, which had been 'deliberately fostered by speeches of responsible statesmen in Éire', and urged Westminster to take positive steps to protect the province:

The position has now been reached when our people require some assurance that the Imperial Government are alive to the dangers which may threaten Northern Ireland. They look to you and your colleagues to take steps to allay any anxiety in the matter, and to let it be known without equivocation that your Government will not tolerate a continuance of the policy of threats and incitement directed against this part of the United Kingdom.[173]

The Unionist case received a sympathetic hearing at Westminster, as Ede and Noel-Baker reminded their cabinet colleagues of the dubious claims made by Éire ministers. During discussions in October and November 1948, they had insisted that their decision to withdraw from the Commonwealth was intended to improve relations between London and Dublin. While the two Labour ministers acknowledged that some of the tension could be attributed to the calling of a Northern Ireland general election in February 1949, there was no doubt that they deplored the actions of cabinet ministers in Dublin.[174] When the cabinet discussed this issue, the extent of the sympathy for Brooke's position came to light: 'The conduct of the Éire Government was far from satisfactory, and it was right that the justifiable anxieties of the people of Northern Ireland should be allayed.'[175] Nevertheless, in spite of this sympathy, Brooke was informed that the Labour cabinet would not endorse his proposal to make direct representation to the government in Dublin, as this would only encourage further statements in support of the anti-partition campaign. Instead, Attlee informed the Unionist leader that a clear and firm statement on the subject of partition could be made during the proceedings on the Ireland Bill which, of course, contained provisions affirming the province's constitutional position.[176] Once again, in the discussion of Brooke's proposal, it was evident that the Labour government attached considerable significance to the possibility of Conservative intervention if a firm line in support of partition were not taken.[177]

In calling a snap general election Brooke had exacerbated the Labour government's difficulties and contributed to a heightening of anti-partition agitation. At the same time, however, he enjoyed partial success in restraining some of his more militant followers, whom Rugby had predicted would seek to exploit the anti-partition campaign. Unionist MPs at Westminster had been especially active in pressing the Labour government for action in response to the intensification of the anti-partition campaign.[178] It was clear to Brooke that this kind of action by the Westminster Unionists only frustrated Attlee and his colleagues. Accordingly, he used his influence to dissuade his party colleagues at Westminster, particularly Professor D.L. Savory, the MP for Queen's University, from pursuing a course which only embarrassed the Stormont premier in his negotiations with the government in London. Once again, Brooke made full use of the services of the Northern Ireland liaison officer at the Home Office in his attempts to curb further moves by Unionists in the House of Commons.[179] While he was not always successful, his efforts to restrain the Westminster MPs were appreciated by Attlee, who informed the Stormont premier: 'I am grateful to you for the efforts which I know you have made to prevent the stirring up of trouble.'[180]

Despite the obvious rise in anti-partition pressure, the authorities at Westminster were convinced that the removal of the border was, by no means, a primary objective of the South's political leaders. In one of his early reports Gilbert Laithwaite, who had succeeded Rugby as United Kingdom representative to Éire in March 1949, noted that he sensed a genuine desire among ministers in the Dublin government to co-operate with London in promoting friendly relations. This was being impeded, however, by the political need to persevere with rhetoric on the border question: 'Partition is represented as the one obstacle to (the) fullest and most intimate understanding, but I suspect that there is much greater appreciation of (the) practical difficulties of solving that issue than any Minister could admit in public.'[181] Indeed, the Labour government won the respect of Éire's political elite, when unexpected congratulatory messages arrived from both Attlee and the king, and these were given prominence at the Easter Monday celebrations marking the official declaration of the republic. The message from the king was a particular surprise, because Noel-Baker had rejected the idea following a meeting in London with Dulanty, the Éire high commissioner, who had in fact made the request 'with some diffidence'.[182] While the message from George VI was regarded as a generous gesture in the South, it caused anger and frustration in the North. The Unionist government was forced to cancel a press statement attacking the new republic, when Brooke learned of the king's message to the new president, Seán T. O'Kelly.[183] While Laithwaite was pleased to report on the goodwill generated by the messages, he also observed that the celebrations were something of an anti-climax, clearly missing the presence of de Valera.[184]

The publication of the Ireland Bill on 3 May 1949 marked the culmination of a sustained period of trust and close co-operation between the Labour government in London and the Unionist government in Belfast. Ministers in the Costello government were obviously shaken by news of the provisions in the bill affirming Northern Ireland's constitutional position and territorial integrity. In early January, when negotiations between Stormont and Westminster were at a vital stage, the astute Boland had tried to anticipate the content of the bill, but he never considered the possible inclusion of any constitutional safeguards for the province.[185] While there had been all kinds of press speculation, most political leaders in Éire were taken by surprise once the details of the new bill were made public. De Valera was in London when he learned of Labour's plans, and he immediately tried to arrange a meeting with Rugby, but his request was refused. In a public statement an angry de Valera claimed that the British government had now made Irish unity 'an impossible task', and he warned that Anglo-Irish relations would sink to a level not seen since the War of Independence.[186] As minister for external affairs, MacBride made protests on behalf of the Dublin government, firstly in an interview with Bevin and Noel-Baker on 5 May, and then formally in an *aide-memoire* on 7 May. Surprisingly, however, MacBride appeared to be the most restrained political leader in the South in his reaction to the Ireland Bill. Boland confirmed this when he informed Laithwaite that both he and MacBride had been genuinely surprised at the extent of the Costello cabinet's reaction to the Ireland Bill, and that since then MacBride had been 'acting as a brake' in cabinet discussions.[187] When leading figures in the government subsequently spoke at a protest rally in Dublin, MacBride's 'relatively calm and reasoned' approach contrasted sharply with the inflammatory contributions of Costello and Norton, though Laithwaite discerned an element of political manoeuvring in MacBride's actions: 'It may be part of his political plan to allow Fine Gael to take the blame for present developments. He is no doubt astute enough to realise that there is unlikely to be much credit.'[188] But perhaps the most interesting observation in this series of reports was Laithwaite's view that while the political atmosphere in Dublin had been deeply disturbed by the constitutional guarantee given to Northern Ireland, there was 'no sign of general excitement or even active public interest'.[189]

When MacBride met Bevin in London on 9 May, he heard a clear exposition of Westminster's attitude to partition. Previously, Bevin had only registered his interest on two matters. He expressed some concern that this sequence of events might create an Irish vote in Great Britain, and he wanted to ensure that relations with Éire, following her secession from the Commonwealth, remained the responsibility of the Commonwealth Relations Office. Now, however, the foreign secretary set out the Labour government's policy on partition in some detail. Responding to MacBride's criticism of the Ireland Bill, Bevin declared:

> Many people in this country and many people in the present Government were in broad sympathy with the ideal of a united Ireland. But we could not ignore the history of the last forty years. Northern Ireland had stood in with us when the South was neutral. Without the help of the North Hitler would unquestionably have won the submarine war and the United Kingdom would have been defeated. That would have brought Hitler at once to Dublin and they would have made the Irish become as slaves. Until the majority of the Northerners were persuaded, therefore, that it was in their interests to join the South, the British people would oblige us to give them guarantees that they would not be coerced.

While outlining the traditional strategic reasons, therefore, Bevin also stressed Labour's determination to ensure that Northern Ireland's constitutional future did not become a party political issue in Britain. The foreign secretary then proceeded to criticize the recent actions of the Dublin government, arguing that these had rendered partition more intractable:

> ... firstly, they had gone out of the Commonwealth, and it was virtually impossible for us to give the impression that we were encouraging or desiring Northern Ireland to go out too. Secondly, they had refused to join the Atlantic Pact. This meant that we had no assurance of the help of the Irish Republic in time of trouble, and after our last experience, people would not be willing to take a chance.[190]

When the Ireland Bill was given its second reading in the House of Commons, Herbert Morrison, who wound up the debate for the government, was even more forthright in his support for the continuation of partition.[191] Although the authorities in Belfast were annoyed by the speeches of Delargy and McGhee, who cited various examples of maladministration in connection with Stormont's treatment of the minority, Brooke and his colleagues were satisfied by the outcome of the debate.[192] Not surprisingly, the Ulster Unionists who contributed to the debate condemned the Dublin government's actions, but they adhered to Brooke's requests to avoid any reference to either the boundary or navigational rights, as this would have embarrassed the Labour government.[193] This was yet another example of Brooke successfully using his influence to restrain Ulster Unionists at Westminster. Clearly, the Stormont premier now enjoyed very close relations with the Labour government, and he was keen to ensure that Attlee and his colleagues were not undermined by ill-judged Unionist speeches in the House of Commons.

During the committee stage of the Ireland Bill fifty-six MPs opposed the constitutional guarantee.[194] Moreover, five parliamentary private secretaries were sacked following their opposition to the bill.[195] At a cabinet meeting on the day after the division on the second reading, comment was also made on the significant number of abstentions among Labour backbenchers. Their concern was giving the Northern Ireland parliament a constitutional veto, when a flawed electoral system in the province could mean that Stormont might not accurately reflect the people's will. In the cabinet discussion that followed, the suggestion was made that after the Ireland Bill had been passed, the Westminster government 'might take steps to satisfy themselves that the Northern Ireland Parliament was, in fact, so constituted as to reflect fairly the views of the electors'. Not surprisingly, however, considering the Labour government's earlier stance on Northern Ireland, there was general agreement that it would be 'ill-advised to appear to be interesting themselves in this matter which fell wholly within the jurisdiction of the Northern Ireland Government'. Furthermore, Ede, the minister responsible for dealing with Northern Ireland, moved the discussion on to the possibility of an impending security threat, following the implementation of the new constitutional arrangements. He told his colleagues that the Home Office had received information suggesting that the authorities in Dublin were intending to relax their efforts to check the illegal activities of the IRA, and, as a consequence, he had ordered precautionary action to be taken in Great Britain.[196] Further backbench criticism of the Belfast administration was raised at the Labour party conference in June 1949, but Morrison refuted all allegations that the province's elections were conducted on an unfair basis.[197] Earlier, the Unionist leadership had expressed its appreciation at the Labour front bench's firm refusal to be drawn into any discussion on controversial issues falling within Stormont's jurisdiction during the passage of the Ireland Bill, even though it was recognized that Westminster had the power to intervene under section 75 of the Government of Ireland Act. Conscious of the Labour administration's desire to avoid unnecessary discussion of the partition issue, the Unionist government resisted the temptation to promote a debate at Stormont on the province's constitutional position following the passage of the Ireland Act and ensured that the issue was not raised separately by any Unionist backbencher.[198]

Naturally, the Unionist government viewed the settlement of the problems created by the South's withdrawal from the Commonwealth with great satisfaction. Moreover, there may also have been a sense of relief among Unionist leaders, following the uncertainty that existed in the period immediately after Costello's Canadian announcement. Colonel S.G. Haughton, the Westminster MP for Antrim, had voiced this concern, when he warned a Unionist meeting that the main danger to Northern Ireland during this period would be 'political expediency at Westminster'.[199] Yet the outcome of the Stormont–Westminster negotiations demonstrated clearly to the Unionist government that it had nothing to fear from the Labour administration. Brooke's persistent prompting following the Dublin government's decision to repeal the External Relations Act had resulted in Labour taking a positive stance in favour of partition. Although an editorial in the *Belfast Newsletter* recognized correctly that the constitutional guarantee contained in the Ireland Act was not binding on successive parliaments, it concluded, nevertheless, that the moral force of the declaration was of 'incalculable value'.[200] The *Irish Times*, on the other hand, chose to emphasize what it regarded as a tragic mistake by the Dublin government, arguing that if Costello had not acted, 'all the odds are that Sir Basil Brooke would have lacked either opportunity or excuse to drive another, and a very formidable, nail into the coffin of Irish unity'.[201]

Undoubtedly, one of the reasons for the Labour administration's decision to declare itself in favour of partition was its belief that the authorities in Dublin were not really serious in their attempts to remove the border.[202] Indeed, the Attlee government never fully understood the reasons behind the Inter-Party government's decision to withdraw from the Commonwealth. Of course, the most obvious explanation was the Costello government's desire to counter de Valera's anti-partition crusade, but Laithwaite, who was still considering the issue towards the end of 1949, believed that the Inter-Party government had also been desperate to draw attention away from its serious economic problems.[203] Previously, Laithwaite had noticed that in spite of the Dublin government's anger at British intransigence on partition, it had displayed 'a wide realism' in its economic and financial relations with the United Kingdom.[204] His assessment of the impact of the Ireland Act in the South also provided his political masters with a shrewd assessment of recent developments. Laithwaite believed that the act had prompted

> a fuller appreciation of the reality of an issue which public and political opinion has been very reluctant to face – that the essential obstacle to the anti-Partition cause is the attitude of the majority in Northern Ireland and that the Government and people of Great Britain cannot ignore the attitude of that majority or forcibly impose on it a settlement of the Partition issue, and particularly one which would involve their extrusion from the Commonwealth.[205]

THE 1949 CHAPEL GATES ELECTION AND THE DECLINE OF THE ANTI-PARTITION LEAGUE

In an effort to exert further pressure on the Westminster authorities during the formulation of the Ireland Bill, Brooke had announced a general election on 20 January, with polling to take place on 10 February. While the Stormont premier understood that this would add to the Labour government's difficulties, he was convinced that this would be outweighed by the advantages to be gained from a snap general election.[206] Certainly, circumstances pointed to a Unionist land-slide. The Inter-Party government's decision to repeal the External Relations Act and the subsequent increase in anti-partition agitation enabled the Unionists to turn the 1949 election into a referendum on the border. Brooke's task was facilitated by a decision taken prior to the election by the main parties in the Dáil to unite in an all-party effort to make progress on the partition issue. The lead-ers of all major parties in the South attended a meeting in the Mansion House on 27 January 1949, and it was agreed that a fund should be established to sup-port anti-partition candidates in the North. Collections for the fund were to be made outside churches on the following Sunday, hence the term 'Chapel Gates' election, and this was quickly exploited by the Unionist party in the knowledge that it could benefit from a bitterly sectarian election.[207] Despite public state-ments to the contrary, it was apparent that the border question had again become entangled in party politics in the South. Under strong pressure from Clann na Poblachta, Costello had summoned party leaders to the Mansion House Conference with the intention of formulating a united strategy on partition in an attempt to prevent de Valera making political capital out of the issue.[208] Moreover, the failure to consult Nationalist MPs in the North, some of whom were fiercely opposed to the election fund, about the conference was a further indication that the Inter-Party government's motives were dominated by domes-tic political considerations.

Nevertheless, the intervention by the southern parties enabled Nationalists standing under the APL banner to fight a record seventeen seats, including a num-ber of safe Unionist seats such as Lisnaskea and South Londonderry which had never before been contested. In the election the APL won over 100,000 votes, the best total by Nationalists in any election since 1921, and this represented a 27.2 per cent share of the total votes cast.[209] Yet in spite of the APL's good showing, the Unionist party increased its overall majority by four seats. The circumstances in which the election was fought ensured that the constitutional issue was the main focus of attention, while potentially divisive issues for the Unionist party, such as education, were easily brushed aside. Three of the gains made by the Unionists (Dock, Oldpark and Pottinger) saw increased turnouts, and this reflected the gen-eral pattern with the turnout rising by almost 10 per cent to 79.3 per cent. Clearly, the Unionist party benefited from the higher poll, and it managed to increase its share of the vote from the 1945 figure of 50.4 per cent to 62.7 per cent. In the party's manifesto Brooke gave full prominence to the border question:

> Our country is in danger ... today we fight to defend our very existence and the heritage of our Ulster children. The British Government have agreed to abide by the decision of the Ulster people. It is therefore imper-ative that our determination to remain under the Union Jack should be immediately and overwhelmingly re-affirmed.[210]

It was no surprise that the 1949 election campaign was a bitterly sectarian affair in which there were numerous outbreaks of violence. Yet in spite of all the negative publicity, the Labour administration in London refused to intervene. Indeed, when complaints about the unfair conduct of the election were subsequently raised at the Labour conference, Morrison rejected all the allegations and prevented further discussion of the subject.

The sectarian nature of the campaign also contributed to the collapse of the NILP, which lost all three of its parliamentary seats. Its nine candidates polled only 26,831 votes compared to the 66,053 polled by fifteen candidates in the 1945 election, and its percentage share of the vote dropped from 18.6 per cent to 7.2 per cent. In truth, the party had been under pressure since the Inter-Party government's decision to withdraw from the Commonwealth. The subsequent surge in anti-partition agitation put the NILP's ambiguous stance on the border under the spotlight. Indeed, the constitutional issue was foremost in delegates' minds at the party's 1948 annual conference, which was held at Warrenpoint in mid-September, and it was apparent that there had been a hardening of attitudes between the pro- and anti-partition factions within the party. Just before the conference, those NILP members who wanted Northern Ireland to remain within the United Kingdom welcomed the appointment of A.A. Johnston, a full-time British Labour party organizer, who worked in Northern Ireland from 1948–52, because the closer association with the British Labour party edged the NILP towards a pro-partition stance.[211] Almost simultaneously, however, members opposed to the British link began to argue the case for a united, socialist Ireland. This led to the convening of a special conference in November 1948, called by the NILP's West Belfast branch, at which protests were made against the move to strengthen links with the British Labour movement. In a swift response the party executive, which had a strong Protestant trade unionist influence, expelled the West Belfast branch, and it subsequently formed an Irish Labour Association which was opposed to partition.[212] The executive's next move was to arrange a meeting with Morgan Phillips, the general secretary of the British Labour party, in an attempt to have the NILP affiliated to the British party. The meeting took place on 18 December, and though the Labour party was keen to help the NILP win Westminster seats in the province, Phillips refused to commit the party to any decision that would result in affiliation.[213] The most immediate consequence of the meeting was the resignation of the NILP chairman, Robert Getgood, who opposed any further moves to bind the party to the British Labour movement.[214]

Matters were finally brought to a head by the Unionist government's decision to call an early general election, and this effectively split the party. While the anti-partition faction prepared to form a northern section of the Irish Labour party, the official party decided to make a formal declaration in support of partition before polling: 'The Northern Ireland Labour Party, being a democratic party, accepts the constitutional position of Northern Ireland and the close association with Britain and the Commonwealth. Furthermore we are not seeking any mandate to change it.'[215] Yet neither this decision nor the candidates' vigorous attempts to emphasize their loyalty to the crown could prevent a humiliating defeat, as the party's hopes for a substantial Protestant working-class vote were not realized. However, the party's poor showing at the polls was not due solely to the bitterly sectarian nature of the 1949 election. The Unionist government had, to some extent, succeeded in limiting the NILP's working-class appeal. In the 1945 Northern Ireland general election many voters had been attracted by the party's progressive welfare programme, but a good number of these demands had been met by the Unionist government which had implemented the Westminster government's welfare legislation with only minor alterations in the immediate post-war period. Consequently, the Unionist party believed that its record on social and economic issues gave it an extra advantage over the NILP during the 1949 election campaign.[216] After 1945 Unionists had recognized that the NILP represented a significant threat, and some effort had been expended in countering this challenge. This was reflected in the selection of younger, more progressive figures for safe Unionist seats in the 1949 contest, and the party leaders hoped that such a move would improve the Unionist party's image. The two most distinguished new candidates were Brian Faulkner and Morris May, who were returned for East Down and Ards respectively, and there is no doubt that the introduction of this new blood helped create a more progressive image for the party.

Although it enjoyed relative success in the 'Chapel Gates' election, the APL soon began to lose ground. The passing of the Ireland Act in May 1949 had angered many Nationalist MPs, and this feeling of resentment towards the Labour government later influenced the decisions taken by the conventions in the new Westminster constituencies of Mid-Ulster and Fermanagh-South Tyrone to support abstention following victories by Mulvey and Healy in the British general election in February 1950. There was also strong support within the movement for abstention from Stormont. A motion proposing this was defeated at the annual conference in May 1950, but Nationalist MPs attended Stormont only infrequently after the 1949 election.[217] The debate over abstentionism highlighted the weaknesses of the APL. After the early burst of enthusiasm it quickly became apparent that the APL was devoid of any clear strategy, while the confusion over abstention from Stormont, with some MPs attending and others not, made it impossible for the movement to enforce any consistent policy.[218] Yet the APL was also frustrated by the actions of the Dublin government. In July 1949 two of the most militant Nationalist MPs, McAteer and Conlon, had their appeals to sit in the Dáil rejected, and a year later McSparran, the APL chairman, saw his appeal meet with a similar refusal.[219] While such requests may have embarrassed the Inter-Party government, it was clear that none of the party leaders in the South wanted unpredictable northern Nationalist MPs in the Dáil. This was certainly true of de Valera, who consistently rejected appeals by Nationalist MPs for admission to the Dáil during the 1950s.[220]

The only highlight for the Nationalists during this period was the expulsion of the Rev. Godfrey MacManaway from both the Westminster and Stormont parliaments. The fiercely sectarian MacManaway had first been returned for the Stormont constituency of Londonderry City at a by-election in June 1947, and he won the Westminster seat in West Belfast by ousting Beattie in an extremely bitter contest in the general election held in February 1950. Bing, however, challenged MacManaway's eligibility to take his seat in parliament under the 1801 House of Commons (Clergy Disqualification) Act, which barred Anglican clergymen from membership of the House of Commons, and the issue was referred to a Judicial

Committee of the Privy Council. Although he had been warned by the attorney general to refrain from participating in parliamentary business until the committee had reported, MacManaway insisted on voting against the Labour government on the controversial issue of the nationalization of the iron and steel industry. When the Privy Council declared him ineligible in October 1950, Morrison expressed his criticism of MacManaway's action. As Labour had an overall majority of only six at that time, it was conceivable that MacManaway's vote could have threatened the survival of the government. Following the Privy Council's ruling, Nationalists subsequently challenged MacManaway's eligibility for his Stormont seat, and he resigned in January 1951 before any official decision had been reached.[221]

Yet this could only have been small consolation for the APL leaders, whose spirits had been deflated by the bleak prospects for progress on the border question.[222] Their association with the Friends of Ireland group had led to some scrutiny of Stormont's treatment of the minority, but it had little impact on the Labour government. To many observers, moreover, the Unionist administration appeared even more intransigent following its sweeping election victory in 1949. In the South the preoccupation with partition in 1948–9 ended abruptly, as more pressing domestic issues demanded attention, and this particularly angered northern Nationalists. In spite of these failings, however, there was no doubt that the Unionist administration had been unsettled by the anti-partition agitation. At the first cabinet meeting in 1951 Brooke emphasized that special publicity in both Great Britain and the United States was essential, because of the 'increasingly tense campaign' that had been conducted over the previous five years in a determined attempt to remove the border.[223] While the authorities at Stormont remained nervous of any perceived threat to the province's constitutional position, it was also true that the Unionist government was prepared to engage in clandestine co-operation with the Dublin government when this was of mutual benefit. Contact between civil servants was a regular occurrence, but on more significant matters, such as the future of the Great Northern Railway, which ran on both sides of the border, there was ministerial engagement. On this occasion, Sinclair and McCleery, the minister of commerce, travelled secretly to Dublin to meet Costello, Norton, McGilligan and Liam Cosgrave, then a junior minister in the Inter-Party government.[224] In fact, contact between the Unionist government and ministers in the Costello administration was not confined to economic projects. On several occasions MacBride had meetings in Dublin with Walter Topping, the Unionist chief whip, during which discussions took place on political relations between North and South.[225]

Despite this secret dialogue, the Unionist party moved swiftly and effectively when presented with an opportunity to discredit the Dublin government. The opportunity arose as the crisis over the 'mother and child' scheme broke in the spring of 1951. This involved the provision of free maternity care for all mothers and expectant mothers, and free medical service for all children up to the age of sixteen. These proposals caused great controversy in the South, and following opposition from the Catholic hierarchy the Inter-Party government abandoned its plans to overhaul the country's health services.[226] Not surprisingly, the Unionist party used these events to argue that 'in any matter' where the Catholic Church decided to intervene, the Dublin government would have no choice but to give way.[227] Indeed, both the government's climb-down and the subsequent fallout from what appeared to be the abandonment of Noel Browne provided Unionists with a huge propaganda advantage. This was exploited by their leaders, who seized on statements and actions by leading political figures in the South to support their contention that unification could not even be considered while the Church exerted such powerful influence in the Republic.[228] It was equally apparent, of course, that during the crisis little attention was paid to the impact that the controversy between church and state would have in Northern Ireland, where Nationalist leaders were dismayed by the actions of southern politicians. MacBride subsequently claimed that he was fully aware of the damage that the affair could inflict on the anti-partition cause, but he had been unable to prevent Browne from pressing ahead with such controversial health proposals.[229]

The mother and child affair had further negative consequences for the APL. It led directly to the fall of the Costello administration, and it proved to be a major factor in the collapse of Clann na Poblachta. The downfall of Clann na Poblachta dealt a severe blow to the League. While no progress had been made on the partition issue in the 1948–51 period, Clann na Poblachta's presence in the administration ensured that the border question featured more prominently in southern politics. MacBride, moreover, was regarded as the principal champion of Irish unity, and his fall from office was regretted by the leaders of the APL.[230] In the subsequent election campaign de Valera took a noticeably cautious line on the partition issue, warning that there was little likelihood of any progress on the border 'in the foreseeable future'.[231] Indeed, in the month following the Inter-Party government's defeat, the silence and lack of interest in partition among politicians in the South was noted, and MacBride was singled out as the only exception.[232] Yet even before the collapse of the Costello administration there were signs that the APL was in decline. While the enthusiasm for the anti-partition cause had been rekindled by the political developments of 1949, it had almost fizzled out by 1951. Certainly, de Valera's return to power offered little encouragement to the Nationalist leaders in the North, as it immediately became clear that there was a cooling of interest on the partition issue. In fact, de Valera deliberately steered clear of the issue, and by early 1953 MacBride noted:

> Partition here (is) in the 'Doldrums': neither de Valera nor Aiken even mentioned (it) in introducing their estimates – which is the usual occasion for a declaration of policy in regard to it. We have only had one meeting of the Mansion House Committee in the last twelve months, and were told by de Valera that it was proposed to wind it up soon.[233]

This silence on partition was not confined to de Valera and his colleagues in Fianna Fáil, because the other major parties were equally reluctant to raise the issue. The eclipse of Clann na Poblachta at the 1951 general election, when they only managed to retain two of their ten seats in the Dáil,[234] removed the need for both Fianna Fáil and Fine Gael to take a more militant position on the border question. Furthermore, the events of the 1948–51 period had clearly reinforced partition, and in such circumstances a much more restrained approach appeared to be the best option open to the new Fianna Fáil administration.

It had been the impact made by MacBride's new party and Fianna Fáil's response to the challenge posed by Clann na Poblachta which had combined to make partition an important issue in southern politics in the 1948–51 period. Although Clann na Poblachta had achieved only limited success in the 1948 general election, MacBride was able to exercise disproportionate influence in the new administration. With his leadership of mainstream Irish nationalism now in question, de Valera gave encouragement to Nationalist leaders in the North by embarking on his world tour against partition, but the campaign was aimed primarily at reasserting de Valera's political position at home, rather than appealing to international opinion for support to end partition. The consequent increase in anti-partition agitation, as both Costello and Norton responded to de Valera's rhetoric, created a situation in which mainstream parties in the South competed with each other in their denunciation of the border's existence.[235] Thereafter, the Inter-Party government's hasty decision to repeal the External Relations Act focused even more attention on the border, leaving little room for leading politicians to adopt a more pragmatic approach to the issue. This new militancy on partition was further illustrated by the South's reaction to the Labour government's move to provide a constitutional guarantee for Northern Ireland in the Ireland Act, and this sparked off the most aggressive anti-partition rhetoric since 1921.[236]

Yet despite this fixation with partition among the Republic's political elite, Laithwaite constantly drew attention to the absence of any strong feeling on partition among the people in the South, adding that party politics alone were responsible for the increased agitation on the border question. Consequently, doubts were expressed at Westminster about the sincerity of the South's political leaders in their attempts to secure the removal of the border, and this knowledge exerted some influence on the Labour government in the handling of its relations with both Dublin and Belfast. The increase in anti-partition rhetoric, following Dublin's decision to leave the Commonwealth, and the skilful exploitation of these developments by Brooke had encouraged the Labour government to take a positive line in support of partition. There is no doubt, moreover, that the authorities at Westminster were angered by the performance of the South's political leaders in promoting anti-partition agitation, and this contributed to their decision to include a constitutional guarantee for Northern Ireland in the Ireland Act. Previously, the Labour government's chief concern had been to ensure that the province did not become an issue at Westminster, because it was thought that such an outcome would bring advantages to the Conservative party.[237] It was also apparent that leading figures in the British civil service were in favour of the government at Westminster openly supporting partition. On several occasions in the discussions preceding the formulation of the Ireland Bill, both Sir Norman Brook, the cabinet secretary, and Sir Frank Newsam, the permanent under-secretary at the Home Office, urged the government to meet at least some of Stormont's demands following Éire's secession from the Commonwealth.[238]

The authorities at Westminster welcomed a return to more normal relations with the government in Dublin, when de Valera returned to power in 1951. Indeed, one official at the Commonwealth Relations Office even speculated on the possibility of the Republic of Ireland renewing her association with the Commonwealth:

> Since Mr. de Valera's return to power, there have been certain indications that his attitude towards the Commonwealth issue does not entirely accord with that of his predecessor. In particular, the Ambassador of the Irish Republic in London, evidently speaking on instructions, has more than once given us to understand that Mr. de Valera, had he been in power, would never have severed the connection with the Commonwealth.[239]

Earlier, at the 1950 Labour party conference, Morrison outlined Labour's official policy on partition, arguing that the province's constitutional future should be determined by Irishmen and 'not be dragged into British politics'.[240] This had clearly been the line taken by the Labour government in the 1945–8 period, and it enabled Attlee and his colleagues to convey the impression that they would support any political agreement between Belfast and Dublin, even if this reduced British influence in the North. Of course, the authorities at Westminster knew that such agreement would be anathema to the Unionists at Stormont, and this ensured that partition would continue. In the immediate post-war period there were numerous references in the British cabinet papers to the lessons of the war and the need to retain control of the North for strategic purposes, and Labour was, therefore, able to conceal its real support for partition by delegating responsibility for its continuation to the Unionists in Northern Ireland. By playing down the border question in this way the Labour administration also ensured that Northern Ireland would not become an issue for debate at Westminster. The events of 1948 and early 1949, however, had forced Westminster to take a positive stance in support of partition, but this represented only a change in its approach to the issue and not a change in actual policy.

The inclusion of a constitutional guarantee for the province in the Ireland Act finally dispelled any remaining doubts about Labour's commitment to partition. Some unease during the first three years of Labour rule had contributed to Stormont's reticence on the border question, but the increase in anti-partition agitation, following the Costello government's repeal of the External Relations Act, enabled the Unionist leadership to become more aggressive in its defence of the province's constitutional position. As the anti-partition rhetoric of political leaders in Dublin became more extreme, Brooke was able to exploit the sympathy for Northern Ireland's position at Westminster, which had resulted from the rise in anti-partition agitation, to win concessions from the administration in London. At the same time, the Unionist party took advantage of the increase in sectarian tension, which accompanied political developments in the South, by calling a snap general election in February 1949 and consolidating its position at Stormont at the expense of the NILP. Meanwhile, the Nationalist party, encouraged initially by Labour's 1945 general election victory, had by 1948 become frustrated by Westminster's lack of interest in partition and dismayed at the failure of the Fianna Fáil government to make a more positive contribution to the anti-partition cause. The increase in agitation following the announcement of Éire's decision to withdraw from the Commonwealth, and the formation of the Mansion House Committee to promote a united strategy on the border question, marked the beginning of a three-year period during which anti-partition pressure rose dramatically. However, this change in approach yielded only adverse results and led to the disintegration of the APL.

NOTES

1. Bowman, *De Valera and the Ulster Question*, p.98. It would not have been difficult to organize on a thirty-two county basis considering Sinn Féin's efforts less than ten years earlier.
2. Ibid., pp.132–5. Éamon Donnelly was an abstentionist MP; NIHC 1925–9, 1942–4 and a Fianna Fáil TD, 1933–7.
3. Ibid., pp.123–37.
4. For a discussion of Nationalist abstention and attendance, see Phoenix, *Northern Nationalism*, pp.337–50 and pp.371–84.
5. See the introduction by Éamon Phoenix to the Healy papers, PRONI, D2991, 'The Nationalist Party in Northern Ireland, 1921–55', p.11.
6. Farrell, *The Orange State*, pp.170–1.
7. Bardon, *A History of Ulster*, p.589.
8. Interviews with James Doherty and Edward McAteer.
9. *Irish Times*, 28 July 1945.
10. PROL, CAB129/2, C.P.(45) 152 annex 1, memo by Maffey, 'The Irish Question in 1945', 21 August 1945.
11. Ibid., memo by Addison, 'Relations with Éire', 7 September 1945. For Addison's relationship with Attlee, see Morgan, *Labour in Power*, p.54.
12. PROL, CAB129/2, C.P.(45) 152, memo by Addison, 7 September 1945.
13. PROL, CAB128/1, C.M. 33, 18 September 1945.
14. PROL, CAB129/2, C.P.(45) 152 annex 1, memo by Maffey, 21 August 1945.
15. Interview with McAteer.
16. Ibid. See also Farrell, *The Orange State*, p.179.
17. Farrell, *The Orange State*, p.179.
18. Interview with McAteer.
19. Farrell, *The Orange State*, p.180.
20. *The Times*, 15 November 1945.
21. PRONI, D1862/F/1, Mulvey papers, McGhee to Mulvey, 3 November 1945. The correspondence contains a list of Labour MPs who attended the inaugural meeting.
22. Ibid., McGhee to Mulvey, 6 December 1945. McGhee expressed satisfaction with the free publicity which the Unionists were giving to the Friends.
23. *Irish Independent*, 8 January 1946.
24. PROL, DO 35/1228/WX101/1/95, 'Political and Constitutional Relations: Friends of Ireland – Request by Sir J Maffey for information', Machtig to Addison, 19 January 1946.
25. Ibid., note by Parker, 30 January 1946.
26. Ibid., Maffey to Machtig, 16 January 1946.
27. Ibid., Parker to Stephenson, 15 March 1946, and Machtig to Parker, 9 April 1946.
28. Ibid., Addison to Whiteley, 12 April 1946, asking the chief whip to consider a second approach to the Friends of Ireland.
29. PROL, DO 35/1228/WX101/146, 'Political and Constitutional Relations: Conversation between Lord Addison and Sir Basil Brooke, May 1946', note on meeting between Brooke and Addison, 29 May 1946.
30. Ibid., Stephenson to Addison, 22 May 1946.
31. *Irish News*, 1 June 1946, 3 June 1946, 4 June 1946 and 6 June 1946.
32. Ibid., 8 June 1946. Lieutenant C.H. Mullan -50,697 and Donnelly -28,846. See also Harbinson, *A History of the NILP*, pp.196–7.
33. PRONI, CAB9A/7/58, note by Brooke, 15 September 1946.
34. NIHC Debates, vol. 30, cols 1964–72, 8 October 1946, and cols 2225–36, 22 October 1946.

35. PROL, CAB129/13, C.P.(46) 381, memo by Morrison, 'Éire and Northern Ireland', 16 October 1946.
36. Ibid. On this occasion Morrison reported one of Brooke's frequent criticisms of extreme Unionists in Northern Ireland.
37. PROL, CAB129/13, C.P.(46) 391, memo by Addison, 18 October 1946.
38. PROL, DO 35/1228/WX101/1/69, 'Political and Constitutional Relations: Irish–American Relations', J.C. Donnelly, an official at the British Information Services in New York, first raised the issue in a letter to W.D. Allen, a first secretary at the Foreign Office, 7 May 1945.
39. See file PROL, DO 35/1228/WX101/1/69.
40. See PROL, DO 35/1231/WX168/4, 'Trade Negotiations General: Northern Ireland's Projection in the United States, June 1946–January 1947 passim', Stephenson to Machtig, 28 November 1945.
41. Ibid., Machtig to Maffey, 29 October 1946, and Maxwell to Gransden, 22 November 1946.
42. Ibid., Sir Charles Dixon, an assistant under-secretary at the Dominions Office, to A.W. Peterson, the private secretary at the Home Office, 18 October 1946.
43. Irish Independent, 19 November 1945.
44. Ibid., 18 March 1946.
45. Ibid., 14 June 1946, report of a public speech in Cork.
46. Ibid., 6 May 1946, report of a public speech by E. Coogan, Kilkenny.
47. Ibid., 9 October 1946.
48. Ibid., 6 November 1946.
49. Irish News, 8 October 1946.
50. PROL, CAB129/10, C.P.(46) 212, which included a memo by Maffey following an interview which he had with de Valera, 18 May 1946.
51. Dáil Debates, vol. 101, col. 1155, 29 May 1946.
52. Irish Independent, 24 June 1946.
53. SPOI, S13710A, 'Internment', cabinet meeting, 12 June 1945.
54. Dáil Debates, vol. 97, col. 2740, 18 July 1945.
55. Ibid., vol. 102, col. 1444, 25 July 1946.
56. PROL, DO 35/1228/WX101/137A, 'Political and Constitutional Relations: Addison's conversation with Dulanty re Partition', note of this meeting, 18 April 1946.
57. PROL, DO 35/1228/WX101/152, 'Political and Constitutional Relations: Éire's position in the Commonwealth. Mr. de Valera's Statement June 1946', Archer to C.R. Price, an assistant secretary at the Dominions Office, 2 July 1946. This followed Archer's meeting with F.H. Boland who wanted Éire to be invited to the forthcoming conference if Commonwealth preferences were being discussed. In fact, an Éire delegation did attend a conference in the spring of 1947.
58. PROL, DO 35/1228/WX101/154, 'Political and Constitutional Relations: General Questions with de Valera', note of meeting between de Valera and Archer, 6 July 1946.
59. Ibid., Stephenson to Machtig, 24 July 1946: cited in Bowman, De Valera and the Ulster Question, p.263.
60. PROL, DO 35/1228/WX101/154, Stephenson to Machtig, 24 July 1946.
61. PROL, CAB129/13, C.P.(46) 391, memo by Addison, 'Éire and Northern Ireland', 18 October 1946. See also Bowman, De Valera and the Ulster Question, pp.263–4.
62. Irish Times, 8 July 1946.
63. E. MacDermott, Clann na Poblachta (Cork, 1998), pp.29–37.
64. Irish Independent, 18 August 1947.
65. Irish News, 6 July 1947.
66. Interview with McAteer.
67. Irish News, 16 December 1946.
68. PRONI, D1862/B/5, Mulvey papers, Delargy to Mulvey, 6 November 1945.
69. Irish News, 15 November 1946.
70. Ibid., 18 November 1946. Although Clann na Poblachta had no formal links with the Nationalist party, informal contact was made, and MacBride had several meetings with Healy. Interview with MacBride.
71. Irish Independent, 10 March 1947, report of a speech to an APL meeting in Chorlton.
72. PRONI, D1862/D/1, Mulvey papers, MacBride to Mulvey,15 March 1947.
73. For examples of attacks on the Labour government, see speeches by McSparran and Mulvey, Irish News, 10 March 1947, and 17 March 1947.
74. Irish News, 12 April 1947.
75. Ibid., see a press statement by the League, 24 September 1947.
76. Interview with McAteer.
77. Ibid. McAteer confirmed this, adding that the most sympathetic home secretary was the Conservative, Rab Butler. See also Irish News, 24 November 1947.

78. Interview with McAteer.
79. For example, see *Irish News*, 10 March 1947.
80. Ibid., 9 January 1946. McGhee's visit coincided with the visit by McEntee and Longden to Dublin.
81. See a speech by Stokes, *Irish Independent*, 24 November 1947. Such an outcome was most unlikely, considering the antipathy of the NILP towards the Labour party in Éire.
82. See an attack by Lemass on Bing's statement of the previous day, *Irish Independent*, 31 October 1947, and 1 November 1947.
83. *Irish Times*, 1 November 1947.
84. MacDermott, *Clann na Poblachta*, pp.54–5.
85. Bowman, *De Valera and the Ulster Question*, p.265.
86. Interview with McAteer.
87. *Irish Independent*, 22 January 1948. MacBride claimed that partition was not an important issue in the 1948 general election. Interview with MacBride.
88. *Irish Independent*, 27 January 1948.
89. Ibid., 20 January 1948.
90. Ibid., 5 January 1948.
91. Ibid., 29 January 1948.
92. Dáil Debates, 24 June 1947: cited in M. Moynihan (ed.), *Speeches and Statements by Éamon de Valera 1917–73* (Dublin, 1980), pp.494–5.
93. Lee, *Ireland 1912–1985*, p.299.
94. MacDermott, *Clann na Poblachta*, p.64. The Clann suffered from a poor vote management strategy, and this cost them a further nine seats.
95. *Belfast Telegraph*, 19 February 1948.
96. For information on the 1947 negotiations, see SPOI, S14134A, 'British Financial Crisis of 1947', and PROL, CAB130/27/GEN194, 'Discussions with Éire Ministers, June–Sept. 1947'. See also P. Bew and H. Patterson, *Seán Lemass and the Making of Modern Ireland 1945–66* (Dublin, 1982), pp.36–44.
97. SPOI, S13743A, 'Civil Aviation Agreement with the British Government', and PROL, DO 35/1110/A272/7, 'U.K.–Éire Air Service: Suggestion for U.K.–Éire Civil Air Agreement', and DO 35/1110/A272/11, 'U.K.–Éire Air Service: Discussions in Dublin between representatives of Civil Aviation Dept. & Éire Authorities'.
98. PRONI, CAB4/664/10, Cab. Conclus., 18 April 1946.
99. See especially PROL, DO 35/1228/WX101/155, 'Use of the term "Ireland" (Éire) in the Agreement relating to Air Services'. When the agreement was formally signed in October 1946, there were two versions: 'Éire' in the London one and 'Ireland' in the Dublin one. See also PRONI, CAB4/668/19, Cab. Conclus., 16 May 1946, and CAB4/672/6, Cab. Conclus., 5 June 1946.
100. PRONI, CAB4/650/15, Cab. Conclus., 3 January 1946. See also CAB4/613/10, Cab. Conclus., 1 February 1945; CAB9A/37/7 and CAB9A/37/18, 'Lough Erne Drainage'; and SPOI, S13314A, 'River Erne (Proposed H.E.P.)'.
101. PRONI, CAB4/745/13, Cab. Conclus., 26 February 1948. The meeting, which was expected to attract 30,000 people and include a special escort for the tricolour, was banned under the Special Powers Act.
102. NIHC Debates, vol. 32, cols 487–8, and col. 492, 2 March 1948. See also Farrell, *The Orange State*, p.199.
103. HC Debates, 5th series, vol. 448, cols 534–5, 4 March 1948. See also B. Purdie, 'The Friends of Ireland: British Labour and Irish Nationalism, 1945–49', in T. Gallagher and J. O'Connell (eds), *Contemporary Irish Studies* (Manchester, 1983), p.87.
104. *Irish News*, 9 March 1948.
105. HC Debates, 5th series, vol. 448, col. 535, 4 March 1948.
106. PROL, HO 45/22028/919703, 'Northern Ireland Parliament: constitutional position in relation to United Kingdom Parliament', Bing to Morrison, 6 March 1948.
107. Ibid., Maxwell to D. Stephens, a private secretary at the Privy Council Office, 11 March 1948. Stephens also acted as Morrison's personal assistant.
108. Ibid., Morrison to Bing, 16 March 1948.
109. Purdie, 'The Friends of Ireland', p.90.
110. In fact, in his study, *Labour in Power 1945–1951*, Kenneth Morgan made no reference to the Friends of Ireland group.
111. Purdie, 'The Friends of Ireland', pp.88–90.
112. Cited in Bew and Patterson, *Seán Lemass and the Making of Modern Ireland*, p.50.
113. See *Irish Press* supplement 1948: 'With de Valera in America and Australia: world appeal against partition'.

114. Bowman, *De Valera and the Ulster Question*, p.274.
115. H. Delargy, 'The man who outlived his memory', *New Statesman*, 5 September 1975.
116. *Irish Independent*, 16 and 17 February 1948.
117. PROL, FO 371/70175/W180, '1948 Commonwealth Liaison: "Relations with Éire"', Rugby to Foreign Office, 9 January 1948. The Dominions Office had changed its name to the Commonwealth Relations Office on 3 July 1947.
118. PROL, FO 371/70175/W1582, Rugby's report of his first meeting with MacBride, 23 February 1948.
119. *Irish Independent*, 8 March 1948, and 17 March 1948. MacBride later noted that Bevin had shown an interest in the economic unity idea, but Attlee was not in favour. Interview with MacBride.
120. *Belfast Telegraph*, 25 February 1948.
121. Ibid., 30 July 1948.
122. PROL, FO 371/70175/W2757, note on Bevin's meeting with MacBride, 16 April 1948.
123. PROL, FO 371/70175/W3831, note on a discussion between Bevin, Ede and Noel-Baker on Northern Ireland and Éire, 16 June 1948.
124. Ibid., note on a talk between Rugby and MacBride, 4 June 1948.
125. Cited in Bew and Patterson, *Seán Lemass and the Making of Modern Ireland*, p.52.
126. PROL, T 236/776/37/11/6A, 'Éire: United Kingdom trade negotiations', E. Rowe Dutton, a third secretary at the Treasury, to C.G.L. Syers, an assistant under-secretary at the Commonwealth Relations Office, not dated.
127. PROL, CAB130/37/GEN225, discussions at the Treasury on 'Economic Relations with Éire', 22 March 1948.
128. R. Fanning, *The Irish Department of Finance 1922–58* (Dublin, 1978), p.466.
129. See M. McInerney, 'J.A. Costello Remembers', *Irish Times*, 7 September 1967.
130. For example, see a New York speech, 3 April 1948 in Moynihan (ed.), *Speeches and Statements by Éamon de Valera*, pp.497–505.
131. See Dáil Debates, vol. 97, cols 2643–9, 18 July 1945, and vol. 107, cols 22–6, 24 June 1947.
132. PROL, CAB129/29, C.P.(48) 205 annex B, 'Éire and the Commonwealth', note by Rugby, 9 August 1948. See also R. Fanning, 'The response of the London and Belfast Governments to the Declaration of the Republic of Ireland, 1948–49', *International Affairs*, 58, 1 (1982), pp.95–114.
133. Ibid., memo by Noel-Baker, 17 August 1948.
134. Interview with MacBride. In particular, the establishment of diplomatic relations with Argentina provided what MacBride felt was a clear signal that Éire was about to leave the Commonwealth. See also *Irish Press*, 2 August 1948.
135. I. McCabe, *A Diplomatic History of Ireland, 1948–49: The Republic, The Commonwealth and NATO* (Dublin, 1991), pp.42–3.
136. Ibid., pp.34–5.
137. Bowman, *De Valera and the Ulster Question*, pp.268–70.
138. Ibid., pp.273–4. See also NLI, Frank Gallagher papers, Ms 21,273, a short biography which was written with de Valera's co-operation.
139. McCabe, *A Diplomatic History of Ireland, 1948–49*, pp.56–63.
140. PROL, CAB128/13, C.M. 74, 18 November 1948.
141. Fanning, 'The response of the London and Belfast Governments to the Declaration', p.99. For the development of India's relationship with the Commonwealth at this time, see N. Mansergh, *The Commonwealth Experience* (London, 1969), pp.334–6. See also S. Gopal, *Jawaharlal Nehru: A Biography, Volume 2, 1947–56* (London, 1979), pp.45–55. MacBride, who was an acquaintance of Nehru, had discussed this with the Indian leader, and both believed that India, though a republic, could remain in the Commonwealth, but that a similar relationship for Éire was impossible because of its proximity to Britain. Interview with MacBride.
142. Ibid. See also Fanning, 'The response of the London and Belfast Governments to the Declaration', p.103.
143. Dáil Debates, vol. 113, col. 350, 24 November 1948.
144. PROL, CAB128/13, C.M. 67, 28 October 1948.
145. PROL, CAB128/13, C.M. 71, 12 November 1948.
146. HC Debates, 5th series, vol. 457, col. 239, 28 October 1948.
147. Bowman, *De Valera and the Ulster Question*, p.270.
148. Cited in McCabe, *A Diplomatic History of Ireland, 1948–49*, p.64.
149. Dáil Debates, vol. 113, col. 508, 25 November 1948.
150. PROL, CAB128/13, C.M. 74, 18 November 1948.
151. PROL, CAB129/31, C.P.(48) 289, 'Republic of Ireland Bill: Effect on Northern Ireland', note by Attlee on his meeting with Brooke, 7 December 1948. See also Fanning, 'The response of the

London and Belfast Governments to the Declaration', pp.103–4. Towards the end of 1948 Brooke demanded, and was given, sole responsibility for the conduct of the negotiations with Westminster by the Unionist Party Standing Committee. Interview with the Second Viscount Brookeborough.

152. PRONI, CAB4/769/11, Cab. Conclus., 25 November 1948.
153. HC Debates, 5th series, vol. 458, col. 1419, 25 November 1948.
154. Ibid., col. 1417, 25 November 1948.
155. Interview with the Second Viscount Brookeborough.
156. Cited in Fanning, 'The response of the London and Belfast Governments to the Declaration', p.105.
157. PROL, CAB128/13, C.M. 81, 15 December 1948, and CAB130/44/GEN262, 'Working Party on Éire', meeting on 23 December 1948.
158. PROL, CAB130/44/GEN262, meeting on 16 December 1948.
159. Cited in Fanning, 'The response of the London and Belfast Governments to the Declaration', p.106.
160. Ibid., pp.106–7.
161. PROL, CAB130/44/GEN262, meeting on 23 December 1948.
162. PROL, CAB129/32, C.P.(49) 4, 'Ireland: Report of Working party', memo by Attlee, 7 January 1949.
163. PROL, CAB130/44/GEN262, minutes of the meeting, 6 January 1949. The following passage is based on this source unless otherwise stated. See also Fanning, 'The response of the London and Belfast Governments to the Declaration', pp.107–9.
164. PROL, FO 371/76369/W665, '1949 Commonwealth Liaison: UK–Éire relations. Éire and the Commonwealth', memo by P. Mason, an acting counsellor at the Foreign Office, 11 January 1949. In connection with the possible military threat to the province, Brooke also drew attention to the activities of the GOC Northern Ireland Command, whose recent Dublin visit during which he engaged in talks of a 'quasi-political nature' with leading personalities in the South had caused embarrassment in the North. In addition, reservations had also been expressed concerning the arrangement to have a number of Éire army officers trained under the Northern Ireland Command, because while Brooke had no objection to the training of Éire officers by the army, he suggested that in the existing circumstances this should not take place in Northern Ireland.
165. PROL, CAB129/32, C.P.(49) 5, memo by Attlee, 'Ireland', 10 January 1949.
166. PROL, CAB128/15, C.M. 1, 12 January 1949. See also B. Purdie, 'The 1949 British Cabinet Papers and Partition', Belfast Bulletin, no. 9, pp.9–12.
167. PROL, CAB128/15, C.M. 1, 12 January 1949.
168. PROL, CAB130/44/GEN262, meeting on 18 January 1949.
169. See Fanning, 'The response of the London and Belfast Governments to the Declaration', pp.111–12.
170. PROL, FO 371/76369/W270, note of Boland's meeting with Brook and Liesching, 7 January 1949.
171. PROL, CAB129/33, C.P.(49) 45 Appendix I, note by Rugby, 'The Anti-Partition Campaign', 21 March 1949.
172. Ibid., extract from Rugby memo, 29 November 1949.
173. PRONI, CAB9B/267/6, 'Éire Propaganda and Political Interference in N. Ireland', Brooke to Attlee, 18 February 1949.
174. PROL, CAB129/33, C. P.(49) 48, memo by Ede and Noel-Baker, 'Ireland: The Anti-Partition Campaign', 4 March 1949.
175. PROL, CAB128/15, C.M. 18, 8 March 1949.
176. PRONI, CAB9B/276/6, Attlee to Brooke, 21 March 1949.
177. PROL, CAB128/15, C.M. 18, 8 March 1949.
178. Interview with the Second Viscount Brookeborough. For example, see HC Debates, 5th series, vol. 461, col. 190, 8 February 1949.
179. PRONI, CAB9B/276/6, McWilliam, an assistant cabinet secretary at Stormont, to Ross, 21 February 1949, and Brooke to Savory, 28 February 1949.
180. Ibid., Attlee to Brooke, 21 March 1949.
181. PROL, FO371/76371/W2248, '1949 Commonwealth Liaison: "UK–Éire relations. Éire and the Commonwealth"', Laithwaite to Syers, 12 April 1949. Although most of his diplomatic career had been spent in India, Laithwaite, a past pupil of Clongowes and a first cousin of the IRA leader, Ernie O'Malley, was an astute observer of Irish politics.
182. Ibid., Noel-Baker to Attlee, 12 April 1949.
183. PRONI, see file, CAB9B/267/4, 'Repeal of External Relations Act: miscellaneous correspondence 1949'.
184. PROL, FO 371/76371/W2402, report by Laithwaite of the celebrations in Dublin marking the declaration of the republic.
185. PROL, FO 371/76369/W270, note on Boland's meeting with Brook and Liesching, 7 January 1949.

186. See Bowman, *De Valera and the Ulster Question*, p.271.
187. PROL, FO 371/76371/W2744, note on meeting between Laithwaite and Boland, 8 May 1949. MacBride later claimed that his response stemmed from his lack of surprise at the Labour government's action in restating its policy on partition. Interview with MacBride. For the content of the Irish *aide-memoire*, see SPOI, S14528, 'British "Ireland Bill, 1949": Attitude of Ireland towards'. The file also contains a memo by MacBride in which he described the Ireland Act as 'an unnecessary and provocative act that can only be destructive', 18 May 1949. MacBride's main criticism of the bill, however, centred on the Labour government's failure to inform Dublin of its intentions. He claimed that an agreement had been reached whereby Westminster would consult with the authorities in Dublin before the introduction of any new bill, but in the event the Inter-Party government only received twenty-four hours warning. Lord Rugby later described this as a 'smokescreen' by MacBride: see PROL, DO 35/3974/X2638/62 Part III, 'The Ireland Bill, 1949', Rugby to Liesching, 4 June 1949.
188. PROL, FO 371/76371/W2744, Laithwaite telegram, 14 May 1949.
189. Ibid., Laithwaite telegram, 9 May 1949. Indeed, the United Kingdom representative had already expressed his opinion to Liesching, stating that he did not believe that there was any 'real feeling in this country' for the anti-British agitation following the publication of the Ireland Bill: see DO 35/3972/X2638/62 Part II, 'The Ireland Bill, 1949', Laithwaite to Liesching, 7 May 1949.
190. PROL, FO 371/76371/W2744, note on MacBride's meeting with Bevin and Noel-Baker, 9 May 1949. See also Fanning, 'The response of the London and Belfast Governments to the Declaration', pp.113–14.
191. HC Debates, 5th series, vol. 464, cols 1956–68, 11 May 1949.
192. Ibid., Delargy speech, cols 1889–94, and McGhee speech, cols 1905–7, 11 May 1949.
193. PRONI, CAB4/784/12, Cab. Conclus., 28 April 1949.
194. HC Debates, 5th series, vol. 465, cols 167–8, 16 May 1949. This figure included two tellers. Among the fifty-six were three Liberals: W. Roberts, T.L. Horabin and Lady Megan Lloyd George.
195. They were F. Beswick (Uxbridge), W.R. Blyton (Houghton-le-Spring), J.P.W. Mallalieu (Huddersfield), R.J. Mellish (Rotherhithe) and G.H.R. Rogers (North Kensington).
196. PROL, CAB128/15, C.M. 34, 12 May 1949.
197. *Irish News*, 8 June 1949.
198. PRONI, CAB4/788/7, notes on the proposed discussion of the Ireland Act in the Northern Ireland Parliament, 3 June 1949, and CAB4/788/14, Cab. Conclus., 3 June 1949.
199. *Belfast Newsletter*, 29 September 1948.
200. Ibid., 4 May 1949.
201. *Irish Times*, 5 May 1949.
202. PROL, DO 35/3974/X2638/62 Part III. Laithwaite continued to insist that there was little public interest in the Ireland Act which had developed into a party issue in the South. A secret appeal by MacBride for party unity on the issue had been spurned by Fianna Fáil, Laithwaite to Liesching, 9 June 1949.
203. PROL, FO 371/76372/W6488, '1949 Commonwealth Liaison: "UK–Éire relations. Éire and the Commonwealth"', Laithwaite to Liesching, 23 November 1949.
204. Ibid., W5298, Laithwaite's review of Irish affairs, April–September 1949, 30 September 1949.
205. Ibid., W3432, report by Laithwaite, 9 June 1949. At this time informed observers in the South, such as Thomas Johnson, the former Labour leader who had learned his politics as a trade unionist in Belfast, were highly critical of the anti-partition campaign. In fact, Johnson described it as having 'undeniably adverse results to date': see NLI, Johnson papers, Ms 17,200, note by Johnson, 8 October 1949.
206. Interview with the Second Viscount Brookeborough.
207. B. Lynn, 'The Irish Anti-Partition League and the political realities of partition, 1945–9', *Irish Historical Studies*, xxxiv, 135 (May 2005), p.330. A total of £46,000 was raised.
208. MacBride has claimed that the idea for a united effort on partition initially took de Valera by surprise, and he found himself in something of a dilemma in deciding if Fianna Fáil should enter into such a partnership. Interview with MacBride.
209. B. Lynn, *Holding the Ground: The Nationalist Party in Northern Ireland, 1945–72* (Aldershot, 1997), pp.46–7.
210. Cited in Farrell, *The Orange State*, p.184.
211. Harbinson, *A History of the NILP*, pp.209–11.
212. Farrell, *The Orange State*, p.193.
213. *Belfast Newsletter*, 18 December 1948. See also Farrell, *The Orange State*, p.194.
214. *Belfast Newsletter*, 20 December 1948. See also Farrell, *The Orange State*, pp.193–4.
215. Farrell, *The Orange State*, p.194.

216. Interview with the Second Viscount Brookeborough.
217. Lynn, *Holding the Ground*, pp.89–93.
218. PRONI, D2991, Healy papers, see Éamon Phoenix's introduction to the Healy calendar, 'The Nationalist Party in Northern Ireland, 1921–55', p.15.
219. McAteer had informed the Costello government that he did not expect equal privileges to other TDs, and that all he wanted was 'a token attendance – right of audience or something of the sort which gives little administrative difficulty'. See UCD Arch. Dept., McGilligan papers, P35b/146, McAteer to MacBride, 5 March 1949. The government asked Lavery, the attorney general, to consider McAteer's proposal, but nothing was done. MacBride, however, was keen to admit northerners to the Senate, and Denis Ireland of the Ulster Union Club was appointed by the Costello government in 1948. Interview with MacBride.
220. Bowman, *De Valera and the Ulster Question*, pp.283–5. De Valera had also angered the APL leaders by refusing to give financial assistance to the League when he was in government. MacBride later claimed that de Valera was to some extent disappointed with the APL, because it did not identify itself more closely with Fianna Fáil. Interview with MacBride.
221. Interview with McAteer. See also Farrell, *The Orange State*, pp.195–6.
222. Interviews with Doherty and McAteer.
223. PRONI, CAB4/833/3, memo by Brooke, 3 January 1951.
224. PRONI, CAB4/834/5A, memo by McCleery, 8 January 1951. In fact, the Stormont ministers spent two days in Dublin.
225. Interview with MacBride.
226. For a full discussion of this complex issue, see J.H. Whyte, *Church and State in Modern Ireland 1923–1979* (Dublin, 1980), pp.196–273.
227. Ibid., p.232.
228. See W.A. Carson, *Ulster and the Irish Republic* (Belfast, 1957).
229. Interview with MacBride. MacBride believed that Browne was motivated by personal ambition, and his intention was to bring down the Costello administration and take MacBride's place as leader of Clann na Poblachta.
230. Interviews with McAteer and MacBride.
231. Bowman, *De Valera and the Ulster Question*, p.279.
232. For example, see a letter written by Eric D. O'Gorman, an ex-British army officer who lived in County Cavan and was interested in partition, PRONI, D2991/A, Healy papers, O'Gorman to Healy, 22 May 1951.
233. Ibid., MacBride to Healy, 26 February 1953.
234. MacBride was only elected on the last count, and he eventually lost his seat at the 1957 general election. Clann na Poblachta struggled on until 1965, when it was formally wound up. By then it had only one TD, John Tully of Cavan, and he continued to sit as an Independent TD until 1969: see MacDermott, *Clann na Poblachta*, pp.162–7. By the time the party was wound up MacBride had developed other interests and had become the secretary general of the International Commission of Jurists. Interview with MacBride.
235. At the time MacBride often thought that Fine Gael was actually ahead of Clann na Poblachta on the partition issue. Interview with MacBride.
236. For example, see a report of a Costello speech on the Ireland Act which Laithwaite described as 'deplorable' and a reminder of 'Hitler's harangues', PROL, DO 35/3974/X2638/62 Part III, Laithwaite to Liesching, 9 June 1949.
237. Indeed, at one stage MacBride, who had an excellent personal relationship with the Labour prime minister, was told by Attlee that if he could ever secure Churchill's agreement to any change in Northern Ireland's status, Attlee would be an enthusiastic supporter. Interview with MacBride.
238. During his period as minister for external affairs, MacBride certainly believed that the Labour government was heavily influenced by leading civil servants. Interview with MacBride.
239. PROL, DO 35/3987/X2638/134, 'Meeting between the Secretary of State for Commonwealth Relations with Minister for External Affairs in the Republic of Ireland, on 14 February 1952', memo by R.R. Sedgwick, an assistant under-secretary at the Commonwealth Relations Office, 27 February 1952. It was also apparent that since 1951 there had been a general feeling of stagnation on the partition issue.
240. PROL, see file DO 35/3988/X2638/136, 'Meeting between Lord Pakenham, Éamon de Valera and Mr. Aiken, in Dublin, May 1952'. Morrison's conference statement, 21 February 1950, is included in this file.

Conclusion

Labour's surprise victory at the 1945 British general election had caused apprehension among cabinet ministers at Stormont, but after a brief period of uncertainty an excellent relationship was established between the governments in London and Belfast. That there should have been this initial period of uncertainty was not surprising, because the Unionist government was bound to encounter some problems in dealing with a new administration which had such a radical social and economic programme. During this early period the government at Stormont came under attack from a section of Unionist backbenchers for allowing Westminster to legislate on transferred services. Many of the wartime economic controls were continued, and new measures which appeared to signal the beginning of much greater state intervention in the economy were introduced. This led to a call for increased devolution as a small group within the party, including Nugent, the minister of commerce, advocated dominion status to give the provincial government virtual independence in dealing with local affairs. Brooke, however, was able to contain the campaign for dominion status, which really only attracted support from members of the province's business community. It was this group that felt most threatened by what they regarded as increased state control of the economy.

The majority of the Unionist cabinet were quick to appreciate the substantial financial benefits that would accrue to Northern Ireland if Stormont followed a policy of close co-operation with the Labour administration. In particular, Sinclair typified the Unionist government's pragmatic attitude to Stormont–Westminster relations in the immediate post-war period, as he consistently urged co-operation with the Labour government. As minister of finance, Sinclair knew that Labour was much more benevolent and flexible in its dealings with the province than any previous Westminster administration. The most positive consequence of Stormont's close financial relationship with the Labour government was the implementation of the welfare state in Northern Ireland on parallel lines to Great Britain. This strengthened the Unionist party's position in the province at a time when its hold on the Protestant working-class vote appeared to be slipping. Yet simultaneously, it increased Unionist dependence on Westminster in a way that was to raise future problems. Indeed, Stormont's adoption of Labour's welfare legislation programme, together with the province's low level of unemployment in the early post-war years, reduced the appeal of the NILP, which had achieved relative success in the 1945 Northern Ireland general election by concentrating its campaign on social and economic issues. Opposition from within the Unionist party to the introduction of the new welfare measures was minimal, and it was not related to the dominion status campaign. The main criticism of Stormont's welfare legislation centred on the activities of the Housing Trust. Grant had created the Trust before the Labour government came to power in an attempt to alleviate the province's serious housing difficulties, but the new government agency lacked the necessary support from the Ministry of Finance. It was treated with suspicion by the Unionist-dominated local authorities, which consistently abused their powers by allocating houses on political grounds. The Housing Trust was attacked because of its detrimental effect on private enterprise building, but opponents never linked the establishment of the new body to the Labour administration at Westminster, and criticism was reserved for the Stormont department responsible.

When the extensive social and economic changes that took place in the province during the 1945–51 period are considered, it is remarkable to note the lack of friction between the Stormont and Westminster administrations, and this bears testament to the harmonious relations existing between the Ministry of Finance in Belfast and the Treasury in London. The Labour government's benevolent treatment provided substantial benefits for the province's population and consequently strengthened Ulster Unionism, which was able to claim credit for the implementation of the Beveridge report. Furthermore, Labour's financial assistance enabled Unionist leaders to focus on the contrast in standards of living between Northern Ireland and Éire, when reaffirming their opposition to any alteration of the province's constitutional position. This was significant, because it carried more weight at Westminster than the traditional Unionist arguments against unification, such as the fear of Protestant civil and religious liberties being abrogated in a Catholic-dominated state.

Still, the close financial relationship which Stormont enjoyed with Westminster in the post-war period should not obscure the uneasiness occasionally felt by the Unionist government during Labour's term of office. In return for the generous financial assistance, the Unionist government had to submit to increased Treasury scrutiny and control which effectively reduced its capacity for independent action on some transferred services. Accordingly, Brooke and his colleagues took every opportunity to emphasize the Belfast government's independence and flexibility in local matters, as they highlighted the differences in Stormont and Westminster legislation. Northern Ireland's separate Agriculture Act, the retention of the Trade Disputes Act and the differences in Stormont's welfare legislation were all cited in public speeches by Unionist cabinet ministers as examples of the regional government's ability to act independently of the Labour administration at Westminster. The embarrassment which the Unionist government occasionally felt when subjected to criticism for being too closely wedded to a socialist administration in London proved insignificant once the advantages of close co-operation with Westminster were considered. On taking office, Brooke and his colleagues realized quickly that radical social and economic changes were inevitable in the immediate post-war period whatever party was in power at Westminster. As these changes did not pose any threat to Unionist domination in the province, they were accepted and used to the party's advantage. In their important work Bew, Gibbon and Patterson have emphasized 'the progressive de-insularisation of the economy, politics and ideology in Northern Ireland during and immediately after the Second World War', and have noted how this 'de-insularisation' was 'weathered' by the Brooke government.[1] One important consequence of this 'de-insularisation' was that the Unionist government was forced to attach much greater significance to the handling of its relations with Westminster, and it appeared as though Labour's 1945 election victory would make the Unionist administration's task more difficult. After some initial problems, however, the Northern Ireland government realized that its fears had been exaggerated, and confidence in the Attlee government soon increased. During the early stages of the war, therefore, a new phase in Stormont–Westminster relations had begun, and the formation of a Labour government in 1945 made little impact on the pattern that had already been established.

Labour's record on what the Unionists liked to emphasize as the crucial question of partition also delighted the Brooke government. The border issue provided the clearest example of the delicate link between Belfast, London and Dublin, because events such as Éire's withdrawal from the Commonwealth had serious repercussions not only for Dublin–Westminster relations but also for Stormont–Westminster relations. Éire's neutrality in the Second World War had entrenched partition and damaged relations with London, while dramatically improving Stormont–Westminster relations. The impact of neutrality largely dictated the Labour government's policy on partition in the post-war period, as the relevant cabinet discussions emphasized the lessons of the war and revealed the desire to retain control of Northern Ireland as part of Britain's defence requirements. Perhaps more interesting, though less significant in the minds of Labour cabinet ministers, was the determination to prevent the province's constitutional position becoming a serious issue in party politics at Westminster, because experience had shown that only the Conservative party would benefit from such an outcome. Consequently, Labour's policy was to play down the border question, ensuring that Northern Ireland did not become an issue, while simultaneously working quietly to restore harmonious relations with Dublin in less controversial areas, such as trade, which might have advantages for both countries. In more general terms, it is possible to fit Northern Ireland into the wider context of the Labour government's colonial and foreign policies. There were numerous examples of how 'national and imperial self-interest, especially in relation to defence and to the needs of the British economy' helped to determine Labour's colonial policy, while the non-appearance of a distinctly socialist foreign policy probably made it easier for Labour to support the existence of a right-wing government in Northern Ireland.[2]

The end of the Second World War saw the Unionist government basking in Churchill's praise for Northern Ireland's war contribution and very confident on the question of partition. This confidence, however, was slightly shaken, firstly by Labour's unexpected election victory, and then, more importantly, by the formation of the Friends of Ireland group within the parliamentary Labour party. The immediate consequence of these developments was Stormont's adoption of a more cautious line on the border, and this assisted the Labour government in its attempts to repair the wartime damage to its relations with Dublin. Yet the Unionists never altered their approach to the province's constitutional position, and once it was clear that the Friends of Ireland group was unable to influence Labour party policy, they vigorously attacked the APL and the anti-partition propaganda emanating from the South. In the immediate post-war period the border issue remained dormant in Éire until interest was stirred by the activities of Clann na Poblachta. Before this, de Valera had usually been content to ignore the continuation of partition. He seemed resigned to the fact that the events of the war had consolidated the North's position within the United Kingdom, and there was, therefore, no likelihood of any progress on partition in the foreseeable future. In addition, neutrality had damaged Éire's international standing, particularly in the United States, and this made it more difficult for the Dublin government to obtain international sympathy for action on partition. Although the border was of minor importance in comparison to other political issues in Éire, the early impact made by Clann na Poblachta forced the other parties to take an active interest in the issue. Each of the parties realized that they had nothing to lose by adopting a firm anti-partition stance, whereas they all feared that a conciliatory approach could result in a loss of electoral support. While it was apparent that the border was relatively unimportant in southern politics, none of the parties felt confident enough to ignore the issue. Consequently, they chose to play safe by taking an uncompromising line on partition. This fear of being left behind on the partition issue was clearly illustrated following the Inter-Party government's decision to withdraw from the Commonwealth. Every political leader in Éire realized that the electorate was pre-occupied with social and economic issues, but they recognized that there was latent, emotional feeling on the border question that might be exploited by one of the other parties.

Éire's secession from the Commonwealth and the subsequent Westminster legislation focused attention in Dublin, Belfast and, unusually, in London on the issue of partition, and this had significant repercussions for relations in the triangle. The Costello administration's decision to establish a republic, and the escalation in anti-partition rhetoric which followed, presented the Unionist leadership with the opportunity to coax the Labour government into taking a positive line in support of partition. In effect, the Inter-Party government's hasty action had resulted in damage to Dublin–Westminster relations and further improvement in Stormont–Westminster relations. The events of 1948–9 confirmed Westminster's suspicions that the Dublin government was not serious in its desire to see the border removed, and that the partition issue should primarily be regarded as a party political issue within the twenty-six counties. While this was too cynical a judgement on the motives of Éire's political leaders in focusing attention on the border question, there is no doubt that their actions strengthened the government in Belfast. Costello and his colleagues had acted impulsively, and their actions highlighted the absence of any clear strategy on the border question. That they should have been without a clear strategy on partition was not surprising, because every political leader in the South recognized that a government in Dublin lacked the capacity to exert any real influence on the issue. Yet when the chain of events was set in motion, none of them felt they could appear inactive on the border question. Consequently, as the anti-partition rhetoric became more aggressive, southern politicians actually contributed to the further consolidation of the Unionist government's position. Therefore, while the ending of partition remained a long-term, if vague, objective of every party in the South, it was clear that the issue was only of minor importance. An indication of this was the refusal by both the Fianna Fáil and the Inter-Party governments to admit Nationalist MPs to the Dáil and the general reluctance of all the parties in the South to work closely with the northern Nationalists. This was emphasized in the 1948 Éire general election when, despite frantic efforts, the northern Nationalists found all the southern parties unwilling to commit themselves to specific proposals on the border issue.[3]

In the 1949 Northern Ireland general election the Nationalists did receive financial assistance from Éire, but the impact of Éire's indirect involvement, together with the intensification of anti-partition propaganda emanating from the South, enabled the Unionists to concentrate more than ever on the province's constitutional position during the election campaign. The Unionist government's call for unity on the fundamental question of the province's constitutional position dealt a major blow to the NILP and left the Belfast government in its strongest position since partition. The Ireland Act which followed the election was regarded by the Unionist government as a very significant expression of Labour's support for Northern Ireland. The Unionists had always doubted any Westminster government's resolution to stand firm on partition in the face of extreme pressure from Dublin, but they seized the opportunity presented by Costello's action in withdrawing from the Commonwealth to commit Westminster on the issue. Unionists had harboured an instinctive suspicion of all London governments from the establishment of the Northern Ireland state, and it was ironic that trust in a Westminster government reached its peak in the immediate post-war years, as initial apprehension about Labour's commitment to the province gave way to genuine confidence. Of course, subsequent events, culminating in the proroguing of Stormont in 1972 by a Conservative administration, demonstrated the fragility of the Ireland Act. At the time of its passage, however, it was regarded in Northern Ireland as a significant gesture by the Attlee government, which carried considerable moral force. In effect, the only change made by the 1949 legislation occurred in the minds of Unionists and Nationalists, as both groups believed that partition had been further entrenched. There was no change of policy in London, because the Ireland Act simply confirmed what the Westminster government of the day was doing anyway – supporting partition. References to the fact that Northern Ireland should be defended, if necessary, against itself indicated that Westminster's self interest was the primary influence on its policy of perpetuating partition. Still, the obstinacy of the Unionist government and Westminster's contention that partition was a matter for the Irish themselves to decide enabled the Labour administration to conceal the real motives behind its strategy on Northern Ireland. This was deemed necessary not only for the conduct of its relations with Dublin, but also to defend British policy should the issue be raised internationally. It is surely no coincidence that

Westminster's general attitude to Northern Ireland changed as the retention of the province became increasingly irrelevant to Britain's defence requirements.

Although there was little likelihood of disagreement between Belfast and London over the border question, the Stormont administration's treatment of the Catholic minority did appear to offer the potential for dissension between the Unionist and Labour governments. The Dublin government also had a crucial role to play here, because it regarded itself as the defender of the minority's interests in the province. During 1938, the de Valera administration had some success in highlighting the minority's grievances. Although its prompting had led to an investigation by both the Home Office and the Dominions Office of alleged maladministration and discrimination by the Stormont authorities, Westminster rejected intervention to implement changes, even though it had reservations about the Unionist government's handling of sectarian issues. The events of 1938 merely confirmed the established convention of Westminster leaving the regional government to manage its own affairs without interference from London. When Attlee took office, however, the Unionist authorities could not be certain that the new Labour administration would refrain from using its sovereign powers under the 1920 act to interfere in Northern Ireland's internal affairs.

In his excellent survey of the post-war Labour government, Kenneth Morgan has summarized Labour's attitude to the government in Belfast: 'Nothing whatsoever was done to overhaul the system of government in Northern Ireland, for all its proven gerrymandering by the Protestant Unionist ascendancy.' Later in the book, he emphasized that Labour 'generally ignored Northern Ireland and left it to its Unionist rulers at Stormont'.[4] Indeed, Morgan's striking lack of reference to the province provides an indication of just how insignificant an issue Northern Ireland was for the Attlee government. Yet his assessment of Labour's impact on Northern Ireland, while being generally correct, requires some qualification, because there were several instances during its early period in office when the application of discreet pressure by the new administration succeeded in forcing Stormont to modify its attitude on particular issues. This was most clearly seen in the controversy over the Education Bill and in Stormont's handling of the Éire labour issue. The latter also provided an example of Éire's involvement in Northern Ireland affairs and demonstrated how rash action by the cabinet in Belfast could influence Westminster's relations with Dublin. In the controversy surrounding both the Education Bill and the Éire labour issue, however, the new Labour administration was merely echoing the concern expressed by the Churchill government. The fact that the Labour government was successful in promoting a more moderate approach by Stormont on these two issues was not because the Attlee administration was prepared to exert a greater degree of pressure, but rather the Unionist government's fears that Labour would be more likely to interfere directly in the province's affairs, using its supreme powers under section 75 of the Government of Ireland Act. Therefore, the Unionist government's action in awarding increased grants to Catholic schools and its decision to shelve proposals for the expulsion of large numbers of Éire workers during 1945–6 should be regarded as attempts to prevent possible confrontation with Westminster.

Nevertheless, the Brooke government's fears of the new administration's intentions proved unfounded, because the Labour cabinet never considered assuming responsibility for Northern Ireland's affairs. The minor successes that it enjoyed were attributable to the Unionist government's fears that if it did not respond to discreet ministerial pressure, Westminster intervention could follow. The Labour government preferred, however, to see responsibility for administering Northern Ireland's affairs remain with Stormont. Despite reminders from the Bevanite, Geoffrey Bing, and other Friends of Ireland MPs that Westminster should exercise its sovereignty to overhaul the system of government in the province, Attlee and his cabinet colleagues never even considered using such powers. Although the Unionist government's treatment of the minority occasionally caused some embarrassment at Westminster, it was never regarded as a major problem and, consequently, the Labour administration could continue to remain aloof. For the most part, therefore, Northern Ireland was off the political radar at Westminster because, minor concerns apart, the Northern Ireland state was from Westminster's perspective a qualified success. For all its faults Stormont kept the Northern Ireland problem off the agenda at Westminster, and, in spite of the efforts made by the Friends of Ireland, Labour was very anxious to keep its distance from the devolved administration. In his biography of Jim Callaghan, Morgan subsequently confirmed Labour's determination to stay out of Northern Ireland affairs: 'Attlee took care not to intervene in Northern Ireland matters in 1945–51, and neither did Wilson in 1964.'[5]

In its early dealings with the new Labour government, the role played by Northern Ireland's 'friends' at the Home Office proved significant. Since the 1920 act, the Home Office had interpreted its responsibilities regarding Northern Ireland in a very narrow light, and instead of acting in a supervisory capacity to safeguard the rights of the Catholic minority its major concern was to ensure that harmonious relations with the Unionist government were maintained.[6]

When the possibility of disagreement with Labour ministers emerged after 1945, Brooke felt confident that he could rely on officials at the Home Office to defend the province's interests. Moreover, the presence of a high-ranking Stormont civil servant at the Home Office proved invaluable. His advice enabled the Brooke government to take steps to avoid potential clashes with Labour during its early period in office. It was ironic that the Unionist government should have an official stationed in Whitehall to report back to Belfast on the activities of the government in London, while no such facility was available to the authorities at Westminster. Again this was an indication of how little importance successive Westminster governments attached to Northern Ireland affairs, and it was not until 1969 that Oliver Wright, an official from the Foreign Office, was dispatched to Stormont with the task of advising the Unionist leadership on British policy.[7] When Westminster intervention did come in the late 1960s, it was primarily because the media had stirred the British public's consciousness and focused international attention on the Northern Ireland problem.

Yet the post-war Labour government had recognized the deficiencies of the Unionist administration, and as it refused to take steps to remedy the situation, it must bear some of the responsibility for the subsequent problems. The unprecedented financial assistance which Northern Ireland received from the Labour administration presented Westminster with the opportunity to negotiate concessions from Stormont on the most controversial issues affecting the minority, but the opportunity was not taken. Of course, any success in promoting fairer government in the province would have depended on Stormont's reaction to this kind of pressure, but it was likely that the application of sustained, but subtle, pressure from Westminster could have achieved some reward. In fact, something of a precedent linking financial assistance from central government to the administration of Northern Ireland's internal affairs had been established in December 1925–January 1926. The then prime minister, Stanley Baldwin, had managed to secure the release of all political prisoners held in the province by threatening to withhold Treasury assistance for the financing of the Ulster Special Constabulary.[8] Without persistent cajoling by Westminster there was no possibility of the Unionist government reforming itself. Although individual members of the Unionist cabinet, notably Brian Maginess, were keen to improve the province's image in Great Britain, the majority of cabinet ministers never saw the need to make any concessions in order to appease the authorities in London.

On the surface, Captain Terence O'Neill's accession to power in 1963 seemed to offer the possibility of a change by Stormont in its approach to relations with the minority. His meetings with his southern counterpart, Seán Lemass, and his attempts to improve community relations created the impression that O'Neill would usher in a new era of more normal politics in Northern Ireland. Yet the changes that did take place during O'Neill's first few years in office were merely cosmetic. The gestures made in his personal crusade to build bridges between the two communities proved meaningless, and the major reforms anticipated by some sections of the nationalist community were not forthcoming. When proposals for these reforms were belatedly advanced in the late 1960s, there was considerable speculation that pressure from the Wilson government at Westminster had been responsible for altering traditional Unionist strategy in relation to the minority. Wilson's presence as leader of the Labour administration certainly added fuel to this speculation. With a large Irish population in his Merseyside constituency it was well known that Wilson subscribed to James Connolly's ideas on nationalism and socialism in Ireland, and the Labour prime minister never concealed his sympathy for a united Ireland. In addition to confronting a hostile prime minister at Westminster who favoured unification, O'Neill's economic policy made Stormont more dependent than ever on Treasury support. In these circumstances the Unionist leader believed that his government was likely to come under pressure from Westminster to implement the reforms sought by the minority. Yet O'Neill probably misjudged Labour's intentions on Northern Ireland, because the Wilson government, like the earlier Attlee administration, did not exert financial pressure to prod Stormont into implementing political reforms. Wilson himself was by no means consistent in his approach to the Northern Ireland problem. More significantly, he lacked support in the cabinet for any initiative on Northern Ireland. The Labour leader's preoccupation with the province has to be regarded as one of his attempts at statesmanship – Vietnam and Rhodesia provided other failures –

because he believed that the achievement of a solution to the Northern Ireland problem would bring him the 'historical immortality' which he desperately sought.[9]

Therefore, before the troubles erupted in 1968 Wilson's approach to the Northern Ireland problem was essentially a personal contribution that did not involve his cabinet colleagues. The other members of the Labour cabinet favoured the continuation of the established Westminster policy of staying out of Northern Ireland's affairs. Consequently, Wilson's ideas were not allowed to influence his government's determination to avoid any form of confrontation with Stormont. It was true that reform was urged on the Unionist government at a series of meetings that he and his home secretary, Roy Jenkins, had with O'Neill,[10] but there was no evidence that Westminster had yet formulated a strategy aimed at goading the Belfast administration into action. It was not until after the outbreak of violence in 1968 that the prospect of Westminster using her supreme powers to implement reforms was even threatened.[11] Other cabinet ministers have confirmed Westminster's reluctance to assume responsibility for Northern Ireland affairs, even when it was clear that the situation was deteriorating rapidly and the regional government was losing control. Richard Crossman, the secretary of state for social services, indicated that the cabinet was dejected by O'Neill's setback at the 1969 Northern Ireland general election, because he had been 'the man we were relying on in Northern Ireland to do our job of dragging Ulster out of its eighteenth-century Catholic–Protestant conflict'.[12] Meanwhile, Barbara Castle, the secretary of state for transport, reflected her colleagues' thinking on Northern Ireland shortly after the 1969 election, when she expressed the view that Westminster should try to exert some influence 'while getting embroiled as little as possible'.[13] Of course, the minister with overall responsibility for Northern Ireland, Roy Jenkins, who had just published his biography of Herbert Asquith in 1964, was acutely aware of the damage that involvement in Irish affairs could cause to opponents of the Tory party at Westminster.[14] Accordingly, even when it was clear that the Unionists had lost control of the situation in the province and intervention by Westminster was inevitable, the Labour cabinet determined that its policy should be based on the minimum intervention possible.[15] Indeed, in his analysis of Tony Benn's detailed diary record for the crucial cabinet meeting of 19 August 1969, Andrew Marr has emphasized the Labour government's 'astonishingly confused and faltering attempt, shortly after the troops had gone in, to understand what had happened'. Jim Callaghan, who was now home secretary, having exchanged office with Jenkins on 30 November 1967, and Denis Healey, secretary of state for defence, were united in their determination to avoid responsibility for implementing changes in Northern Ireland, warning that this must be left to the Unionist government. Callaghan's other concern, as Benn records, was his fear that Unionists would exploit the situation in conjunction with the Tories to undermine Labour's position at Westminster.[16]

Wilson apart, therefore, the Labour cabinet was determined to see responsibility for handling the province's affairs remain at Stormont. In effect, Labour's approach to Northern Ireland in the 1960s was precisely the same as it had been in the 1945–51 period. Yet O'Neill had taken risks to conciliate opinion in Britain, because he feared the prospect of intervention by the Wilson government. The Labour leader's personal interest in Ireland and his well-known sympathy for Irish unity contributed to O'Neill's anxiety, but the Stormont premier's ignorance of the lack of support, and indeed interest, which the rest of the cabinet expressed in Wilson's designs on Ireland led him to exaggerate the potential dangers facing the Unionist government. The existence of a civil rights pressure group, the Campaign for Democracy in Ulster (CDU), which was formed in June 1965 by Labour backbenchers, increased O'Neill's worries that some form of interference from Westminster to promote political reforms was likely to be forthcoming. The CDU, a more vociferous body than the old Friends of Ireland group, could on occasion rely on the support of 100 Labour MPs, and it was given more impetus by Gerry Fitt's return for West Belfast in the 1966 Westminster general election.[17] In the changing circumstances confronting the Unionist government, O'Neill probably assumed that the CDU would arouse the Labour government's interest in what was happening in Northern Ireland. Certainly, Fitt's criticism of the Unionist government's shortcomings made an immediate impact at Westminster, and he became the bridge between sympathetic Labour backbenchers and the province's minority community. But perhaps more significantly, O'Neill's major concern was that his new economic policy, which was totally dependent on substantial Treasury support, left the Unionist government vulnerable to the use of financial pressure by a hostile government at Westminster, demanding the introduction of political reforms. The Unionist leader's response was to take pre-emptive action by implementing what he considered to be the minimum amount of progressive measures necessary to prevent Westminster interference. Again, comparisons can be made with the Attlee era, when Brooke attempted to improve the image of the state by making a few minor concessions to the minority in order to prevent possible intervention by the Labour government. The shock, and more significantly, the scale of Labour's victory in 1945 had raised doubts among Unionist leaders about the Conservative party's ability to regain office in the foreseeable future, and it was the comprehensive nature of Labour's election triumph that was responsible for creating the initial apprehension and concern over the development of Stormont–Westminster relations in the immediate post-war period.[18] In the 1960s, however, the threat of intervention appeared more real to O'Neill, even though Labour had no intention of deviating from the non-intervention policy of previous Westminster governments. His anticipation of a Labour administration meddling in the province's affairs resulted in Stormont making concessionary gestures, designed to placate the government in London, which eventually split the Unionist party.

Thus between 1945 and 1969, the two main parties at Westminster shared a desire to prevent Ireland becoming the divisive issue in British politics which it had been after the First World War. If anything, Labour was the more determined to avoid interference in Northern Ireland, but successive Unionist leaders failed to see this. As long as the Unionist government was able to maintain stability in the province, the authorities at Westminster were content to overlook the deficiencies of the local administration in relation to its treatment of the Catholic minority. It was not until the imposition of direct rule by a Conservative government in 1972 that Westminster finally, if reluctantly, took full responsibility for administering the province, but the continued perseverance with Unionist rule between 1969 and 1972 merely aggravated an already deteriorating situation.

The essential difference between the 1945–51 period and the 1964–70 period was the effective organization of the nationalist community in the North during the 1960s. Labour's return to power in 1964 and the formation of the CDU created the conditions for the establishment of the Civil Rights movement which was able to draw on almost universal Catholic support within Northern Ireland.[19] Inspiration for the new reform group came not from Dublin, where de Valera's successor, Seán Lemass, contributed nothing to the debate on the North,[20] but from the American civil rights movement led by Martin Luther King. The effective political mobilization of the minority by the Civil Rights movement contrasted sharply with the lack of direction and decisive leadership given by the APL during the 1945–51 period. An additional important difference was that the Civil Rights movement formulated specific demands, and it was clear that the movement was seeking reforms within the existing political system in Northern Ireland. Previously, the APL had concentrated on the complete overthrow of the system of government in Northern Ireland rather than on securing reforms within that system. While northern Nationalists had been painfully slow to come to terms with the fact that the population in the South was less than enthusiastic about unification, their decision to focus on specific grievances and frequently ignore Stormont by appealing directly to the authorities at Westminster provided the Catholic minority with real leverage for the first time since partition. Ultimately, this led directly to the formation of the Social Democratic and Labour Party (SDLP) in August 1970, and, unlike its predecessor, the SDLP enjoyed solid support in both rural and urban areas.

Yet the emergence of this more effective Catholic voice was more a product than a cause of O'Neill's reform agenda. The Unionist leader's initiative was a manoeuvre to outflank a resurgent NILP and, more significantly, an attempt to appease the largely disinterested authorities at Westminster, whom he wrongly suspected were poised to embark on a crusade on behalf of the North's minority community. Successive Unionist leaders had, of course, conducted relations with London with the disadvantage of a guilty conscience linked to the treatment of the Catholic minority, but this had been more of a feature of O'Neill's premiership than it had been of Brooke's. By the mid-1960s, moreover, Unionists had frittered away the advantages of the Attlee years. The 1945–51 period was marked by a growing level of trust in the London government, as Unionists overcame their natural suspicion of Westminster. O'Neill, however, was nervous of a Labour administration whose sympathies, he judged incorrectly, lay with the nationalist community. Unfortunately, O'Neill, who lacked Brooke's common touch and political skills, was unable to convince the Unionist party of the merits of his liberal reform programme. It had been Stormont's fear of Westminster intervention, therefore, that led directly to the disintegration of Unionism and indirectly to the collapse of the Stormont regime.

NOTES

1. Bew et al., *Northern Ireland 1921–1996*, p.82 and p.106.
2. For a summary of Labour's foreign and colonial policies, see Morgan, *Labour in Power*, pp.188–277.
3. Bowman, *De Valera and the Ulster Question*, p.265.
4. Morgan, *Labour in Power*, p.56 and pp.199–200.
5. K.O. Morgan, *Callaghan: A Life* (Oxford, 1997), p.345.
6. See Canning, *British Policy towards Ireland*, p.52. For a summary of the Northern Ireland functions of the home secretary in the early 1950s, see F. Newsam, *The Home Office* (London, 1955), pp.168–70.
7. J. Callaghan, *A House Divided: The Dilemma of Northern Ireland* (London, 1973), p.66.
8. See Buckland, *The Factory of Grievances*, pp.211–12.
9. Bew et al., *Northern Ireland 1921–1996*, pp.163–4. For more recent comment on the Wilson government's relationship with the Stormont administration, see G. Warner, 'Putting pressure on O'Neill', *Irish Studies Review*, 13, 1 (2005), and G.K. Peatling, 'Unionist divisions, the onset of the Northern Ireland conflict, and pressures on O'Neill reconsidered', *Irish Studies Review*, 15, 1 (2007).
10. J.H. Wilson, *The Labour Government, 1964–70: A Personal Record* (London, 1971), p.270 and p.670.
11. Ibid., p.672.
12. R.H.S. Crossman, *The Diaries of a Cabinet Minister: Secretary of State for Social Services, 1968–70 Volume 3* (London, 1977), p.381.
13. B. Castle, *The Castle Diaries 1964–70* (London, 1984), p.640.
14. See R. Jenkins, *Asquith* (London, 1964).
15. Bew et al., *Northern Ireland 1921–1996*, p.165.
16. *The Independent*, 14 December 1987.
17. T. Hennessey, *Northern Ireland: The Origins of the Troubles* (Dublin, 2005), p.111.
18. Interview with the Second Viscount Brookeborough.
19. For the formation of the Civil Rights movement, see B. Purdie, *Politics in the Streets: The Origins of the Civil Rights Movement in Northern Ireland* (Belfast, 1990), pp.82–97.
20. Bew and Patterson, *Seán Lemass and the Making of Modern Ireland*, p.11.

Bibliography

PRIMARY SOURCES

Public Record Office, London (PROL)

I <u>Cabinet papers</u>:

CAB 65	War Cabinet Conclusions, 1939–45
CAB 66	War Cabinet memoranda and supporting papers, 1939–45
CAB128	Cabinet Conclusions, 1945–52
CAB129	Cabinet memoranda and supporting papers, 1945–52
CAB130–134	Cabinet Committees: minutes and memoranda

II <u>Departmental papers</u>:

DO 35	Dominions Office and Commonwealth Relations Office: Original Correspondence
DO 35/893/X11/123	U.K.–Ireland Political and Constitutional Relations: Treatment of the Catholic minority in N. Ireland, March 1938
DO 35/893/X11/251	U.K.–Éire Political and Constitutional Relations: Allegations made by Éire Govt. as to the maltreatment of the minority in Northern Ireland, arising out of the Partition Question, November 1938
DO 35/1110/A272/7	U.K.–Éire Air Service: Suggestion for U.K.–Éire Civil Air Agreement
DO 35/1110/A272/11	U.K.–Éire Air Service: Discussions in Dublin between representatives of Civil Aviation Dept. & Eire Authorities
DO 35/1228/WX101/1/69	Political and Constitutional Relations: Irish–American Relations

DO 35/1228/WX101/1/95   Friends of Ireland – Request by Sir J. Maffey for information, 1943–1946

DO 35/1228/WX101/137A   Political and Constitutional Relations: Addison's conversation with Dulanty re Partition

DO 35/1228/WX101/146   Political and Constitutional Relations: Conversation between Lord Addison and Sir Basil Brooke, May 1946

DO 35/1228/WX101/152   Political and Constitutional Relations: Éire's position in the Commonwealth. Mr. de Valera's Statement, June 1946

DO 35/1228/WX101/154   Political and Constitutional Relations: General Questions with de Valera

DO 35/1228/WX101/155   Political and Constitutional Relations: Use of the term 'IRELAND' (ÉIRE) in the Agreement relating to Air Services

DO 35/1229/WX123/2   Labour – Conditions of residence in the six Irish Counties, 1943–1946

DO 35/1229/WX123/5   Discarding of Éire Labour in N. Ireland, 1943–1946

DO 35/1231/WX168/4   Trade Negotiations General: 'Northern Ireland's Projection in the U.S.'

DO 35/3972/X2638/62   Republic of Ireland: Political and Constitutional Relations: Parts I, II and III 'The Ireland Bill, 1949!'

DO 35/3987/X2638/134   Meeting between the Secretary of State for Commonwealth Relations with Minister for External Affairs in the Republic of Ireland, on 14 February 1952

DO 35/3988/X2638/136   Meeting between Lord Pakenham, Éamon de Valera and Mr Aiken, in Dublin, May 1952

DO 35/3996/X2650/1   Meeting between United Kingdom Ambassador to Republic of Ireland, Sir W.C. Hankinson and Éamon de Valera in Dublin, December 1951

FO 371	Foreign Office General Correspondence: Political. Each of the following major files contain a large number of sub files marked 'W' in the notes
FO 371/70175	1948 Commonwealth Liaison: 'Relations with Eire'
FO 371/76369	1949 Commonwealth Liaison: 'UK–Éire relations'. 'Éire and the Commonwealth'
FO 371/76370	1949 Commonwealth Liaison: 'UK–Éire relations'. 'Éire and the Commonwealth'
FO 371/76371	1949 Commonwealth Liaison: 'UK–Éire relations'. 'Éire and the Commonwealth'
FO 371/76372	1949 Commonwealth Liaison: 'UK–Éire relations'. 'Éire and the Commonwealth'
HO 45	Home Office: Original Correspondence
HO 45/21265/916605	Trade Disputes and Trade Union Act (Northern Ireland), 1927: repeal rejected by Northern Ireland House of Commons. Imperial Parliament not empowered to intervene, 1946–1947
HO 45/21985/900542	Infiltration and Immigration into Northern Ireland: control, 1942–1948
HO 45/21996/915158	Elections and Franchise Bill (Northern Ireland) 1946; Elections and Franchise (Amendment) Act (Northern Ireland) 1948, 1945–1948
HO 45/22028/919703	Northern Ireland Parliament: constitutional position in relation to United Kingdom Parliament, 1948
PREM 4	Prime Minister's Office
PREM 4/53/6	Teeling to Churchill, 25 April 1944
LAB 43	Private Office Papers
LAB 43/28	C.R. Attlee CH, MP: personal minute about unemployment in Northern Ireland, 1950

T 160	Treasury Finance
T 160/l194/14464/043/03	Northern Ireland: Memoranda on financial relations with Great Britain
T 160/1277/F18624	Post-War Financial Relations with the Government of Northern Ireland, 1943–1944
T 160/1327/F14464/043/04	Post-war reconstruction, 1941–1945
T 233	Treasury Home Finance Division
T 233/170/9/28/03	Papers leading up to the Northern Ireland Health Services Bill
T 233/172/13/9/01	Papers leading up to the Industries Development Bill, 1945
T 233/173/13/9/02	Northern Ireland: Treatment as a Development Area, 1946–1947
T 233/l74/9/469/05A	(1) Northern Ireland Comprehensive Reinsurance Agreement, 1946 (2) Papers leading up to Unemployment and Family Allowances (N.I.) Agreement Act 1946, ratifying agreement, 1946–1947
T 233/440/9/270/01A	Financial Arrangements: submission of supplementary estimates: expenditure over £50,000: annual agreements of Northern Ireland budget 1939–1949
T 233/441/9/270/01B	Financial arrangements; submission of supplementary estimates: expenditure over £50,000: annual agreements of Northern Ireland budget, 1949–1950
T 233/442/9/332/01	Northern Ireland Housing Trust: formation and financing, 1944–1950
T 236	Treasury Overseas Finance Division
T 236/776/37/11/6A	Éire: 'United Kingdom trade negotiations', 1948

Public Record Office of Northern Ireland (PRONI)

I <u>Cabinet papers</u>:

CAB4/1–861	Cabinet	Conclusions and memoranda, 1921–1951

II <u>Cabinet papers relating to</u>

Ministry of Finance:

CAB9A/3/5   Financial position, January 1933–November 1937

7/58   Visit of the Right Hon. and Mrs Herbert Morrison, 1946

30/4   Miscellaneous financial matters, 1937–43

37/7, 18   Drainage: Memoranda and correspondence concerning Lough Erne drainage, 1933–45

61/2   Shipbuilding questions, 1932–45

95/5   Local Government (Finance) Bill: derating. Report of Committee on Finance of Local Authorities 1942–50

Ministry of Home Affairs:

CAB9B/125/1   Equal franchise: Representation of the People Bill. Correspondence and memoranda concerning the laws governing elections in N. Ireland, 1928–37

125/2   Equal franchise: Representation of the People Bill. Correspondence and memoranda on the question of the inclusion of N. Ireland within the direct scope of the new Westminster franchise bill, 1924–8

125/3   Correspondence and memoranda regarding the franchise in N. Ireland, 1942–9

258   Proposed Ministry of Health and Reconstruction, 1942–44

264	Correspondence with Attorney General concerning the playing of the National Anthem, 1946–7
267/4	Repeal of External Relations Act: miscellaneous correspondence, 1949
267/6	Éire propaganda and Political Interference in N. Ireland, 1949

Ministry of Labour:

CAB9C/1/7	Unemployment Insurance Agreement, January 1928–June 1948
13/3	Unemployment relief schemes and grants, 1939–43
22/2	Arbitration in strikes and industrial disputes, 1943–7
27/2	National Health Insurance Bills, 1939–49
47/2	Infiltration of Éire workers into N.I., 1934–43
47/3	Infiltration of Éire workers into N.I., 1946–7
51/2 Part 1	Post-war employment, 1945
51/2 Part 2	Post-war employment, 1945–7

Ministry of Education:

CAB9D/1/10	Religious education in schools, 1942–4
1/11	Religious education in schools, 1942–4
1/12	Educational reconstruction, 1944–5
1/15	Education Act: proposals for new legislation, 1946
1/16	Religious education in schools, 1946
1/17	Education Act, 1946–51

Ministry of Agriculture:

CAB9E/150/1	Correspondence and memoranda in connection with the Agriculture Bill, 1946–7

Ministry of Commerce:

CAB9F/ 165/4 — Correspondence about the broadcast 'The Week in Stormont', 1945–6

188/1 — Correspondence relating to industrial development in Northern Ireland and measures taken by the British Government in relation to same, 1949–50

Ministry of Health and Local Government:

CAB9N/4/11 — Correspondence, memoranda, etc. re rural housing, 1945–50

III Departmental papers:

COM7 — Post-War Planning Committee

State Paper Office of Ireland (SPOI)

Cabinet minutes and memoranda in the Taoiseach's Department:

S 5750/5 — Northern Prisoners: Representations made to Sir James Craig, July 1943

S 11306 — Censorship of mails between the six and the twenty-six counties, August 1941

S 11582A — Transfer to Great Britain of Irish workers waiting to migrate, March 1941

S 12432 N.I. — (conscription), May 1941

S 12533 — Discussions with Great Britain: Establishment of Inter-Departmental Committee, July 1941

S 12939 — Admission of Evacuees from Derry, August 1942

S 13314A — River Erne: proposed Hydro–electric scheme, August 1943

S 13710A — Internment

S 13743A — Civil Aviation Agreement with the British Government, 1945

S 14134C   Taoiseach's paper for meeting with British Prime
                  Minister and other British ministers, London, 19
                  September 1947

S 14333A   Conference of Dominion Prime Ministers, London,
                  1948–June 1951

S 14528   British 'Ireland Bill, 1949': Attitude of Ireland towards
                  others

Private Papers

Frank Gallagher papers
National Library of Ireland, Dublin

Cahir Healy papers
Public Record Office of Northern Ireland, Belfast

Thomas Johnson papers
National Library of Ireland, Dublin

Frank MacDermot papers
Public Record Office of Ireland, Dublin

Patrick McGilligan papers
Archives Department, University College Dublin

Anthony Mulvey papers
Public Record Office of Northern Ireland, Belfast

W.B. Spender papers
Public Record Office of Northern Ireland, Belfast

Interviews and Correspondence

Lord Brookeborough (Second Viscount)
James Callaghan
James Doherty
Seán MacBride
Edward McAteer
I also conducted several interviews with a prominent figure in the Orange Order
who was close to the Unionist party organization for much of the post-war period.
He has asked that he remain anonymous.

Newspapers

Belfast Newsletter

Belfast Telegraph
Cork Examiner
Irish Independent
Irish News
Irish Times
Northern Whig
The Times

SECONDARY SOURCES

Akenson, D. H. *Education and Enmity: The Control of Schooling in Northern Ireland, 1920–50* (Newton Abbot, 1973).

Allen, K. *Fianna Fáil and Irish Labour: 1926 to the Present* (London, 1997).

Arthur, P. *Special Relationships: Britain, Ireland and the Northern Ireland Problem* (Belfast, 2000).

Barrington, R. *Health, Medicine and Politics in Ireland 1900–1970* (Dublin, 1970).

Barton, B. *Brookeborough: The Making of a Prime Minister* (Belfast, 1988).

Barton, B. 'Relations between Westminster and Stormont during the Attlee pre-miership', *Irish Political Studies*, vol. 7 (1992).

Barton, B. *Northern Ireland in the Second World War* (Belfast, 1995).

Barton, B. 'Northern Ireland, 1925–39', in J.R. Hill (ed.), *A New History of Ireland: Vol. VII, Ireland, 1921–1984* (Oxford, 2003), pp.161–98.

Barton, B. 'Northern Ireland, 1939–45', in J.R. Hill (ed.), *A New History of Ireland: Vol. VII, Ireland, 1921–1984* (Oxford, 2003), pp.199–234.

Bew, P. 'The political history of Northern Ireland since partition: The prospects for North–South co-operation', in A.F. Heath, R. Breen and C.T. Whelan (eds), *Ireland North and South: Perspectives from Social Science* (Oxford, 1999), pp.401–18.

Bew, P. and Patterson, H. *Seán Lemass and the Making of Modern Ireland 1945–66* (Dublin, 1982).

Bew, P., Darwin, K. and Gillespie, G. *Passion and Prejudice: Nationalist–Unionist Conflict in Ulster in the 1930s and the Founding of the Irish Association* (Belfast, 1993).

Bew, P., Gibbon, P. and Patterson, H. *Northern Ireland 1921–1996: Political Forces and Social Classes* (London, 1996).

Birrell, W.D. and Murie, A.S. *Policy and Government in Northern Ireland: Lessons of Devolution* (Dublin, 1980).

Birrell, W.D., Hillyard, P.A.R., Murie, A.S. and Roche, D.J.D. *Housing in Northern Ireland* (London, 1971).

Black, R.D.C. *Economic Thought and the Irish Question* (Cambridge, 1960).

Blake, J.W. *Northern Ireland in the Second World War* (Belfast, 1956).

Blanshard, P. *The Irish and Catholic Power: An American Interpretation* (Boston, 1953).

Bleakley, D.W. *Faulkner: Conflict and Compromise in Irish Politics* (London, 1974).

Boal, F.W. and Douglas, J.N.H. (eds), *Integration and Division: Geographical Perspectives on the Northern Ireland Problem* (London, 1982).

Bowman, J. *De Valera and the Ulster Question 1917–1973* (Oxford, 1982).

Boyce, D.G. and O'Day, A. (eds), *Englishmen and Irish Troubles: British Public Opinion and the Making of Irish Policy 1918–1922* (Cambridge, 1972).

Boyce, D.G. *The Making of Modern Irish History: Revisionism and the Revisionist Controversy* (London, 1996).

Brady, C. (ed.), *Interpreting Irish History: The Debate on Historical Revisionism* (Dublin, 1994).

Brand, C.F. *The British Labour Party* (California, 1964).

Brennan, R. *Ireland Standing Firm: My Wartime Mission in Washington and Éamon de Valera – A Memoir* (Dublin, 2002).

Brewer, J.D. and Higgins, G.I. *Anti-Catholicism in Northern Ireland 1600–1998: The Mote and the Beam* (London, 1998).

Bromage, M.C. *De Valera and the March of a Nation* (London, 1956).

Bromage, M.C. *Churchill and Ireland* (Indiana, 1964).

Browne, N. *Against the Tide* (Dublin, 1986).

Brown, T. *Ireland: A Social and Cultural History 1922–79* (London, 1981).

Buckland, P. *Irish Unionism 2: Ulster Unionism and the Origins of Northern Ireland, 1886 to 1922* (Dublin, 1973).

Buckland, P. *The Factory of Grievances: Devolved Government in Northern Ireland 1921–1939* (Dublin, 1979).

Buckland, P. *James Craig* (Dublin, 1980).

Buckland, P. *A History of Northern Ireland* (Dublin, 1981).

Budge, I. and O'Leary, C. *Belfast: Approach to Crisis: A Study of Belfast Politics 1613–1970* (London, 1973).

Bullock, A. *The Life and Times of Ernest Bevin* (2 Vols) (London, 1967).

Callaghan, J.A. *House Divided: The Dilemma of Northern Ireland* (London, 1973).

Calvert, H.G. *Constitutional Law in Northern Ireland: A Study in Regional Government* (London, 1968).

Campbell, T.J. *Fifty Years of Ulster 1890–1940* (Belfast, 1941).

Canning, P. *British Policy towards Ireland 1921–1941* (Oxford, 1985).

Carroll, J.T. *Ireland in the War Years 1939–45* (Newton Abbot, 1975).

Carson, W.A. *Ulster and the Irish Republic* (Belfast, 1957).

Carter, C.J. *The Shamrock and the Swastika: German Espionage in Ireland in World War II* (California, 1977).

Castle, B. *The Castle Diaries 1964–70* (London, 1984).

Chester, D.N. (ed.), *The Organisation of British Central Government 1914–56* (London, 1957).

Chubb, B. *Cabinet Government in Ireland* (Dublin, 1974).

Chubb, B. *The Government and Politics of Ireland* (Oxford, 1974).

Cochrane, F. '"Meddling at the crossroads": The decline and fall of Terence O'Neill within the unionist community', in R. English and G. Walker (eds), *Unionism in Modern Ireland: New Perspectives on Politics and Culture* (London, 1996), pp.148–68.

Cohan, A.S. *The Irish Political Elite* (Dublin, 1972).

Coogan, T.P. *Ireland Since the Rising* (London, 1966).

Coogan, T.P. *The IRA* (Glasgow, 1980).

Coogan, T.P. *De Valera: Long Fellow, Long Shadow* (London, 1995).

Cook, C. and Peele, G. (eds), *The Politics of Reappraisal: 1918–1939* (London, 1975).

Cook, J.I. 'Financial relations between the exchequers of the United Kingdom and Northern Ireland', in D.G. Neill (ed.), *Devolution of Government: The Experiment in Northern Ireland* (London, 1953), pp.18–44.

Cooney. J. *John Charles McQuaid: Ruler of Catholic Ireland* (Dublin, 1999).

Corkey, W. *Episode in the History of Protestant Ulster, 1923–47: History of the Struggle of the Protestant Community to maintain Bible Instruction in their Schools* (Belfast, not dated).

Cowling, M. *The Impact of Labour 1920–1924* (Cambridge, 1971).

Cradden T. *Trade Unionism, Socialism and Partition: The Labour Movement in Northern Ireland 1939–53* (Belfast, 1993).

Cronin, M. *The Blueshirts and Irish Politics* (Dublin, 1997).

Crossman, R.H.S. *The Diaries of a Cabinet Minister: Secretary of State for Social Services, 1968–70 vol. 3* (London, 1977).

Cruise O'Brien, C. *States of Ireland* (London, 1972).

Cunningham, M.J. *British Government Policy in Northern Ireland, 1969–1989: Its Nature and Execution* (London, 1991).

Curran, J.M. *The Birth of the Irish Free State 1921–1923* (Alabama, 1980).

Daly, M.E. (ed.), *County and Town: One Hundred Years of Local Government in Ireland* (Dublin, 2001).

Darby, J. *Conflict in Northern Ireland: The Development of a Polarised Community* (Dublin, 1976).

Darby, J. (ed.), *Northern Ireland: The Background to the Conflict* (Belfast, 1983).

Delaney, E. *Demography, State and Society: Irish Migration to Britain, 1921–1971* (Liverpool, 2000).

De Paor, L. *Divided Ulster* (Harmondsworth, 1970).

Devlin, P. *Yes We Have No Bananas: Outdoor Relief in Belfast 1920–39* (Belfast, 1981).

Ditch, J. *Social Policy in Northern Ireland 1939–1950* (Aldershot, 1998).

Doherty, G. and Keogh, D. (eds), *De Valera's Irelands* (Cork, 2002).

Doherty, R. *Irish Men and Women in the Second World War* (Dublin, 1999).

Donohue, L.K. 'Regulating Northern Ireland: The Special Powers Acts 1922–1972', *Historical Journal*, 41, 4 (1988).

Donoughue, B. and Jones, G.W. *Herbert Morrison: Portrait of a Politician* (London, 2001).

Douglas, J.N.H. and Boal, F.W. 'The Northern Ireland problem', in F.W. Boal and J.N.H. Douglas (eds), *Integration and Division: Geographical Perspectives on the Northern Ireland Problem* (London, 1982), pp.1–18.

Dudley Edwards, O. *The Sins of our Fathers* (Dublin, 1970).

Dudley Edwards, R. *The Faithful Tribe: An Intimate Portrait of the Loyal Institution* (London, 1999).

Duggan, J.P. *Neutral Ireland and the Third Reich* (Dublin, 1985).

Duggan, J.P. *Herr Hempel at the German Legation in Dublin 1937–1945* (Dublin, 2003).

Dunphy, R. *The Making of Fianna Fáil Power in Ireland 1923–1948* (Oxford, 1995).

Dwyer, T.R. *Irish Neutraility and the USA 1939–47* (Dublin, 1977).

Dwyer, T.R. *Éamon de Valera* (Dublin, 1980).

Dwyer, T.R. *De Valera's Finest Hour: In Search of National Independence 1932 –1959* (Cork, 1982).

Dwyer, T.R. 'Éamon de Valera and the partition question', in J.P. O'Carroll and J.A. Murphy (eds), *De Valera and his Times* (Cork, 1983), pp.74–91.

Elliott, M. *The Catholics of Ulster: A History* (London, 2000).

Elliott, S. *Northern Ireland Parliamentary Election Results 1921–1972* (Chichester, 1973).

English, R. *Radicals and the Republic: Socialist Republicanism in the Irish Free State 1925–1937* (Oxford, 1994).

English, R. *Armed Struggle: A History of the IRA* (London, 2003).

Ervine, St-J. *Craigavon: Ulsterman* (London, 1949).

Fallon, B. *An Age of Innocence: Irish Culture 1930–1960* (Dublin, 1998).

Falls, C. 'Northern Ireland and the defence of the British Isles', in T. Wilson (ed.), *Ulster Under Home Rule* (Oxford, 1955), pp.79–90.

Fanning, R. *The Irish Department of Finance 1922–58* (Dublin, 1978).

Fanning, R. *Independent Ireland* (Dublin, 1983).

Fanning, R. 'The rule of order: Éamon de Valera and the IRA, 1923–1940', in J.P. O'Carroll and J.A. Murphy (eds), *De Valera and his Times* (Cork, 1983), pp.160–72.

Farrell, B. *Chairman or Chief? The Role of the Taoiseach in Irish Government* (Dublin, 1971).

Farrell, M. *Northern Ireland: The Orange State* (London, 1976).

Farrell, M. *Arming the Protestants: The Formation of the Ulster Special Constabulary and the Royal Ulster Constabulary 1920–27* (London, 1983).

Farren, S. *The Politics of Irish Education 1920–65* (Belfast, 1995).

Faulkner, B. *Memoirs of a Statesman* (London, 1978).

Feiling, K. *The Life of Neville Chamberlain* (London, 1946).

Ferriter, D. *The Transformation of Ireland 1900–2000* (London, 2004).

Fisk, R. *In Time of War: Ireland, Ulster and the Price of Neutrality 1939–45* (London, 1983).

Fitzgerald, G. *Towards a New Ireland* (London, 1972).

Fitzpatrick, D. *The Two Irelands 1912–1939* (Oxford, 1998).

Foster, R.F. *Modern Ireland 1600–1972* (London, 1988).

Freer, L.G. P. 'Recent tendencies in Northern Ireland administration', in D.G. Neill (ed.), *Devolution of Government: The Experiment in Northern Ireland* (London, 1953), pp.57–85.

Gailey, A. *Crying in the Wilderness. Jack Sayers: A Liberal Editor in Ulster 1939–1969* (Belfast, 1995).

Gallagher, F. *The Indivisible Island* (London, 1957).

Gallagher, T. and O'Connell J. (eds), *Contemporary Irish Studies* (Manchester, 1983).

Garner, J. *The Commonwealth Office* (London, 1978).

Garvin, T. *The Evolution of Irish Nationalist Politics* (Dublin, 1981).

Gaughan, J.A. *Thomas Johnson* (Naas, 1980).

Gibbon, P. *The Origins of Ulster Unionism: The Formation of Popular Protestant Politics and Ideology in Nineteenth-Century Ireland* (Manchester, 1975).

Gilbert, M. *Winston S. Churchill: Finest Hour vol. vi* (London, 1983).

Girvin, B. *The Emergency: Neutral Ireland 1939–45* (London, 1996).

Girvin, B. and Roberts, G. (eds), *Ireland and the Second World War: Politics, Society and Remembrance* (Dublin, 2000).

Gopal, S. *Jawaharlal Nehru: A Biography vol. 2, 1947–56* (London, 1979).

Gray, T. *The Lost Years: The Emergency in Ireland 1939–1945* (London, 1998).

Gwynn, D.R. *The History of Partition, 1912–25* (Dublin, 1950).

Hanley, B. *The IRA, 1926–1936* (Dublin, 2002).

Harbinson, J.F. *The Ulster Unionist Party, 1882–1973: Its Development and Organisation* (Belfast, 1973).

Harkness, D.W. *The Restless Dominion: The Irish Free State and the British Commonwealth of Nations, 1921–31* (London, 1969).

Harkness, D.W. 'England's Irish Question', in C. Cook and G. Peele (eds), *The Politics of Reappraisal 1918–1939* (London, 1975), pp.39–63.

Harkness, D.W. *Northern Ireland Since 1920* (Dublin, 1983).

Harris, K. *Attlee* (London, 1982).

Harris, M. *The Catholic Church and the Foundation of the Northern Irish State 1912–1930* (Cork, 1993).

Harrison, H. *Ulster and the British Empire 1939* (London, 1939).

Harrison, H. *The Neutrality of Ireland: Why it was Inevitable* (London, 1940).

Hayes, M.N. 'Some aspects of local government in Northern Ireland', in E. Rhodes (ed.), *Public Administration in Northern Ireland* (Londonderry, 1967), pp.77–99.

Hayes McCoy, G.A. 'Irish defence policy, 1938–51', in K.B. Nowlan and T.D. Williams (eds), *Ireland in the War Years and After* (Dublin, 1969), pp.39–51.

Heath, A.F., Breen, R. and Whelan, C.T. (eds), *Ireland North and South: Perspectives from Social Science* (Oxford, 1999).

Hennessey, T. *Northern Ireland: The Origins of the Troubles* (Dublin, 2005).

Hepburn, A.C. (ed.), *The Conflict of Nationality in Modern Ireland* (London, 1980).

Hepburn, A.C. *A Past Apart: Studies in the History of Catholic Belfast 1850–1950* (Belfast, 1996).

Hepburn, A.C. *Ireland 1900–25, Volume 2* (Newtownards, 1998).

Heslinga, M.W. *The Irish Border as a Cultural Divide: A Contribution to the Study of Regionalism in the British Isles* (Assen, 1962).

Hezlet, A. *The 'B' Specials: A History of the Ulster Special Constabulary* (London, 1973).

Hill, J.R. (ed.), *A New History of Ireland: Vol. VII, Ireland, 1921–1984* (Oxford, 2003).

Horgan, J. *Noel Browne: Passionate Outsider* (Dublin, 2000).

Horgan, S. *Seán Lemass: The Enigmatic Patriot* (Dublin, 1997).

Hull, P.H. *The Irish Triangle: Conflict in Northern Ireland* (Princeton, 1976).

Hyam, P. and Martin, G.W. (eds), *Reappraisals in British Imperial History 1921–49* (London, 1975).

Isles, K.S. and Cuthbert, N. 'Ulster's economic structure' and 'Economic policy', in T. Wilson (ed.), *Ulster Under Home Rule* (Oxford, 1955), pp.91–114 and pp.137–82.

Isles, K.S. and Cuthbert, N. *An Economic Survey of Northern Ireland* (Belfast, 1957).

Jackson, A. 'Unionist history', *Irish Review*, no.7 (autumn 1989).

Jackson, A. 'Unionist myths, 1912–85', *Past and Present*, no.136 (1992).

Jackson, A. *Ireland 1798–1998: Politics and War* (Oxford, 1999).

Jackson, A. 'Local government in Northern Ireland, 1920–1973', in M.E. Daly (ed.), *County and Town: One Hundred Years of Local Government in Ireland* (Dublin, 2001), pp.56–76.

Jackson, A. *Home Rule: An Irish History 1800–2000* (London, 2003).

Jackson, T.A. *Ireland Her Own: An Outline History of the Irish Struggle* (London, 1976).

Jenkins, R. *Asquith* (London, 1964).

Jenkins, R. *Churchill* (London, 2001).

Johnson, D.S. 'Northern Ireland as a problem in the Economic War 1932–38', *Irish Historical Studies*, xxii, 86 (September 1980).

Johnson, D.S. 'Partition and Cross-Border Trade', in P. Roebuck (ed.), *Plantation to Partition: Essays in Ulster History in Honour of J.L. McCracken* (Belfast, 1981), pp.229–46.

Johnson, D.S. 'The Northern Ireland economy 1914–1939', in L. Kennedy and P. Ollerenshaw (eds), *An Economic and Social History of Ulster 1820–1939* (Manchester, 1985), pp.184–223.

Keatinge, P. *The Formulation of Irish Foreign Policy* (Dublin, 1973).

Keatinge, P. *A Place among the Nations: Issues in Irish Foreign Policy* (Dublin, 1978).

Kennedy, D. 'Catholics in Northern Ireland, 1926–1939', in F. MacManus (ed.), *The Years of the Great Test* (Cork, 1967), pp.138–49.

Kennedy, D. 'Ulster during the war and after', in K.B. Nowlan and T.D. Williams (eds), *Ireland in the War Years and After* (Dublin, 1969), pp.52–66.

Kennedy, D. *The Widening Gulf: Northern Attitudes to the Independent Irish State 1919–1949* (Belfast, 1988).

Kennedy, L. and Ollerenshaw, P. (eds), *An Economic and Social History of Ulster 1820–1939* (Manchester, 1985).

Keogh, D. 'De Valera, Hitler and the visit of condolence, May 1945', *History Ireland*, 5, 3 (autumn 1987).

Keogh, D. 'Éamon de Valera and Hitler: An Examination of international reaction to the visit to the German minister, May 1945', *Irish Studies in International Affairs*, 3, 1 (1989).

Keogh, D. *Twentieth-Century Ireland: Nation and State* (Dublin, 1994).

Keogh, D. *Ireland and the Vatican: The Diplomacy of Church–State Relations, 1922–60* (Cork, 1995).

Keogh, D. and O'Driscoll, M. (eds), *Ireland in World War Two: Neutrality and Survival* (Cork, 2004).

Lawlor, S. *Britain and Ireland 1914–23* (Dublin, 1983).

Lawrence, R.J. *The Government of Northern Ireland: Public Finance and Public Services 1921–1964* (Oxford, 1965).

Lee, J.J. (ed.), *Ireland 1945–70* (Dublin, 1979).

Lee, J.J. *Ireland 1912–1985: Politics and Society* (Cambridge, 1989).

Longford, Earl of and McHardy, A. *Ulster* (London, 1981).

Longford, Earl of and O'Neill, T.P. *Éamon de Valera* (Dublin, 1970).

Loughlin, J. *Ulster Unionism and British National Identity Since 1885* (London, 1995).

Loughlin, J. *The Ulster Question Since 1945* (London, 1998).

Lynch, J. *Speeches and Statements on Irish Unity, Northern Ireland and Anglo-Irish Relations* (Dublin, 1971).

Lynch, P. 'The Irish economy since the war, 1945–51', in K.B. Nowlan and T.D. Williams (eds), *Ireland in the War Years and After* (Dublin, 1969), pp.185–200.

Lynn, B. *Holding the Ground: The Nationalist Party in Northern Ireland 1945–72* (Aldershot, 1997).

Lynn, B. 'The Irish Anti-Partition League and the political realities of partition, 1945–9', *Irish Historical Studies*, xxxiv, 135 (May 2005).

Lyons, F.S.L. 'The years of readjustment, 1945–51', in K.B. Nowlan and T.D. Williams (eds), *Ireland in the War Years and After* (Dublin, 1969), pp.67–79.

Lyons, F.S.L. *Ireland Since the Famine* (London, 1973).

Lyons, F.S.L. *Culture and Anarchy in Ireland 1890–1939* (Oxford, 1979).

Macardle, D. *The Irish Republic* (London, 1968).

MacDermott, E. *Clann na Poblachta* (Cork, 1998).

MacDonagh, O. *Ireland: The Union and its Aftermath* (London, 1977).

MacDonald, M. *Titans and Others* (London, 1972).

Mackintosh, J.P. *The British Cabinet* (London, 1962).

Mackintosh, J.P. *The Devolution of Power* (London, 1968).

MacManus, F. (ed.), *The Years of the Great Test 1926–39* (Cork, 1967).

Magee, J. *Northern Ireland: Crisis and Conflict* (London, 1974).

Maltby, A. *The Government of Northern Ireland: A Catalogue and Breviate of Parliamentary Papers* (Shannon, 1974).

Manning, M. *The Blueshirts* (Dublin, 1970).

Manning, M. *Irish Political Parties: An Introduction* (Dublin, 1972).

Manning, M. *James Dillon: A Biography* (Dublin, 1999).

Mansergh, N. *The Government of Northern Ireland: A Study in Devolution* (London, 1936).

Mansergh, N. *Survey of British Commonwealth Affairs: Problems of External Policy 1931–39 vol. 2* (Oxford, 1952).

Mansergh, N. *Documents and Speeches on British Commonwealth Affairs 1931–1952, Volumes I & II* (Oxford, 1953).

Mansergh, N. *The Commonwealth Experience* (London, 1969).

Mansergh, N. 'Irish foreign policy, 1945–51', in K.B. Nowlan and T.D. Williams (eds), *Ireland in the War Years and After* (Dublin, 1969), pp.134–46.

Mansergh, N. *The Unresolved Question: The Anglo-Irish Settlement and its Undoing, 1912–1972* (London, 1991).

Martin, G.W. 'The Irish Free State and the Evolution of the Commonwealth, 1921–49', in Hyam and Martin (eds), *Reappraisals in British Imperial History 1921–49* (London, 1975), pp.201–23.

McAllister, I. *The Northern Ireland Social and Democratic Labour Party* (London, 1977).

McAllister, I. 'Political parties: Traditional and modern', in Darby (ed.), *Northern Ireland: The Background to the Conflict* (Belfast, 1983), pp.61–78.

McBirney, A.M. 'Stormont–Westminster relations', in E. Rhodes (ed.), *Public Administration in Northern Ireland* (Londonderry, 1967), pp.7–13.

McCabe, I. *A Diplomatic History of Ireland, 1948–49: The Republic, The Commonwealth and NATO* (Dublin, 1991).

McCracken, J.L. *Representative Government in Ireland: A Study of Dáil Éireann 1919–48* (Oxford, 1958).

McCracken, J.L. 'Northern Ireland, 1921–46', in T.W. Moody and F.X. Martin (eds), *The Course of Irish History* (Cork, 1967), pp.313–41.

McCracken, J.L. 'The political scene in Northern Ireland, 1926–1937', in F. MacManus (ed.), *The Years of the Great Test 1926–39* (Cork, 1967), pp.150–61.

McCrone, G. *Regional Policy in Britain* (London, 1969).

McDowell, R.B. *The Church of Ireland, 1869–1969* (London, 1975).

McGarry, F. (ed.) *Republicanism in Modern Ireland* (Dublin, 2003).

McGarry, F. *Eoin O'Duffy: A Self-Made Hero* (Oxford, 2005).

McKay, S. *Northern Protestants: An Unsettled People* (Belfast, 2000).

McMahon, D. *Republicans and Imperialists: Anglo-Irish Relations in the 1930s* (New Haven, 1984).

McQueen, N. 'Ireland's entry to the United Nations, 1946–56', in T. Gallagher and J. O'Connell (eds), *Contemporary Irish Studies* (Manchester, 1983), pp.65–79.

Meenan, J. 'The Irish economy during the war', in K.B. Nowlan and T.D. Williams (eds), *Ireland in the War Years and After* (Dublin, 1969), pp.28–38.

Meenan, J. *The Irish Economy Since 1922* (Liverpool, 1970).

Miliband, R. *Parliamentary Socialism* (London, 1973).

Miller, D.W. *Queen's Rebels: Ulster Loyalism in Historical Perspective* (Dublin, 1978).

Moody, T.W. and Martin, F.X. (eds), *The Course of Irish History* (Cork, 1967).

Moody, T.W. *The Ulster Question 1603–1973* (Cork, 1974).

Morgan, A. *Harold Wilson* (London, 1992).

Morgan, K.O. *Labour in Power 1945–1951* (Oxford, 1984).

Morgan, K.O. *Callaghan: A Life* (Oxford, 1997).

Morrison, H. *Herbert Morrison: An Autobiography* (London, 1960).

Moynihan, M. (ed.), *Speeches and Statements by Éamon de Valera 1917–73* (Dublin, 1980).

Mulholland, M. *Northern Ireland at the Crossroads: Ulster Unionism in the O'Neill Years* (London, 2000).

Murphy, J.A. 'The Irish party system, 1938–51', in K.B. Nowlan and T.D. Williams (eds), *Ireland in the War Years and After* (Dublin, 1969), pp.147–66.

Murphy, J.A. *Ireland in the Twentieth Century* (Dublin, 1975).

Neill, D.G. (ed.), *Devolution of Government: The Experiment in Northern Ireland* (London, 1953).

Nevin, D. 'Industry and Labour', in K.B. Nowlan and T.D. Williams (eds), *Ireland in the War Years and After* (Dublin, 1969), pp.94–108.

Newark, F.H. 'The Constitution of Northern Ireland', in D.G. Neill (ed.), *Devolution of Government: The Experiment in Northern Ireland* (London, 1953), pp.7–17.

Newark, F.H. 'The Law and the Constitution', in Wilson (ed.), *Ulster Under Home Rule* (Oxford, 1955), pp.14–54.

Newsam, F. *The Home Office* (London, 1955).

Nowlan, K.B. and Williams, T.D. (eds), *Ireland in the War Years and After* (Dublin, 1969).

Nowlan, K.B. 'On the eve of the war', in K.B. Nowlan and T.D. Williams (eds), *Ireland in the War Years and After* (Dublin, 1969), pp.1–13.

O'Carroll, J.P. and Murphy, J.A. (eds), *De Valera and his Times* (Cork, 1983).

O'Connor, E. *A Labour History of Ireland* (Dublin, 1992).

O'Connor, F. *In Search of a State: Catholics in Northern Ireland* (Belfast, 1993).

O'Dowd, L., Rolston, B. and Tomlinson, M. *Northern Ireland: Between Civil Rights and Civil War* (London, 1980).

Ó Drisceoil, D. *Censorship in Ireland 1939–1945* (Cork, 1996).

O'Driscoll, M. *Ireland, Europe and the Marshall Plan* (Dublin, 2004).

Officer, D. 'In search of order, permanence and stability: Building Stormont 1921–1932', in R. English and G. Walker (eds), *Unionism in Modern Ireland: New Perspectives on Politics and Culture* (London, 1996), pp.130–47.

Ó Gráda, C. *Ireland: A New Economic History* (Oxford, 1994).

Ó Gráda, C. *A Rocky Road: The Irish Economy Since the 1920s* (Manchester, 1997).

O'Halloran, C. *Partition and the Limits of Irish Nationalism* (Dublin, 1987).

O'Halpin, E. *Defending Ireland: The Irish State and its Enemies Since 1922* (Oxford, 1999).

O'Leary, C. *Irish Elections, 1918–1977: Parties, Voters and Proportional Representation* (Dublin, 1979).

O'Leary, C. 'Northern Ireland, 1945–1972', in J.J. Lee (ed.), *Ireland 1945–70* (Dublin, 1979), pp.152–65.

Oliver, J.A. *Working at Stormont* (Dublin, 1978).

O'Malley, P. *The Uncivil Wars: Ireland Today* (Belfast, 1983).

O'Neill, T. *Ulster at the Crossroads* (London, 1969).

O'Neill, T. *The Autobiography of Terence O'Neill* (London, 1972).

Ó Nualláin, L. *Ireland: Finances of Partition* (Dublin, 1952).

Ó Tuathaigh, M.A.G. 'De Valera and sovereignty: A note on the pedigree of a political idea', in O'Carroll and Murphy (eds), *De Valera and his Times*, pp. 62–72.

Pakenham, F. (Lord Longford) *Peace by Ordeal* (London, 1962).

Patterson, H. 'Brian Maginess and the limits of liberal unionism', *Irish Review*, vol. 25 (1999/2000).

Patterson, H. *Ireland Since 1939: The Persistence of Conflict* (London, 2006).

Peatling, G.K. 'Unionist divisions, the onset of the Northern Ireland conflict, and pressures on O'Neill reconsidered', *Irish Studies Review*, 15, 1 (2007).

Phoenix, É. *Northern Nationalism: Nationalist Politics, Partition and the Catholic Minority in Northern Ireland 1890–1940* (Belfast, 1994).

Pimlott, B. *Harold Wilson* (London, 1992).

Pritt, D.N. *The Labour Government 1945–51* (London, 1963).

Probert, B. *Beyond Orange and Green* (London, 1978).

Purdie, B. 'The Friends of Ireland: British Labour and Irish nationalism, 1945–49', in T. Gallagher and J. O'Connell (eds), *Contemporary Irish Studies* (Manchester, 1983), pp.81–94.

Purdie, B. *Politics in the Streets: The Origins of the Civil Rights Movement in Northern Ireland* (Belfast, 1990).

Rafferty, O.P. *Catholicism in Ulster 1603–1983* (Dublin, 1994).

Rafter, K. *The Clann: The Story of Clann na Poblachta* (Dublin, 1996).

Rees, M. *Northern Ireland: A Personal Perspective* (London, 1985).

Regan, J.M. *The Irish Counter Revolution 1921–1936* (Dublin, 1999).

Roberts, G. 'The British offer to end partition', *History Ireland*, 9, 1 (spring 2001).

Roche, P. and Barton, B. (eds), *The Northern Ireland Question: Myth and Reality* (Aldershot, 1991).

Roebuck, P. (ed.), *Plantation to Partition: Essays in Ulster History in Honour of J.L. McCracken* (Belfast, 1981).

Rose, P. *Governing Without Consensus: An Irish Perspective* (London, 1971).

Roskill, S.W. *The War at Sea 1939–1945 vol. 1* (London, 1954).

Roskill, S.W. *Churchill and the Admirals* (London, 1977).

Rumpf, E. and Hepburn, A.C. *Nationalism and Socialism in Twentieth-Century Ireland* (Liverpool, 1977).

Sayers, J.E. 'The political parties and their social background', in T. Wilson (ed.), *Ulster Under Home Rule* (Oxford, 1955), pp.55–78.

Shea, P. *Voices and the Sound of Drums: An Irish Autobiography* (Belfast, 1981).

Shearman, H. *Northern Ireland 1921–1971* (Belfast, 1971).

Shinwell, E. *I've Lived Through it All* (London, 1973).

Simpson, J. 'Economic development: Cause or effect in the Northern Ireland conflict', in J. Darby (ed.), *Northern Ireland: The Background to the Conflict* (Belfast, 1983), pp.79–109.

Sloan, G.R. *The Geopolitics of Anglo-Irish Relations in the Twentieth Century* (Leicester, 1988).

Staunton, E. 'The Boundary Commission debacle 1925: Aftermath and implications', *History Ireland*, 4, 2 (summer 1996).

Staunton, E. *The Nationalists of Northern Ireland 1918–1973* (Dublin, 2001).

Stephan, E. *Spies in Ireland* (London, 1965).

Stewart, A.T.Q. *The Narrow Ground: Aspects of Ulster, 1609–1969* (London, 1977).

Sunday Times Insight Team, *Ulster* (Harmondsworth, 1972).

Taylor, A.J.P. *English History 1914–45* (Oxford, 1965).

Townshend, C. *The British Campaign in Ireland 1919–1921: The Development of Political and Military Policies* (Oxford, 1975).

Townshend, C. (ed.), *Consensus in Ireland: Approaches and Recessions* (Oxford, 1988).

Townshend, C. *Ireland: The 20th Century* (London, 1999).

Walker, B. *Dancing to History's Tune: Myth and Politics in Ireland* (Belfast, 1996).

Walker, G. 'The Commonwealth Labour Party in Northern Ireland 1942–47', *Irish Historical Studies*, xxiv, 93 (May, 1984).

Walker, G. 'Protestantism before party: The Ulster Protestant League in the 1930s', *Historical Journal*, 28, 4 (1985).

Walker, G. *The Politics of Frustration: Harry Midgley and the Failure of Labour in Northern Ireland* (Manchester, 1985).

Wall, M. 'Partition: The Ulster Question (1916–26)', in T.D. Williams (ed.), *The Irish Struggle, 1916–26* (London, 1966), pp.84–93.

Wallace, M. *Northern Ireland: 50 Years of Self-Government* (Newton Abbot, 1971).

Warner G. 'Putting pressure on O'Neill', *Irish Studies Review*, 13, 1 (2005).

Whyte, J.H. 'Church, state and society, 1950–70', in J.J. Lee (ed.), *Ireland 1945–70* (Dublin, 1979), pp.73–82.

Whyte, J.H. *Church and State in Modern Ireland 1923–1979* (Dublin, 1980).

Whyte, J.H. *Interpreting Northern Ireland* (Oxford, 1980).

Whyte, J.H. 'How much discrimination was there under the Unionist regime, 1921–68?' in T. Gallagher and J. O'Connell (eds), *Contemporary Irish Studies* (Manchester, 1983), pp.1–35.

Whyte, J.H. 'Economic crisis and political cold war, 1949–57', in J.R. Hill (ed.), *A New History of Ireland: Vol. VII, Ireland, 1921–1984* (Oxford, 2003), pp.278–93.

Whyte, J.H. 'To the declaration of the Republic and the Ireland Act, 1945–9', in J.R. Hill (ed.), *A New History of Ireland: Vol. VII, Ireland, 1921–1984* (Oxford, 2003), pp.261–77.

Wichert, S. *Northern Ireland Since 1945* (London, 1991).

Williams, F. *Ernest Bevin* (London, 1952).

Williams, T.D. (ed.), *The Irish Struggle, 1916–26* (London, 1966).

Williams, T.D. 'Ireland and the war', in K.B. Nowlan and T.D. Williams (eds), *Ireland in the War Years and After* (Dublin, 1969), pp.14–27.

Williams, T.D. 'Irish foreign policy, 1949–69', in J.J. Lee (ed.), *Ireland 1945–70* (Dublin, 1979), pp.136–51.

Wilson, J.H. *The Labour Government 1964–70: A Personal Record* (London, 1971).

Wilson, T. (ed.), *Ulster Under Home Rule* (Oxford, 1955).

Wilson, T. 'Devolution and public finance' and 'Conclusion: Devolution and partition', in T. Wilson, (ed.), *Ulster Under Home Rule* (Oxford, 1955), pp.115–36 and pp.183–211.

Younger, C. *A State of Disunion* (London, 1972).

Index

Labour and the Northern Ireland Problem
1945–51
The Missed Opportunity

Russell Rees
Foreword by Paul Bew

This book provides the first comprehensive analysis of the impact made by Clement Attlee's post-war Labour government on the triangular relationship between Belfast, London and Dublin. The Stormont government had finished the war on a high note, but Labour's shock general election victory in July 1945 shook the confidence of Unionist party leaders who were unsure of the new Labour administration's intentions towards Ireland. The prospect of closer scrutiny by Westminster, particularly in relation to Stormont's treatment of the Catholic minority, troubled the Unionist government. At the same time, the anticipation of radical socialist legislation, some of which was likely to override Stormont's powers, was an additional source of concern.

March 2009   208 pages
978 0 7165 2970 5 cloth €60.00/£45.00/$74.95

Ringside Seats
An Insider's View of the Crisis in Northern Ireland

Robert Ramsay
Foreword by Paul Bew

Provides an insider's first-hand account of many of the most turbulent moments in Northern Ireland's recent history. The author rose to the rank of Deputy Secretary in the Northern Ireland Civil Service, having been Principal Private Secretary to the Prime Minister and experienced and recorded such events as the Civil Rights campaign; the rise of the provisional IRA; the fall of O'Neill; the Faulkner institutional initiatives; internment; Bloody Sunday, the introduction of Direct Rule, the last days of the old Stormont and Edward Heath's decision to prorogue the Northern Ireland Parliament.

An often personal account of events as they unfolded, the author also paints pen portraits of the principal personalities involved, their actions and motivations. The personalities described are not only those in the political limelight, but also senior officials, whose behind-the-scenes influence has frequently made a significant impact on government policies and decisions. The author also gives an informed commentary on the development of the overall situation, drawing on sources within the administrative machine and the security forces.

The second half of Ramsay's career took him to the top of the administrative tree in Brussels and his account of that period traces the tortuous path from Common Market towards integration, via the stages of the constitutional treaties. Uniquely, the author's role brings together the macro political world of the EU and the micro situation in Northern Ireland, in the preparation of the European Peace and Reconciliation Programmes of the 1990s.

May 2009   288 pages illus
978 0 7165 3020 6   cloth €60.00/£45.00/$69.95
978 0 7165 3021 3   paper €24.95/£19.95

William Monsell of Tervoe
1812–1894
Catholic Unionist, Anglo-Irishman

Matthew Potter
Foreword by Gearóid Ó Tuathaigh

William Monsell, first Baron Emly of Tervoe (1812–94) is one of the most significant yet now also one of the most overlooked political figures of nineteenth century Ireland. His political career spanned sixty years, starting in the 1830s when Daniel O'Connell was at the height of his powers, until the 1890s, when Eamon de Valera was a boy. Monsell's extraordinary life saw him move from being an Anglican Tory to a Catholic Liberal and his dual conversion was greatly influenced by the terrible events of the Great Famine. His long period in the House of Commons (1847–74) was marked by service in a number of administrations under four Prime Ministers. He was the most prominent lay Catholic in Ireland and the chief spokesman for a large and influential, but now forgotten political group, the Catholic Unionists. He was also the key liaison between the British establishment and the Irish Catholic Bishops.

This rich contextual biography offers a challenging re-appraisal of the received picture of nineteenth-century Ireland. It is a fascinating portrait of a man whose entire political life was devoted to reconciling the various dilemmas inherent in his ideology. He was a Liberal Catholic devoted to an authoritarian Church, a reforming landlord opposed to the land agitation of the 1880s and 1890s and a patriotic Irishman who staunchly supported the union with Britain. Catholic, Liberal and Unionist; Irishman, Briton and adopted Frenchman; friend of Gladstone, Gavan Duffy and of Pope Pius IX; of Cardinal Newman, Lord Acton and of Cardinal Cullen, William Monsell was a major player in Ireland, Britain and Europe for many decades, whose undeserved slide into obscurity is reversed in this fascinating book.

March 2009   256 pages illus
978 0 7165 2989 7 cloth €35.00/£29.95/$49.95

NEW DIRECTIONS IN IRISH HISTORY SERIES

The Glory of Being Britons
Civic Unionism in Nineteenth-Century Belfast

John Bew

At a moment when British Prime Minister Gordon Brown has excluded Ireland from his version of modern Britishness, John Bew's book could not be more timely. Covering a period of almost ninety years, Bew demonstrates how a strongly held British national identity took hold in nineteenth-century Belfast, a town which was once regarded as the centre of republicanism and rebellion in Ireland. Starting with the impact of the French Revolution – a cause of huge celebration in Belfast - this book describes how political and civic culture in the town became deeply immersed in the imagined community of the British nation after the Act of Union of 1801, allowing the author to provide a new perspective on the roots of Ulster's opposition to Home Rule.

What caused this shift from 'Liberty, Equality, and Fraternity' to 'God save the Queen'? While entirely aware of the sectarian division in Ulster, Bew places these developments in the wider context of the Westminster political system and debates about the United Kingdom's 'place in the world', thus providing a more balanced and sophisticated view of the politics of nineteenth-century Belfast, arguing that it was not simply dominated by the struggle between Orange and Green. The book breaks new ground in examining how the formative 'nation-building' episodes in Britain – such as war, parliamentary reform, and social, economic and scientific advancement – played out in the unique context of Belfast and the surrounding area. Ultimately, however, it also explains how the exponents of this civic unionism struggled to make their voices heard as Britain and Ireland entered the age of mass democracy and traditional modes of identification began to reassert themselves, even before the Home Rule crisis began.

2008   272 pages
978 0 7165 2974 3   cloth   €39.95/£45.00/$59.95

Buying Irish Patriotism for a Five-Pound Note
The Real Inspector Mallon

Donal P. McCracken

This is the biography of the famous Irish detective and security policeman, John Mallon (1839–1915). Son of a small Catholic farmer in republican south Armagh, Mallon rose to be assistant commissioner of the Dublin Metropolitan Police and for 30 years used the G men (the Detective Division) to subvert revolutionary activity in Dublin. He was remarkably successful; his greatest triumph was bringing to the gallows the Invincibles, who had carried out the Phoenix Park murders. Mallon became a legend in Dublin, mentioned in Joyce's Ulysses, very popular with his detectives, always courteous, never resorting to violence in dealing with suspects and a master of interrogation who personally controlled an army of paid informers – the Lord Lieutenant once remarking, 'Without Mallon, we would have no one worth a row of beans'.

June 2009   256 pages illus
978 0 7165 2993 4   cloth   €60.00/£45.00/$69.95
978 0 7165 2994 1   paper €24.95/£19.95